Strikes

Strikes

Michael P. Jackson

Senior Lecturer in Sociology,
University of Stirling

WHEATSHEAF BOOKS · SUSSEX

ST. MARTIN'S PRESS · NEW YORK

First published in Great Britain in 1987 by
WHEATSHEAF BOOKS LTD
A MEMBER OF THE HARVESTER PRESS PUBLISHING GROUP
Publisher: John Spiers
16 Ship Street Brighton, Sussex
and in the USA by
ST. MARTIN'S PRESS, INC.
175 Fifth Avenue, New York, NY 10010

© Michael P. Jackson, 1987

British Library Cataloguing in Publication Data

Jackson, Michael P.
　Strikes.
　1. Strikes and lockouts
　I. Title
　331.89′2　　　HD5306

　ISBN 0-7450-0041-X
　ISBN 0-7450-0209-9 Pbk

Library of Congress Cataloging-in-Publication Data

Jackson, Michael Peart.
　Strikes
　Bibliography: p.
　Includes index.
　1. Strikes and lockouts. 2. Strikes and lockouts —
Australia. 3. Strikes and lockouts — United States.
4. Strikes and lockouts — Great Britain. I. Title.
HD5306. J33　1987　331.89′2　87-14376

Typeset in Times 11/12 point by
Quality Phototypesetting Ltd., Bristol

Printed in Great Britain by Billing & Sons Ltd, Worcester

Contents

Tables

Preface

This book has been designed as an introduction to the study of strikes. Trends and explanations are reviewed in an attempt to give the reader a better understanding of the nature of strike activity. It is, though, pitched at the level of an introduction and no assumptions have been made about prior knowledge of the area.

I am grateful for the comments received from a number of colleagues, in particular John Leopold and Bob Hart. I am also grateful for the work of Dorothy Anderson and Rachel Haigh who helped enormously with the preparation of the manuscript.

1 Introduction: Strikes and Industrial Conflict

The focus of this book is on strikes. However, it is difficult, and often not profitable, to attempt to distinguish rigidly between strikes and industrial conflict. The latter is clearly broader. Kornhouser's definition of industrial conflict, that it is 'the total range of behaviour and attitudes that express opposition and divergent orientations between individual owners and managers on the one hand and working people and their organisations on the other',[1] makes this apparent.

The discussion of strikes clearly gains something from a recognition that it is part of a wider phenomenon. It can be argued that different manifestations of conflict may be alternatives, the choice between which may be dependent more on the opportunities available than anything else. Thus, the use of the strike weapon by a group of workers may not be dependent simply on the level of discontent but may also be dependent on whether they believe they can contemplate this kind of action (for example, do they have the financial resources to allow them to embark on a strike?). If a decision is taken that a strike is not possible then the discontent will not disappear and it may be manifest in other ways, say through output restriction or absenteeism.

Such a view finds some support in the literature.[2] On the other hand, so does the view that where there is a high incidence of one form of industrial conflict, other forms are likely to be high as well. It might be, for instance, that a particular kind of industrial relations climate is one in which conflict of all kinds is likely to occur. The debate on this matter is far from concluded[3] and it is not necessary to try to resolve it here. Both views assert a link

1

between strikes and industrial conflict: the debate is about its nature.

The argument that there is a link between strikes and industrial conflict does not imply that all types of industrial conflict need to be viewed and approached in the same way, nor even that all kinds of what are often referred to as 'organised' conflict (essentially group behaviour, as opposed individual behaviour which is seen as 'unorganised' conflict) should be seen in the same way. Industrial conflict is not a unitary phenomenon. However, discussion of strikes clearly loses something if it is attempted without recognition that there are other ways in which workers can express their discontent with say working conditions, or a wage offer.

It would anyway be difficult to enforce a rigid distinction between strikes and industrial conflict from the point of view of the academic material that needs to be looked at. In many instances material which has a broad industrial conflict focus has obvious relevance for a discussion of strikes. The same, it should be said, is true in the other direction.

The subject matter of the book, then, is broad in the sense that a study of strikes cannot be narrowly interpreted; it is also broad in another sense in that an attempt will be made both to describe and to explain. Description of strike activity, by itself, raises many problems, particularly on an international scale. The coverage of strike statistics varies from country to country, the definitions used for computational purposes vary, and the conventions adopted for presentation differ. Even within one country it is often difficult to find a consistent set of statistics over a reasonable time period: comparison between countries makes the task enormously more complicated.

In an attempt to ease this problem, though not to deal with it entirely, a strategy has been adopted which involves a two-stage approach. The first stage is the broad coverage of strikes in Western industrial nations. This allows general issues and comparisons to be made but little in the way of detail to be considered. The second stage is the more detailed analysis of strike activity in just three countries, Australia, USA and Britain. The claim is not made that these three countries are representative of the broad range looked at earlier. Such a claim would be bogus and it is doubtful if it would be other, no matter which three countries were chosen. The choice has been much more pragmatic. The claim would be made, though, that the comparison of the strike trends in these three countries is interesting and worthwhile in its own right. There are significant differences between them in terms of their industrial relations systems. Australia, with its emphasis on compulsory arbitration, the USA with its relatively low rate of unionisation (the lowest of any country in the Western World), alongside the generally high profile of the law on industrial relations, and the UK with its high rate of unionisation but a tradition of minimum state involvement (though this has changed somewhat in recent years), present different industrial relations backgrounds for the consideration of strikes. There are also major social/political differences between the three countries, with the USA standing out because of the absence of a mainstream labour party linked to the trade unions. At the same time, of course, there are some similarities between the countries, particularly historical and language links.

The description of strike trends, especially of differences between countries, inevitably raises questions. At a very basic level, how can we explain the differences that can be highlighted? Why does one country consistently experience more strikes than another? When one looks at the strike patterns, the variations between individual countries and groups of countries are quite marked, not simply in terms of current patterns but also in terms of trends over time. Questions such as these lead one to consider explanations, both for particular situations and for strike activity in general.

Attempts at explanation have been sought from within different disciplines and using a variety of approaches. Variations between countries have been explored using statistical techniques, in some cases quite sophisticated ones, relating strike patterns to factors like economic conditions and political structure. There is an extensive literature primarily, though not exclusively, from within economics that has sought explanations in this way. Other traditions have sought to explain variations between countries by reference to differences in the institutions of industrial relations and by reference to socio-political considerations. Writing from within such traditions has less frequently relied on statistical analysis, though this is not a universal rule and the traditions anyway are not entirely distinct.

There is, though, another body of writing which can help one to understand strikes and strike behaviour which frequently is ignored by writers who focus more narrowly on variations in strike activity between countries. This is writing which sometimes talks specifically about strikes but often discusses industrial conflict more generally. It is writing which is clearly relevant to an understanding of strikes even when it is not restricted in its coverage. This writing is more likely to come from within subjects like sociology and politics than from within economics, though this is nothing like a clear and unambiguous distinction.

★(Strikes are a subject of regular public debate, more than anything else, because of their impact, particularly because of the impact of some of them, on the consumer. A major transport strike, for example, will bring inconvenience to a large number of people. The passions raised in such circumstances can be enormous, and the popular call for a solution more than just a media creation. Even people who themselves have been on strike, and in normal circumstances would uphold the right of others to withdraw their labour, can be incensed. Popular discussion of strikes is also heightened when there are claims that such action is the cause of serious damage to the national economy. A dock strike which hampers a country's exports when the balance of payments is in deficit, or a power workers' strike that leads to the partial shutdown, even if only on a temporary basis, of other sections of industry, can lead to heightened discussion of action, sometimes specific, sometimes more general, to reduce the incidence of strike activity.)★

In practice most estimates of the impact of strike action raise more questions than they answer. Estimates of production lost as the result of strikes, for example, cannot be based simply on a calculation of the number of days' work lost. If one looks at the impact on employees, similarly, the economic impact cannot simply be based on the wages lost. Estimates of the economic impact of strike action raise formidable methodological problems; estimates of other kinds of impact, such as on managerial and employee attitudes and behaviour, have rarely been attempted at a sophisticated level. The discussion in this book on the impact of strikes looks at some of the major studies in the area, yet the conclusions have to be very tentative. In many cases the important message is the need to treat popular claims with caution, rather than any suggestion that a precise calculation of impact can be offered.

There are, of course, many other issues that one could discuss relating to strikes. One might look, for example, at methods of conflict resolution. For some this will be the most important aspect of the subject and the absence of a full examination of this issue a disappointment. If strikes are viewed as an indication of a failure on the part of the industrial relations system, and a failure that has to be corrected, then it would not be surprising if this attitude were taken. Similarly this attitude might well be taken if strikes are viewed as the result of the work of agitators: such people, maybe for political motives, would be seen to whip up discontent where it did not really exist.

Strikes, though, do not have to be seen in this fashion. This is not the place to embark on a lengthy discussion of different approaches to industrial relations.[4] However, it is clear that a view that industrial relations take place in a context where both sides of industry share the same basic aims and objectives and where consequently any serious dispute must indicate some malfunctioning of the system, need not go unchallenged. There is an alternative which finds extensive support in the literature. In practice, the alternative embraces a number of different traditions, from the pluralist to the Marxist, and quite different emphases within them. Nevertheless, the link between them is a recognition that some level of conflict, at least, is to be expected within a capitalist system. The level of conflict, the causes and the ways of dealing with it, will all find different expressions from the different traditions, but the notion that conflict is to be expected in capitalist society will provide a link and a contrast to the view that interests of different groups should be assumed to converge.

In so far as explanations of strikes help one to understand their causes better, then the discussion in this book will not be irrelevant to those who wish to find ways of reducing levels of overt conflict. There is a difference, nevertheless, between a greater understanding of causes and a concentration on institutional mechanisms for the resolution of conflict, and it is a difference which in part relates to basic assumptions about the nature of industrial relations.

The organisation of the book follows fairly closely the order of the discussion in this introduction. The first part of the book concentrates on a description of strike patterns and trends. In Chapter 2 the position in the major Western industrialised nations is looked at. Attention is focussed on the problems of comparability between statistics from different countries: problems of definition, of categorisation and of presentation. In Chapter 3 this broad focus is narrowed down so that just three countries, Australia, USA and the UK, are looked at. Even though the focus is narrower it is still relatively broad so that nothing like a full account of strike trends and patterns in these three countries can be attempted. Nevertheless more detail is possible and some of the issues which could not be covered in the earlier chapter are explored. In the next two chapters attention is turned to explanations. The aim is to review a range of explanations some of which have been developed from studies of specific countries, others of which have been based on more general comparative work, to see what lessons can be learnt. The aim is stated in this general way rather than say as a specific attempt to explain in a direct and detailed fashion just the strike trends in Australia, USA and the UK. Chapter 4 focusses very much on explanations for variations in strike trends and patterns between countries. Three different categories of explanations are examined: one that refers to the institutions of industrial relations, another that refers to political factors and a third that centres on economic factors. Chapter 5 moves away from studies that have focussed attention on explaining variations towards others which have been based much more on an understanding of industrial conflict in a broader sense, often including but not being exclusively related to strikes. In Chapter 6 the impact of strikes is examined. It is argued that strikes can have an impact not simply on the directly involved participants but, in many instances, also on others like customers, suppliers and the general public. It is the perceived impact of strikes on society in general that accounts for many of the policy initiatives in industrial relations though the impact of strikes on the general public is no easier to measure than it is on the participants themselves. Chapter 7 is a conclusion reviewing the earlier discussions and suggesting priorities for further work.

The book has been written as an introduction to an area of study. A variety of disciplines have been drawn on but no assumption has been made about prior knowledge of them by the reader. The book touches on many issues that cannot be dealt with in full here. The study of strikes is but part of the study of industrial conflict which is but part of the study of industrial relations.

NOTES

1. A. Kornhouser, R. Dubin and A.N. Ross (eds), *Industrial Conflict,* McGraw-Hill, New York, 1954, p.13.
2. See, for example, W.H. Scott, *Coal and Conflict,* Liverpool University Press, 1963.
3. For a review of this area see N. Nicholson, 'Strikes and other Forms of Industrial Action', *Industrial Relations Journal,* November/December 1980, Vol. II, No. 5, pp 20–31.
4. For a fuller discussion see M.P. Jackson, *Industrial Relations,* Croom Helm, Beckenham, Kent, 1985.

2 Comparisons between Industrial Nations

All major industrialised nations publish statistics on strikes. Although the hopes of the International Labour Organisation[1] have not been met, virtually all countries collect data on the number of stoppages, the number of workers involved in stoppages and the number of working days lost through stoppages. These statistics enable some comments to be made about the broad trends within countries (and in certain instances for Western nations in general) and comparisons to be made between them. Strike statistics, however, need to be interpreted with care. Attention needs to be paid to differences in the method of collection, different practices used in the consideration of statistics, and differences in the definitions used for strikes. It may be wise before examining trends, to make a brief comment on the collection of strike statistics and what they are intended to show. Other matters like differences in practice and definition will be discussed along with the trends.

COLLECTION OF STRIKE STATISTICS

What are often referred to in shorthand as strike statistics are more accurately described as stoppages of work resulting from industrial disputes. They therefore include both strikes and lock-outs. The latter are believed to be less important than the former, though only West Germany publishes separate figures. In West Germany over the period 1972 to 1981 lock-outs accounted for 24 per cent of all workers involved in disputes and 44 per cent of working days lost. However, many claim that such percentages are unusually high. They include two years, 1978 and 1979, during which the proportion of disputes accounted for by lock-outs was exceptional by normal West German experience. Three lock-outs occurred: one in the printing industry in 1978 involving 55,000 workers, one in the engineering industry in 1978 involving 177,000 workers, and one in the steel industry in 1978–9 involving 40,000 workers. There is also a view that West Germany is unusual in the extent to which the lock-out is used compared to other European nations and in the way in which it is used to counter strike action.[2] Thus Walsh, in a study of strikes in France, West Germany, Italy and the United Kingdom argued that it

would be wrong to assume that the other three countries experience lockouts in the same proportion as West Germany since German employers seem to have been more ready to use the lockout against intransigent workers than those in the three other countries, but in the absence of separate statistics proportions are not known.[3]

It needs to be borne in mind, as well, that the distinction between a strike and a lock-out, and between a strike and other kinds of industrial action, is not easily made. Many disputes involve a mixture of different forms of action, the balance between which varies over time. A dispute that starts with a strike may conclude with a lock-out; a strike may be linked to other action by employees such the occupation of the workplace so that machinery cannot be moved by the employer. Batstone records a dispute which illustrates this matter well.

In support of their claim, a group of workers went out on strike. Other workers were instructed not to handle work, formerly done by the group but now done by an outside agency. When they refused they were suspended. This occurred several times, and finally the whole staff agreed to strike and did so.

Here we have a number of collective suspensions which are related to refusals to carry out management orders and which therefore involve stoppages of work. It is difficult to decide on the basis of conventional definitions, whether these situations should be seen as suspensions, a form of lock-out, or strikes, or a combination of these.[4]

Whether a dispute is a strike or a lock-out, or should be classified as another form of industrial action, anyway, may depend as much on who is doing the defining as on the particular course of events. It is by no means unknown for workers to define a dispute as a lock-out at the same time as the employers are defining it as a strike.[5]

In this context, then, the method of collection of strike statistics and the sources used become important. The normal practice is for the state employment or labour relations agency to be responsible for the collection and publication of information. However, there are exceptions. In Belgium and Italy the police are the responsible agency, and in Denmark the state is only responsible for publication not collection. In Denmark information is collected by employers' federations and there are fears that reliance on the federations for information may not only affect the kind of information received but also the extent of reporting. Many employers are not members of an employers association and therefore do not have a regular focus for the presentation of information on disputes. In most countries employers are the principal source of information (in West Germany employers are legally obliged to report strikes to the local office of the federal Employment Service) though in a small number of countries information is collected solely from trade unions. This is the case in Iceland and Austria. In practice most countries claim that they use a number of different sources of information. For example, in the USA information is collected 'largely from newspaper accounts',[6] though these accounts are also supplemented by information from local offices of the state social security agencies, state and federal mediation and conciliation agencies as well as trade unions, individual employers and employers' federations. In Australia, the Australian Bureau of Statistics relies heavily on weekly disputes lists from officers of the Department of Employment and Industrial Relations, but this is supplemented by information from newspapers and trade union journals and the ABS has legal powers to compel the provision of information from the parties involved in a dispute.

One of the difficulties in any analysis of strike statistics is the extent of under-reporting. In most instances information is provided on a voluntary basis, and even where there is a legal obligation to report it is far from clear that this has a significant impact. Evidence of the extent of under-reporting is limited. However, some is available from West Germany, the United

Kingdom and Sweden. In West Germany Kalbitz found that 'a considerable proportion of strikes which occurred during the period he was investigating were neither declared nor registered.'[7] In a study of manufacturing establishments in the United Kingdom Brown reports that the official statistics only recorded 68 per cent of stoppages that were eligible (this figure, therefore, does not take account of different criteria of eligibility that might be used).[8] The percentage recorded rose with duration and establishment size. Korpi has reported a study in Sweden which suggested that a higher proportion of stoppages might fail to be reported.[9] The study referred to was commissioned by the Swedish Metal Workers' Union and involved 48 plants in the metal working industry. An attempt was made to determine what proportion of stoppages was reported to the headquarters of the central union and employers' associations. He suggested, on the basis of this evidence, that probably more than a half of strikes are not reported. He also noted some differences between the reported and the unreported strikes. 'The immediate issues in dispute in the unreported strikes differ to some extent from the issues involved in the reported strikes.' They 'involve a smaller proportion of issues related to wages and earnings, a greater proportion of alleged improper behaviour of management representatives and a somewhat greater proportion related to health hazards'.[10] There were also differences in the case of size (a higher proportion of small strikes were not reported) but on the whole such differences were not significant. Although he does not quantify his statement Korpi also argues that the 'lack of reporting and recording of strikes is not unique to Sweden'.[11]

The classification of a dispute as industrial, compared to say political, can also cause problems. In a number of countries political stoppages are excluded from dispute statistics. This is the case in France, Japan, New Zealand and the United Kingdom. In the USA and Canada political stoppages may be included but only if they are designed to influence government policy over pay or other conditions of employment, while in West Germany political strikes are illegal. Most assessments suggest that the different treatment of political stoppages is not a major problem, since such disputes account for a relatively small proportion of the total, but this does not mean that the issue can be totally ignored. It is clear that in some countries political strikes are more frequent than in other countries: Italy is mentioned by a number of authors as having more political strikes than is typical elsewhere and there is some support from an analysis of their statistics.[12]

TRENDS

Many studies of trends using strike statistics are based not on all industries and services but on the mining, manufacturing, construction and transport sectors. The argument for such concentration in part is that these sectors have dominated strike activity; in part, though, it is also that it aids comparability between countries, for without the use of such a restricted point of departure variations in strike figures might tell the reader more about the industrial structure of the country than about its strike record. This point of view has been put forward by the International Labour Organisation.

However, by no means all studies have adopted such an approach, and there are arguments for not doing so. One is that the main industrial sectors are becoming less important in terms of employment opportunities. In many countries the service sector dominates or is coming to dominate. Predictions suggest an increasing role for service and a decreasing role for manufacturing industry as far as employment is concerned. While it is clearly true that in general most strike activity occurs outside the service sector, the growth of white-collar unionisation, and changes in the aims and methods of professional organisations, make it important to examine their record in industrial disputes. In some particular cases the strike propensity in the service sector is greater than in some other traditional sectors of the economy. Walsh notes,[13] for instance, that in Italy, between 1970 and 1979, while 430 working days were lost through strikes per 1,000 workers in the primary sector, and 608 in the construction industry, 662 were lost in the service industries; the manufacturing industry total of 1,647 per 1,000 workers was well above that for the service industries, but this does not detract from the surprisingly high ranking for service industries in Italy. Similarly in France, service industries with 90 working days lost per 1,000 employees experienced more strike activity than the primary sector and the construction industry. This suggests that in particular instances failure to take account of the service sector could give a totally misleading impression of strike activity.

Such arguments are gaining increasing recognition. A number of individual academics have sought to produce statistics for the broader range of all industries and services, while the EEC has started to produce such statistics for member countries. This discussion of trends is based on all industries and services, though some reference will also be made to the measure of major industrial groupings as a point of comparison.

Table 2.1 shows the number of stoppages in 20 major Western industrial nations[14] over the period 1962 to 1984.[15] The information is standardised to take account of the number of workers in each country and is grouped in five-year periods.

Table 2.1: Stoppages per 100,000 Employees, 1962–1984

	1962–66	1967–71	1972–76	1977–81	1982–84
Australia	37	47	50	47	37
Austria	NA	NA	NA	NA	—
Belgium	2	4	7	7	NA
Canada	8	8	12	11	7
Denmark	2	2	7	10	8
Finland	5	17	93	90	81
France	14	18	22	19	18
Federal Republic of Germany	NA	NA	NA	NA	NA
Iceland	61	105	87	79	8
Ireland	12	17	22	17	19
Italy	28	31	29	17	12
Japan	5	6	9	3	2
Netherlands	2	1	1	1	—
New Zealand	11	23	31	42	33
Norway	1	1	1	1	1
Spain	2	8	23	20	21
Sweden	1	1	2	3	3
Switzerland	—	—	—	—	—
United Kingdom	10	12	11	9	6
United States	6	8	7	5	NA

— indicates less than 1
Sources and Notes: See Note 19, p. 29.

From Table 2.1 it can be seen that there were considerable variations in the number of stoppages between countries. In each period either Iceland or Finland experienced the highest number of stoppages, and a group of countries, including Sweden, Norway, the Netherlands and Switzerland, experienced very few at all. Another group of countries, including Australia, France, Ireland, Italy and New Zealand, regularly experienced more than 10 stoppages per 100,000 workers but did not reach the total for Iceland or, in the later periods, for Finland.

There was a relatively stable pattern in terms of the number of stoppages between countries. The rank ordering of countries has changed on occasions. The most dramatic example is provided by Finland. In general, though, the rank ordering has not fluctuated markedly.[16] In some countries the number of strikes has increased over time: in the majority of cases there were more strikes in the 1970s than the 1960s though there were a number of exceptions to this, so that general trends are more difficult to identify.

Table 2.2. shows the number of workers involved in stoppages, again related to the number of workers in each country and expressed over a five-year period. From Table 2.2 it can be seen that Italy had the highest total in each period. Two other countries, Australia and Iceland, regularly experienced more than 100 workers involved in stoppages per 1,000 employees while a number of other countries, West Germany, the Netherlands and Switzerland, experienced stoppages involving 10 workers or less per 1,000 employees in every period.

There was again some stability over time in terms of the ranking of countries, although this statement masks some significant changes in the case of particular countries. The Austrian, Canadian, Finnish and Spanish positions are worth noting in this context. In the case of Austria the 1962–6 period appears to have been atypical, in the case of Canada the same can be said for the 1972–6 period, while in the case of Finland and Spain there was a marked increase between the 1960s and 1970s.

The interpretation of these figures, however, needs to be made while recognising that there are some important variations in the way that the figures are tabulated between countries which

Table 2.2: Workers Involved per 1,000 Employees, 1962–1984

	1962–66	1967–71	1972–76	1977–81	1982–84
Australia	126	239	309	242	111
Austria	46	3	1	3	—
Belgium	10	19	24	19	NA
Canada	29	38	91	40	33
Denmark	6	15	65	35	24
Finland	29	93	225	218	192
France	159	138	123	51	27
Federal Republic of Germany	6	8	6	8	10
Iceland	146	252	221	204	179
Ireland	41	54	45	44	36
Italy	229	353	650	841	373
Japan	47	43	63	14	5
Netherlands	4	6	5	6	10
New Zealand	32	66	83	130	147
Norway	3	1	7	4	11
Spain	9	30	95	495	212
Sweden	2	6	3	46	4
Switzerland	—	—	—	—	—
United Kingdom	64	68	56	81	65
United States	25	42	28	18	NA

— indicates less than 1

Sources and Notes: See Note 19, p. 29.

are likely to affect the totals significantly. One of the important distinctions here is between the number of workers directly and those indirectly involved. Workers directly involved are usually taken to be those engaged in the initial dispute at the establishment where the stoppage first began, whereas workers indirectly involved include those who had to cease work because of the stoppage either at the same or another establishment. Many countries cover indirect effects at the same establishment, though some do not, and none cover the indirect effects of other establishments. Countries which do not cover any workers indirectly involved include Austria, Canada, France, West Germany, Iceland, Italy, Japan and Sweden.

It is impossible to be sure of the exact impact of excluding workers indirectly involved from the figures. However, some guide can be obtained by looking at the position in countries where workers both directly and indirectly involved are counted, but where these figures are published separately. In the UK, for example, such figures are published, and around 20 per cent of all workers involved in stoppages have been indirectly involved at the same establishment. The position in the UK varies in detail from year to year and there are variations between different countries. Nevertheless this at least provides some guide as to the order of magnitude.

The other problem with this measure of strike activity concerns the way that the number of workers involved in a stoppage is calculated. The ILO guidelines suggest it should be based on the average number of workers affected by the stoppage each day for the duration of the stoppage. Many countries base their calculations on this procedure, but not all do so. The countries that do not use this procedure include the USA, Canada and the United Kingdom. In the latter case the calculation involves taking the maximum number of workers involved in the stoppage, even if some of them were only involved for part of it. In the USA and Canada the maximum figure on the day when the stoppage involved most workers is used for the calculations. These different methods of calculation, of course, will all give different results. The detail is examined more closely by Walsh though he recognises that it is impossible to provide a precise account of the effect.[17]

Table 2.3 shows the number of working days lost through stoppages, as in the other two cases, related to the number of workers in each country and expressed over a five-year period. From Table 2.3 it can be seen that Italy and Iceland had the highest totals except for the years 1977 to 1981 when the highest total was recorded by Spain. A number of other countries regularly recorded more than 200 working days lost per 1,000 employees; specifically, Australia, Canada, Finland, Ireland and the United States. Some other countries, like Belgium, France and the United Kingdom, came close to meeting that target but others, like West Germany, the Netherlands and Switzerland regularly lost few working days (in almost all cases no more than 50 working days per 1,000 employees in any period, the only exception being West Germany for 1982–4).

There was some stability in the rank order of countries over time, as with the other two measures of stoppage activity.

Table 2.3: Working Days Lost per 1,000 Employees, 1962–1984

	1962–66	1967–71	1972–76	1977–81	1982–84
Australia	203	421	749	615	324
Austria	81	7	17	8	—
Belgium	113	228	213	199	NA
Canada	400	770	1,111	777	489
Denmark	37	24	455	132	50
Finland	224	468	558	542	411
France	198	202	236	146	97
Federal Republic of Germany	23	50	21	47	88
Iceland	1,401	2,167	1,208	850	1,414
Ireland	640	784	539	818	454
Italy	1,122	1,447	1,697	1,122	958
Japan	143	112	170	28	11
Netherlands	9	21	38	32	39
New Zealand	77	184	205	354	363
Norway	60	16	61	28	76
Spain	22	76	407	1,852	602
Sweden	26	64	26	249	6
Switzerland	7	1	2	1	—
United Kingdom	131	347	491	576	569
United States	358	715	445	378	NA

— indicates less than 1
Sources and Notes: See Note 19, p. 29.

However, there were nevertheless some notable variations. Spain is a good example where the number of working days lost increased quite dramatically. In other instances the variations were less marked but worthy of comment. For example, in the case of Canada the number of working days lost in 1972–6 was almost three times what it had been in 1962–6, but in the following two five-year periods it fell back again although its ranking changed nothing like as dramatically (in 1962–6 and 1967–71 it ranked fourth from the top, in 1972–6 third, while in 1977–81 and 1982–4 it ranked fifth).

The comments that were made about the problems caused by variations in the way strike figures are calculated between countries when discussing the number of workers involved in strikes apply in this case as well. The number of working days lost will be affected in the same kind of way by differences in the inclusion of workers indirectly involved in stoppages, and by differences in the way the number of workers involved in a stoppage are calculated.

On the basis of these measures of strike activity some comparisons clearly can be made and there is a degree of overlap between the conclusions that might be reached on individual measures. A number of countries, such as Australia, Iceland and Italy, appear to be relatively highly strike-prone whichever measure is used whereas others, like West Germany, the Netherlands, Norway and Switzerland, seem relatively lowly strike-prone, again whichever measure is used. However, in some cases there are significant variations between the different strike measures. This has frequently given rise to questions about which measure, if there are differences between them, should be used. As always with this kind of question there is not one agreed answer. Academics have debated the relative importance of the different measures, and some attempts have been made to produce composite measures.[18] Broadly, the use of the number of stoppages is seen to give more weight to short stoppages whereas the use of the number of working days lost is seen to give a clearer guide to the production lost. However, it is not quite as simple as that. Problems arise, for example, with the distinction between a number of related stoppages: under what conditions are they seen as the same and under what conditions are they seen as different stoppages? To what extent do different conventions on this matter affect the figures? When one turns to working days lost, to what extent should part-time workers be treated differently to full-time workers, should some account be taken of overtime, and are hours worked (a measure used by Italy for instance) a better guide than days lost when considering production losses? Added to this are the difficulties recorded earlier about different practices in the basis of calculating the number of workers involved and the treatment of workers indirectly involved.

One issue which has not yet been raised but which can affect judgement on such matters is the criterion used for the inclusion of stoppages in national statistics. Practice varies on this matter. In some countries, like France, Italy, the Netherlands and Spain, no criteria are published; in others, like Belgium, Japan,

Switzerland, Norway and Sweden, the criteria centre on the duration of the stoppage; in others like Australia, Denmark and New Zealand, the criterion centres on the number of days lost; and in still others, like West Germany and the United Kingdom, a mixture of criteria are used. Table 2.4 summarises the precise position in the major Western industrial nations.

The position of the USA is worthy of special mention in this context. In 1982 the basis of the criteria for the inclusion of stoppages in the statistics was changed. Previously all strikes and lock-outs which lasted for a full day or shift and involved six or more workers were counted. Since 1982 only stoppages which last 1 day (or shift) and involve 1,000 workers have been counted. Some guide to the impact of the change can be gained by looking at the extent to which stoppages over the new limit were reflected in the pre-1982 statistics. This particular issue is examined in the next chapter, when the USA statistics are looked at in more detail, though at this stage it might be noted that the new criteria would have excluded the overwhelming majority of strikes previously counted but only a minority (though a substantial minority) of days lost.

The effect of the changes in criteria for inclusion in stoppage statistics in the USA clearly is important for the interpretation of those statistics. However, it also points to a more general lesson: the number of stoppages is much more sensitive than the number of workers involved or the number of working days lost to variations in criteria for inclusion. Thus, the argument has been made that the latter two measures are much more useful than the first as a basis for international comparison of stoppages.

In the discussion so far, most attention has focussed on variations between countries rather than on trends over time either within countries or over all countries (although some comments have been made on this matter in passing). This latter issue is very difficult to discuss for there is not one general time trend which covers all countries: for example, there is not a general trend towards either an increase in strike incidence or a decrease, no matter which of these measures is looked at. Within individual countries the matter is somewhat easier to discuss though there are few general and consistent trends. The only really consistent trend one can point to is in the case of New

Table 2.4: Industrial Disputes: Comparisons of Coverage and Methodology

	Minimum criteria for inclusion in statistics	Are political stoppages included?	Are indirectly affected workers included?	Sources and Notes
Australia	10 or more days lost	Yes	Yes	Information gathered from arbitrators, employers and unions
Austria	No restrictions on size	Yes	No	Trade unions provide information
Belgium	More than one working day's duration	Yes	No	Local police reports sent to National Conciliation Service. Follow-up questionnaires sent from National Statistical Institute
Canada	10 or more days lost, or of more than half a day's duration	Yes	No	Reports from Canada Manpower Centres also Press and Provincial Labor Depts
Denmark	100 or more days lost	Yes	Yes	Voluntary reports from employers' organisations sent annually to Statistical Office
Finland	More than 4 hours' duration unless 100 or more working days lost	Yes	Yes	Returns from mail questionnaires to employers and employees
France	No restrictions on size. However, public sector and agricultural employees are excluded from statistics	No	No	Labour inspectors' reports
Germany (FR)	More than 10 workers involved and more than 1 days' duration, unless 100 or more working days lost	Yes	No	Compulsory notification by employers to Labour Offices
Ireland	10 or more days lost, or of more than one day's duration	Yes	Yes	Reports from local employment office
Italy	No restrictions on size	Yes since 1975	No	Local police reports sent to Central Institute of Statistics

	Definition			Method of collection
Japan	More than half a day's duration	No	No	Interviews by Pretectorial Labour Policy section or local Labour Policy Office of employers and employees
Netherlands	No restrictions on size	Yes	Yes	District Employment Offices informs Central Bureau of Statistics. Public servants are forbidden to strike
New Zealand	More than 10 working days lost. Statistics exclude Public sector strikes	No	Yes	Information gathered by district offices of Dept of Labour
Norway	More than one day's duration	Yes	No	Questions to employees' and employers' organisations
Portugal	No restrictions on size. However, statistics exclude disputes which involve more than one company	Not known	No	
Spain	No restrictions on size	Yes	Yes	Monthly returns made by local province delegates of Ministry of Labour Statistics. Figures exclude Catalonia
Sweden	More than one hour's duration	Yes	No	Press reports compiled by State Conciliation Service are checked by employers' organisations and sent to Central Statistical Office
Switzerland	More than one day's duration	Yes	Yes	Federal Office for industry, crafts, occupations and employment collects press reports, and checks with trade unions and employers
United Kingdom	More than ten workers involved and of more than one day's duration, unless 100 or more working days lost	No	Yes	Local unemployment benefit offices make reports to Department of Employment HQ, which also checks press, unions and large employers
United States	More than one day's or shift's duration and more than 1,000 workers involved	No	Yes	Reports from press, employers, unions and agencies, followed up by questionnaires

Sources: July 1986 Employment Gazette, p. 268, reproduced with the permisson of HMSO.

Zealand where there has been an increase in the number of workers involved and working days lost between each of the five-year periods examined in the tables (there is not the same consistency in the case of the number of stoppages, with 1977–81 being the high point). In some other countries there is some consistency between the different measures of strike activity in that the same five-year period is the high point for strike incidence for all of those measures, though this is the case in less than half of all the countries looked at. In most countries the 1970s were more strike-prone than the early 1960s though there are a number of exceptions to this statement. If one looks, for example, at the number of working days lost in Iceland (see Table 2.3) the lowest totals for any of the five-year periods examined were recorded in 1977–81.

The three measures of stoppages that have been discussed above are the ones most regularly referred to. They give some indication with, as has been suggested, many qualifications, of the extent of strike action. They do not show though the nature of strike action, say in terms of duration. In fact, simply by examining the statistics discussed so far more fully one can get some idea of the average duration of stoppages in different countries. One can calculate for instance the average number of working days lost per worker involved in stoppages. This is shown in Table 2.5. On the basis of this kind of calculation one can note some quite significant variations between countries. There are a number of countries where the average number of working days lost per worker involved has been high (particularly Canada and the USA but also in countries like Ireland and, in the 1960s, Norway and Switzerland) while the average in other countries has been much lower (Australia, Austria, France and New Zealand). The differences between these figures range from 2 days at one extreme to 17 days at the other.

Some countries publish separate more detailed statistics on the duration of stoppages. These aim to show more directly the length of time stoppages last in the countries concerned. They tend to confirm the image produced from the other figures, though they differ in detail and they do not cover all of the countries. In the USA, between 1972 and 1981 64 per cent of all stoppages and 96 per cent of all working days lost through

Table 2.5: Average Number of Working Days Lost per Worker Involved, 1962–1984

	1962–66	1967–71	1972–76	1977–81	1982–84
Australia	1.6	1.7	2.5	2.6	2.9
Austria	1.5	2.1	1.4	3.4	2.5
Belgium	10.7	10.3	9.0	10.0	NA
Canada	14.4	20.1	14.5	19.4	14.8
Denmark	5.2	1.7	4.0	5.0	2.1
Finland	4.9	6.5	2.1	2.1	2.1
France	1.2	1.5	2.0	3.4	3.6
Germany	4.5	3.8	3.0	3.8	8.8
Iceland	11.9	10.7	9.1	10.1	7.9
Ireland	15.3	15.1	11.4	17.7	12.6
Italy	5.1	4.0	3.0	1.3	1.7
Japan	2.9	2.6	2.7	2.1	2.2
Netherlands	2.9	3.3	4.3	4.1	3.9
New Zealand	2.5	3.2	2.5	2.8	2.5
Norway	24.3	16.7	8.0	7.8	6.9
Spain	3.2	2.5	3.5	4.0	2.8
Sweden	11.3	7.8	5.2	4.0	1.6
Switzerland	18.7	14.0	5.3	3.1	5.2
United Kingdom	2.9	5.5	8.0	8.3	8.8
United States	14.8	17.0	15.8	21.6	NA

Sources and Notes: See Note 19, p. 29.

stoppages were accounted for by stoppages of 7 days duration or more. If a cut-off point much higher is used, then almost 30 per cent of all stoppages and 78 per cent of days lost were accounted for by stoppages of 30 days duration or more. This might be compared to the position in the Netherlands, where over 65 per cent of all stoppages were accounted for by stoppages lasting for less than 5 days. Of course, it is important to recognise that these statistics are subject to the same problems as other strike statistics, and figures for the duration of stoppages will be particularly affected by use of a minimum duration for inclusion.

It has long been recognised that there are major variations in strike incidence between industries. This is one of the reasons why, as was noted earlier, some commentators argue that comparisons of strikes between countries should concentrate on certain industries, or groups of industries, rather than try to look at all industries and services.

Table 2.6: *Stoppage Incidence: Annual Averages 1962–1984 in Mining, Manufacturing, Construction and Transport per 1,000 Employees*

	1962–66	1967–71	1972–76	1977–81	1982–84
Australia	366	796	1,507	1,135	677
Belgium	182	394	390	398	NA
Canada	766	1,687	2,203	1,569	980
Denmark	106	64	1,028	258	110
Finland	388	886	1,028	946	433
France	322	313	338	232	197
Germany (FR)	32	80	32	86	170
Ireland	1,199	952	780	1,977	610
Italy	1,393	1,697	2,001	1,513	1,380
Japan	250	194	294	48	20
Netherlands	16	42	82	80	50
New Zealand	166	350	506	798	837
Norway	98	20	116	64	153
Sweden	26	76	18	470	NA
Switzerland	10	2	4	1	—
United Kingdom	230	600	968	1,125	1,303
United States	790	1,649	1,054	900	NA

Sources and Notes: See Note 19, p. 29.

It has already been indicated that while this argument is recognised there is a contrary perspective which may have more force. It is not intended therefore to look in a comprehensive fashion at strike records between countries using a restricted range of industrial groups. However, a rather more limited look at this issue might be valuable. The most frequently discussed industrial group in these terms is that of mining, manufacturing, construction and transport. Table 2.6 looks at the record of different countries (because of difficulties with available data some countries covered in earlier tables are not dealt with in Table 2.6, specifically Austria, Iceland and Spain) for this industrial grouping over the period 1962–84 as far as the number of working days lost through disputes is concerned. On this basis Italy has a consistently high number of working days lost through stoppages in the industries concerned; in each five-year period more than 1,000 days were lost per 1,000 workers. A number of other countries came close to that position, including Canada and the USA. Others, like Switzerland, the Netherlands and West Germany, came at the opposite end of the spectrum. The comparison with Table 2.3 which looked at the same information on an all-industry basis is interesting. In almost all cases, the totals for the mining, manufacturing, construction and transport group are higher than those for all industries (the exception is Sweden for 1962–66 and 1972–6). This is what one would expect given knowledge of the industrial distribution of stoppages. In most cases the concentration on the restricted industry grouping makes very little difference to the rank order, though in some instances this is not the case. A number of examples can be given to illustrate broad consistency of ranking. When all industries and services were looked at, Italy and Iceland headed the league table. Iceland was not covered in Table 2.6 but, as has been noted, Italy was consistently high in that table (it was at the top in three five-year periods, second for one and third for one). The next group of countries when all industries and services were looked at was Australia, Canada, Finland, Ireland and the United States. They occupy a somewhat similar position when just mining, manufacturing, construction and transport are looked at. The group of countries that lost fewest days when all industries and services were looked at was West Germany, the Netherlands and Switzerland. This was generally the case if the restricted range of industries is looked at (West Germany's record was worse in 1982–4 than it had been in earlier periods in both tables). The relationship between stoppage rates by all industries and services and those by the mining, manufacturing, construction and transport, though, varies in detail from country to country and from time period to time period. For example, in the case of the USA the stoppage rate for the restricted industrial grouping was more than double that for all industries and services for all of the five-year periods covered. In the case of the UK the restricted industry grouping stoppage rate was less than double that for all industries and services for the first four time periods considered: for the last time period it was more than twice as great. The ratio between the two sets of figures was more stable in the case of Australia (the restricted industry grouping rate was always more than 80 per cent higher than that for all industries and services in the time periods looked at and in two time periods, was marginally more than 100 per cent higher), whereas in West Germany the restricted industrial grouping stoppage rate generally showed less of an increase over the all industries and services figure than it did in many other countries (between 1962 and 1966 it was only 39 per cent higher) though the variation between time periods was greater than in the case of Australia (the 1982–4 rate for the restricted grouping was 93 per cent higher than the all industries and services rate). The variations in the relationship between the two sets of figures between countries are in part a reflection of the different industrial complexions of the countries concerned, though variations over time in industrial strike propensities within countries complicate matters. In a particular time period the relationship between the two sets of figures in one country also may be affected markedly simply by one major strike or a series of strikes.

The above discussion has developed from an assessment of variations in stoppage incidence between industries. It is important to record also that such variations on some occasions may be so important that in practice individual industries can dominate strike activity in a country. This has been most notable in the case of the coal-mining industry. In some countries over a number of years strikes in the coal-mining industry have been greater in number and intensity than those in all other industries and services put together. In the case of this particular industry as well there have been major variations in strike activity over time so that while the coal mining industry has dominated strike activity for long periods of time, on other occasions it has been less important. This domination of strike activity by individual industries can mean that general strike trends are critically affected by developments in just that one industry. This has led some people to argue that strike trends need to be looked at with dominant industries both included and excluded. Such an argument has considerable merit though it obviously complicates the exercise of discussing trends enormously. It cannot be taken on board in this general review though it will be looked at again in the next chapter when a more detailed discussion of the experience of individual countries is attempted.

CONCLUSION

Differences in the collection, definition and practice of handling strike statistics between countries make comparison difficult. The more one looks at the matter the more complex it seems. Some of the differences that have been highlighted are major ones and significantly distort any comparisons one might try to make. However, in most cases the problems caused by such matters are not so great that general trends and comparisons cannot be made. Major differences in strike propensity between some countries and some groups of countries remain that are not simply a reflection of the basis on which the statistics have been collected or presented.

Inevitably these differences between countries lead one to seek explanations. If the explanations are not simply to be found in the definitions used or the basis of the collection and presentation of the statistics, then where should one look? This issue will be turned to in a later chapter. First, though, more detailed examination of strike trends and records will be attempted for simply three countries, Australia, USA and the UK, so that some of the issues that could not be addressed in this chapter can be approached.

NOTES

1. The ILO established guidelines for member nations in 1926. The guidelines are discussed by K. Walsh, *Strikes in Europe and the United States,* Frances Pinter, London, 1983 and T.G. Sweet and D. Jackson, *The Classification and Interpretation of Strike Statistics: An International Comparative Analysis,* University of Aston Management Centre, Working Paper No. 97, 1978.
2. See T. Kennedy, *European Labor Relations* (D.C. Heath, Lexington, 1980), p. 181 for a discussion of the 1978 lock-out when the printers' union struck in six companies and the industry responded with a lock-out in all newspaper firms in the country.

3. K. Walsh, 'Industrial Disputes in France, West Germany, Italy and the United Kingdom: Measurement and Incidence,' *Industrial Relations Journal,* Vol. 13, No. 4 (Winter 1982) p. 68.
4. E. Batstone, I. Boranston and S. Frenkel, *The Social Organisation of Strikes,* Blackwell, Oxford, 1978, p. 18.
5. *Ibid.,* for further discussion.
6. *Monthly Labor Bulletin,* March 1986, p. 55.
7. R. Kalbitz, *Aussperrungen in der Bundesrepublic.* E.V.A., Köln-Frankfurt, 1979. Quoted by W. Muller-Jentsch, 'Strikes and strike trends in West Germany, 1950–78', *Industrial Relations Journal,* Vol. 12, No. 4 (July/August 1981), pp. 36–5).
8. W. Brown (ed.), *The Changing Contours of British Industrial Relations,* Blackwell, Oxford, 1981.
9. W. Korpi, 'Unofficial Strikes in Sweden', *British Journal of Industrial Relations.,* Vol. 19, No. 1 (March 1981), pp. 66–8.
10. *Ibid.,* p. 73.
11. *Ibid.,* p. 74.
12. In 1975 a category was introduced in the Italian strike statistics which referred to stoppages that have no connection with terms and conditions of employment. Stoppages classified in this way would range wider than a narrow definition of political strikes, but this category can be taken as giving some guide to the importance of political strikes in Italy. In the five years after the introduction of this category in excess of 20 per cent of all days lost through strikes were classified within it.
13. K. Walsh (1982), *loc. cit.,* p. 11.
14. Although the 20 major Western industrial nations are covered in this table and in subsequent ones in the same series the information is not complete because in a number of instances it has not been ·published. The information is based on that published by the International Labour Organisation. See Note 19 for more details of the basis of the preparation of this series of tables.
15. The period 1962–84 has been chosen to allow the current position to be set in a reasonable historical context, though a fuller examination of the topic would necessitate a longer series.
16. For a full discussion of the rank ordering for 1962 and 1981 see S.W. Creigh and G. Poland, *Differences in Strike Activity Between Industrial Countries in the Post-War Period,* National Institute of Labour Studies, Flinders University of South Australia, Working Paper No. 59, 1983. This working paper presents a comprehensive analysis of strike statistics over this period in a way that could not be attempted in this chapter.
17. Walsh (1983), *op. cit.*
18. For a review of this discussion relating to British material see S.W. Creigh, 'Research Note: Stoppage of Work Incidence in the United Kingdom, 1913–1977', *International Journal of Social Economics,* Vol. 7, No. 5 (1980) pp. 296–300; E.W. Evans, 'Research Note: On Some Recent Econometric Models of Strike Frequency', *Industrial Relations Journal,* Vol. 7, No. 3 (1976), pp. 72–6; E.W. Evans and S.W. Creigh (eds) *Industrial Conflict in Britain,* Cass, London, 1977; D. Sapsford, 'On

Some Recent Econometric Models of Strike Frequency: A Reply, *Industrial Relations Journal,* Vol. 8, No. 1 (1977), pp. 70–1.

19. The tables of stoppages have been assembled using the basis established by S.W. Creigh and G. Poland, *Op. cit.* and updating their data. Information on stoppages is taken from the ILO *Yearbook of Labour Statistics,* while information on employment has been taken from Organisation for Economic Co-operation and Development, *Labour Force Statistics,* (wage earners and salaried employees). In a number of individual cases problems have arisen within the statistics. No stoppage figures are available for France for 1968, for France monthly averages were produced for years 1983 and 1984 for the number of stoppages and the number of workers involved, and for the Netherlands data was not available for 1984.

The published French statistics exclude agriculture and public administration. West Germany does not collect statistics on the number of stoppages as such, though the number of establishments involved in stoppages is calculated.

3   Strikes in Australia, USA and the United Kingdom

In the last chapter the pattern of strikes in Western industrial nations was examined in a very general fashion. Major trends and variations were noted but the coverage was too broad to allow detailed investigation of individual issues or developments. The aim of this chapter is to move some way to redress the balance. The strike records of just three countries are examined: Australia, USA and the United Kingdom. The concentration on three countries permits more discussion of detail and allows aspects of strike records which were not examined in the last chapter to be covered. Nevertheless, it must be accepted at the outset that what is presented must still be a summary. Books could be, and have been, written about simply one period of the strike activity of just one of these countries. Certainly far more could be said than could possibly be covered in one chapter.

AUSTRALIA

There is relatively little written material on the pre-Second World War stoppage record of Australia. Possibly the best known piece of work is an article by Oxnam[1] which was built on subsequently by the same author. More has been written in recent years, both about general trends and about more specific matters.[2] The statistics themselves are reasonably comprehensive though Wooden and Creigh note that because the Australian Bureau of Statistics has to regard the information it obtains as confidential, 'raw information' cannot be disclosed to third parties and this limits the analysis researchers can undertake.[3]

Table 3.1: Stoppages of Work in Australia, 1913–1984 (five-yearly periods)

Period	Number of Stoppages	Number of Workers Involved in Stoppages (000s)	Number of Working Days Lost through Stoppages (000s)
1913–17	371	109	1,715
1918–22	476	130	2,117
1923–27	416	144	1,244
1928–32	198	65	1,441
1933–37	201	57	406
1938–42	462	181	933
1943–47	904	313	1,462
1948–52	1,247	386	1,419
1953–57	1,378	415	943
1958–62	1,000	336	529
1963–67	1,303	462	749
1968–72	2,233	1,162	2,101
1973–77	2,385	1,398	3,577
1978–82	2,345	1,217	3,153
1983–84	1,876	516	1,474

Sources: Commonwealth Bureau of Census and Statistics, *Labour Report;* Australian Bureau of Statistics, *Industrial Disputes*

Table 3.1 supplements the information given in the last chapter about the major trends in Australia's strike record. It shows the number of stoppages, the number of workers involved in stoppages and the number of working days lost through stoppages by five-year periods. From this table it can be seen that prior to the Second World War the number of stoppages varied from an average of around 200 to almost 500 a year. After the Second World War the number of stoppages increased, so that by 1943–7 the number recorded was almost twice as high as it had been in 1938–42. The number continued to rise in the mid-1950s and although it dipped in the late 1950s (the 1959 total was exactly the same as that recorded in 1946) it rose again in the 1960s and 1970s and continued at a high level into the 1980s. The total collapsed, however, in 1982 to a level more reminiscent of the 1960s.

The trends with regard to workers involved in stoppages showed some similarities though the details differed. In the pre-Second World War years the annual averages varied from just over 50,000 to over 180,000. The number rose in the immediate post-Second World War years and into the 1950s. The 1953–7 annual average was more than twice as great as the highest annual average for any pre-war five-year period. The total fell back again in the following five-year period though there was considerable variation from year to year (the 1960 figure, at 603,000 was a post-war high). The most significant increase, though, occurred in the early 1970s: in two years the total exceeded two million. The total fell back a little in the late 1970s and in the 1980s fell back quite markedly.

The number of working days lost through stoppages in the first 20 years of the table varied from an average of little more than one million a year to more than double that number. The total declined in the 1933–37 period although it rose again over the following fifteen years. The averages for the 1950s and most of the 1960s were at historically low levels and it wasn't until the end of the 1960s that the trend was reversed. The totals in the 1970s and early 1980s were significantly higher than they had been in earlier years, averaging over three million working days (the highest total for a single year was in 1974 when over six million working days were lost) though in 1982 the number of working days lost, like the number of strikes and workers involved, fell back dramatically.

For most of the period under discussion Australia's strike pattern has been dominated by disputes in just one industry, coal mining. The industrial distribution of strike activity is dealt with in more detail later: for the moment the need is to record the effect that changes in the strike record of one industry can have on the general trends. In the inter-war years stoppages in coal mining accounted for up to 80 per cent of all strikes, and over 60 per cent of all working days lost through strikes. If stoppages in coal mining are excluded from the overall figures, then the general trends look rather different. For example, if coal mining is included in the overall total then the average number of days lost in Australia fell from 1,441 a year in 1928–32 to 749 in

1963–7. However, if coal mining is excluded from the overall total then over the same period the average number of days lost rose from 563 to 700 a year. If the number of stoppages are considered, then the impact of the exclusion of coal mining is different. The contrast is between a rise from 198 to 1,309 (with coal mining included) and a rise from 66 to 1,008 (with coal mining excluded) over the period 1928–32 and 1963–7. If, though, a different time period is considered then the impact of the exclusion of coal mining is more dramatic. If the 1948–52 and the 1963–7 periods are examined then the overall total, with coal mining included, falls from 1,419 to 1,309, but with coal mining excluded it rises from 479 to 1,008. The coal mining industry is an extreme case which points to the importance of recognising that general trends mask considerable variations between component parts, and at times changes in the component parts have a significant impact on the general trends.

The changes and developments noted so far have to be seen in the context of changes in the size of the Australian labour force. At the beginning of the period under discussion the labour force stood at around 1.6 million: by the end of the period it had risen to about 7 million. Of course, there have been changes in the size of the labour force in other countries since the beginning of the century, but the Australian changes are particularly dramatic and need to be taken into account in assessing strike trends. The greater than threefold increase in the labour force offers some explanation for the increase in the number of strikes (it does not though explain the whole of the increase, for the strike frequency per worker was still about twice as high in the 1970s as it was in the early 1920s and about five times as high as it had been during the depression). The increase in size of the labour force similarly modifies the apparent increase in the number of workers involved between the 1920s and 1970s and more than accounts for the increase in days lost. The variations over shorter periods of time are less influenced by changes in the labour force but still need to be taken into account.

There has been discussion by a number of writers (such as Oxnam and Bentley and Hughes[4]) about how these trends might be examined in terms of strike cycles. This discussion, particularly the links made between strike cycles and economic conditions, will be examined more closely in a later chapter. However, Wooden and Creigh,[5] in their discussion of strike cycles, also drew attention to a recent trend in Australian strike statistics which is not obvious given the presentation in Table 3.1 (by five-year periods) but which is clearly relevant at this point. They noted 'a dramatic collapse of strike activity' in 1982 and 1983 which they linked to record post-war unemployment levels. This collapse in strike activity can be seen, in part, from Table 3.1 by looking at the figures for 1983, but cannot be seen in full from that source because the 1982 figure is masked by the rest of the 1978–82 five-year period.

Table 3.2: Size and Duration of Stoppages of Work in Australia, 1913–1984 (five-yearly periods)

Period	Average Number of Workers Involved in Each Strike	Average Duration of Each Strike (days)
1913–17	293	16
1918–22	273	16
1923–27	346	9
1928–32	328	22
1933–37	284	7
1938–42	392	5
1943–47	346	5
1948–52	310	4
1953–57	301	2
1958–62	336	2
1963–67	355	2
1968–72	520	2
1973–77	586	3
1978–82	519	3
1983–84	275	3

Sources: Commonwealth Bureau of Census and Statistics, *Labour Report;* Australian Bureau of Statistics, *Industrial Disputes*

Table 3.2 shows one measure of the size and duration of stoppages in Australia between 1913 and 1984. Although they are fairly crude averages and need to be used with caution they at least give a guide to trends. From this table it can be seen that the size of strikes stayed fairly constant at around 300 workers for most of the period, though 1968–82 was an exception, when the figure rose above 500. The average duration of strikes rose in the 1928–32 period though subsequently the decline in duration that had been established prior to the depression was seen once again. The average duration of strikes dropped to only two days for much of the post-Second World War period though it rose a little in the 1970s and 1980s.

A more detailed analysis of the duration of stoppages is presented in Table 3.3 The first part of the table looks at duration in terms of the number of stoppages. In his commentary on these statistics, looking at the period up to 1950, Oxnam pointed out that over 50 per cent of all stoppages were very short, lasting for only one day or less. He also noted that with 'the exception of the depression years from 1931–34, the proportion of strikes of a day or less has increased continously over the years, and in 1946–50 was almost double what it was in 1913–18.'[6] The dominance of short strikes continued through the 1950s and into the 1960s. However, although during this period more than 50 per cent of all stoppages were of one day or less the upward trend in the proportion of short stoppages had already been reversed. Bentley notes that in the early 1970s there was 'a period of heightened strike activity' which was 'marked by an increase in the length of strikes'[7] (from Table 3.3 it can be seen that the proportion of stoppages lasting for more than two days increased from 31.3 per cent to 39.3 per cent between the periods 1966–70 and 1971–5). The proportion of lengthy stoppages declined somewhat after 1976 but it remained markedly higher than it had been in the 1960s.

In the second part of Table 3.3 the duration of stoppages is looked at from the point of view of the number of days lost. As one would expect, the position is different in detail from the discussion of the first part. Whereas for most of the period 1913–82 more than 40 per cent of all stoppages lasted for a day or less, at no time did strikes of this duration account for more than 30 per cent of all days lost. Nevertheless, the pattern established from a discussion of the first part of the table is broadly confirmed. The general trend from 1913–60 was for an increase in the proportion of days lost through short strikes (there were variations in the trend over this period but the

Table 3.3: Duration of Stoppages in Australia, 1913–1982

Period	1 day & less %	2 days & more than 1 day %	Over 2 days & less than 1 week %	1 week & less than 4 weeks %	4 weeks & over %	Total %
			Number of Stoppages			
1913–15	36.6	13.2	18.8	21.3	10.1	100.0
1916–20	33.9	11.7	19.8	21.6	13.0	100.0
1921–25	43.2	13.5	16.6	18.3	8.4	100.0
1926–30	40.6	13.2	16.9	21.0	8.3	100.0
1931–35	34.7	14.8	20.0	22.4	8.1	100.0
1936–40	49.8	16.1	16.8	13.0	4.3	100.0
1941–45	58.3	14.3	13.8	11.8	1.8	100.0
1946–50	65.3	13.3	11.8	7.7	1.9	100.0
1951–55	62.8	15.8	10.4	9.0	2.0	100.0
1956–60	59.9	16.6	12.5	9.3	1.7	100.0
1961–65	55.8	18.7	16.6	8.4	0.5	100.0
1966–70	49.8	18.9	19.5	11.1	0.7	100.0
1971–75	43.5	17.2	19.9	17.4	2.0	100.0
1976–80	44.6	19.1	17.9	16.2	2.2	100.0
1981–82	46.1	18.2	16.8	16.6	2.3	100.0
			Number of Days Lost			
1913–15	3.1	2.0	4.8	25.1	65.0	100.0
1916–20	1.4	0.8	2.4	10.3	85.1	100.0
1921–25	6.1	3.8	6.6	26.9	56.6	100.0
1926–30	2.2	1.1	2.4	12.8	81.5	100.0
1931–35	4.7	3.4	11.3	34.9	45.7	100.0
1936–40	7.9	3.6	7.2	17.7	63.6	100.0
1941–45	13.2	6.7	11.8	37.8	30.5	100.0
1946–50	11.8	3.5	11.1	20.3	53.3	100.0
1951–55	23.9	11.9	10.4	28.9	24.9	100.0
1956–60	28.6	11.6	12.8	31.6	15.4	100.0
1961–65	26.8	15.7	17.5	23.7	16.3	100.0
1966–70	23.3	24.4	18.4	27.7	6.2	100.0
1971–75	13.7	10.4	16.4	47.9	11.6	100.0
1976–80	17.9	18.8	22.7	26.1	14.5	100.0
1981–82	7.2	8.8	23.0	48.2	12.8	100.0

Sources: Commonwealth Bureau of Statistics, *Labour Report;* Australian Bureau of Statistics, *Industrial Disputes.*

general pattern is clear). The proportion of days lost through short strikes declined in the 1961–75 period with this trend being reversed between 1976 and 1980. In the last time period the proportion of days lost through short stoppages was lower than at any time in the post-Second War period.

The discussion of trends of the size and duration of stoppages is further complicated if it is recognised that the overall patterns are a reflection, sometimes, of moves in a different direction, say in particular industries. Waters, for example, notes how trends in the coal mining industry in the late 1940s were different to those in all industries and services. Waters also notes other variations in the components in the overall trends as far as duration is concerned. 'In the 1970s both the frequency and the duration of strikes covering wage issues showed marked rises. Frequency rose from 9.2 per 100,000 workers in the 1960s to 18.9 in the 1970s, and duration increased from 1.75 man-days lost per striker to 3.11.' At the same time, however, the frequency of strikes over 'other issues' reduced, and the duration, rather than rising, in line with the trend for wage disputes, 'stabilized at about one man-day lost per striker'.[8]

The variations in strike propensity between industries are presented in Tables 3.4 and 3.5. Table 3.4 shows a detailed breakdown of the share in stoppages and days lost through stoppages by industry over the whole of the 1913–82 period. This table allows an impression to be gained of the relative importance of different industries in terms of stoppages. The dominance of the mining industry up until the immediate Second World War years which was referred to earlier is clear and has been noted by many commentators.[9] No other industry came anywhere near the record of mining. The position started to change, though, from the early 1950s onwards: this has been seen by many as a crucial development for Australian industrial relations. The proportion of stoppages accounted for by the mining industry declined from 76 per cent in 1948–52 to 11 per cent in 1968–72. The comparable figures for working days lost were 33 per cent and 9 per cent. The position changed a little after the mid-1970s but mining has never regained its dominant position. It is also worthwhile recording that while coal mining has generally dominated the record of this group (between 1928 and 1948 less than 4 per cent of all stoppages and working days lost in mining were accounted for by non coal-mining activities) there have been changes in recent years. Between 1975 and 1982 there were more stoppages in the non-coal-mining than the coal-

Table 3.4: Stoppages of Work by Industry in Australia, 1913–1982
A: 1913–1967

	Wood, Saw-mill, Timber	Engine-ering, Metal Works	Food, Drink	Clothing, Hats, Boots	Books, Printing	Other Manu-facturing	Building
% of stoppages in:							
1913–17	1.6	6.3	4.4	0.7	0.3	6.3	3.2
1918–22	1.4	3.1	6.3	0.8	0.3	4.7	2.3
1923–27	1.2	4.8	2.9	0.7	0.5	2.0	3.6
1928–32	1.3	2.8	5.8	1.2	0.4	1.1	2.3
1933–37	0.6	6.4	2.8	1.0	0.1	2.6	0.9
1938–42	0.3	8.4	2.1	1.2	0.1	1.9	1.7
1943–47	0.4	7.4	4.0	0.7	0.3	2.9	1.1
1948–52	0.1	4.4	2.0	0.2	0.2	1.7	1.3
1953–57	0.0	6.1	3.6	0.2	0.2	3.6	4.3
1958–62	0.1	13.8	7.9	0.4	0.5	6.5	8.5
1963–67	0.0	27.9	8.1	0.4	1.3	7.4	14.1
% of working days lost in:							
1913–17	2.4	7.5	3.0	0.1	0.0	5.1	2.1
1918–22	0.3	4.7	3.3	1.2	1.2	2.2	2.7
1923–27	1.0	9.5	2.0	0.1	0.3	0.6	6.8
1928–32	26.3	0.7	1.5	0.6	0.3	0.1	0.1
1933–37	0.6	20.7	2.4	1.9	0.1	2.8	0.2
1938–42	0.2	14.1	2.3	7.5	0.0	4.1	2.0
1943–47	1.0	27.9	11.1	1.1	2.6	4.3	4.2
1948–52	0.0	13.9	3.5	0.2	0.4	3.2	1.0
1953–57	0.0	16.7	9.1	0.3	0.6	6.9	6.0
1958–62	0.1	20.9	10.5	0.2	1.1	8.4	7.3
1863–67	0.0	28.3	11.3	0.8	2.2	9.3	10.9

(table continues)

mining part of the group and while in the case of the number of working days lost coal mining still dominated the group it did not do so to the same extent as it had in, say, the pre-Second World War years.

At the same time as the mining industry was figuring less in the strike statistics other industries were becoming more important. In the 1950s and early 1960s shipping and stevedoring and water transport came to account for a higher proportion of stoppages but this trend was reversed in later years (in 1967 moves were made to stabilize employment in the industry though it is

Table 3.4: Stoppages of Work by Industry in Australia, 1913–1982
A: 1913–1967

Mining	Rail & Tramway Services	Other Land Transport	Shipping Steve- doring	Agricult- ural, Pastoral	Domestic Hotels	Miscel- laneous	TOTAL
50.8	7.7	1.3	6.7	2.8	0.4	7.7	100.00
60.6	3.9	0.4	6.9	3.7	0.7	4.9	100.00
70.0	2.0	0.3	5.4	0.9	0.2	5.6	100.00
69.9	1.2	0.7	4.6	1.1	0.5	7.3	100.00
69.5	0.5	0.3	3.2	1.6	0.1	10.4	100.00
80.1	0.9	0.2	1.1	0.1	0.1	1.9	100.00
75.6	2.1	0.4	3.5	0.2	0.3	1.1	100.00
76.0	1.7	0.7	10.2	. 0.1	0.1	1.2	100.00
55.7	2.6	1.1	21.0	0.1	0.1	1.4	100.00
33.5	2.0	2.2	22.5	0.1	0.6	1.4	100.00
17.3	1.6	2.5	16.5	0.0	1.0	1.9	100.00
42.9	12.4	3.2	15.9	2.1	0.1	3.2	100.00
42.2	2.1	0.2	31.1	1.1	0.1	7.6	100.00
63.8	6.0	0.1	6.0	0.2	1.1	2.5	100.00
62.3	0.9	0.1	5.5	1.0	0.0	0.6	100.00
55.5	0.7	0.4	5.2	3.8	0.0	5.7	100.00
66.3	0.5	0.1	2.3	0.0	0.0	0.6	100.00
30.1	6.5	0.6	8.6	1.4	0.2	0.4	100.00
33.7	31.6	0.6	10.8	0.0	0.1	1.0	100.00
27.9	2.0	1.7	27.0	0.4	0.1	1.3	100.00
23.9	4.2	2.1	18.7	0.1	0.7	1.8	100.00
11.7	6.2	5.2	10.4	0.0	1.2	2.5	100.00

difficult to determine the precise link between such moves and strike activity). The rise in the proportion of stoppages and the proportion of working days lost through stoppages in the engineering and metal works category has been more marked and consistent.

It is, of course, important to relate the strike incidence in different industries to the size of those industries and the number of employees in them. In some cases major changes have taken place in the number of employees in industries over a relatively short period of time. If one looks, for example, at the period 1973–84 then there has been a significant decline in the number of people employed in construction (from 503,200 to

Table 3.4: (continued) *Stoppages of Work by Industry in Australia, 1913–1982*

B: 1968–1982

	Number of Stoppages			Number of Days Lost		
	1968–72 %	1973–77 %	1978–82 %	1968–72 %	1973–77 %	1978–82 %
Agriculture, forestry, fisheries & hunting	—	0.2	0.3	—	0.2	1.2
Mining—coal	8.9	8.4	11.8	6.0	4.8	12.3
other	2.7	7.5	13.2	3.5	4.4	6.8
Manufacturing— food, beverages, tobacco	9.7	7.9	5.6	7.2	10.2	10.7
textiles, clothing, footwear	0.6	0.5	0.4	0.9	0.9	1.0
Wood, wood products, furniture	0.1	0.6	0.3	0.1	0.5	0.5
paper, printing, publishing	1.2	1.6	1.7	1.7	2.4	3.4
chemical, petroleum & coal products	0.0	2.3	1.8	0.0	1.3	1.5
metal products, machinery & equipment	30.0	26.2	28.9	28.0	33.0	23.9
other manufacturing	6.3	3.3	1.6	4.6	2.5	1.8
Electricity, gas & water	1.2	1.6	3.4	3.0	3.7	2.8
Construction	11.8	12.5	8.5	24.0	16.1	8.8
Wholesale and retail trade	0.0	2.4	2.0	0.0	3.9	4.0
Transportation and Communication —road transport, other transport & storage, communication	3.0	3.0	3.4	4.2	4.2	4.0
railway transport, air transport	2.9	3.0	3.0	5.8	2.5	4.6
stevedoring	14.2	9.6	4.6	4.5	1.6	2.5
water transport	2.0	2.4	1.9	0.5	0.6	0.5
Recreation, personal and other services	1.6	1.5	1.2	1.9	2.7	2.2
Other industries	3.7	5.5	6.4	4.0	4.5	7.5
TOTAL	100.0	100.0	100.0	100.0	100.0	100.0

Note: The categorisation of industries was changed from 1968, though in many cases the change did not have a major impact.
— = less than 0.1
Sources: Commonwealth Bureau of Census and Statistics, *Labour Report;* Australian Bureau of Statistics, *Industrial Disputes.*

433,400) and a significant increase in some of the service industries (there was an increase in finance, property and business services from 401,300 to 615,000). There was also an increase in the number of employees in the mining group as a whole, from 69,500 to 100,000. It is not possible within the space available to look at this issue in full over a long time period. Nevertheless, the most recent time period, 1973–84, is covered in Table 3.5 and this takes account of the number of workers engaged in an industry by standardising the days lost through stoppages according to the number of employees.

It can be seen from Table 3.5 that in every year, except 1978 and 1983, coal mining lost more working days through stoppages than any other industry: in those two years it came next in the ranking. Thus, despite the decline in the proportion of stoppages and working days lost through stoppages accounted for by mining in the economy as a whole, mining, and particularly coal mining, remains a comparatively highly strike-prone industry in Australia. A similar picture emerges in stevedoring. Throughout the 1973–84 period, when the number of employees is taken into account, a high number of working days is seen to have been lost in this industry through stoppages (in 1978 higher than mining, and frequently second only to mining): the exceptions are the comparatively low figures for 1982 to 1984, but in those three years the total was still higher than the all-industry average and these figures were available only as part of a larger grouping. In earlier discussion the growth in the percentage of stoppages, and days lost through stoppages, in a number of other industries was noted. Nevertheless, Table 3.5 shows that despite this growth only metal manufacturing and construction generally lost more working days than the all-industry average (construction failed to do so in 1978) and the 'other industry' category was significantly lower than the all-industry total for all of the period.

Tables 3.6 and 3.7 show the officially recorded causes of stoppages in Australia between 1913 and 1982. The basis of this classification changed on a number of occasions over this period but a comparable series can be constructed if only the broad categories are examined.[10] From Table 3.6 it can be seen that most stoppages were apparently caused by 'physical working conditions and managerial policy'. In the 1950s, the proportion

Table 3.5: *Number of Working Days Lost through Stoppages in Australia, by Industry, per 1,000 Employees, 1973–1983*

	Mining		Manufacturing		Construction	Transport & Storage: Communication:		Other Industries	All Industries
	Coal	Other	Metal Products, Machinery & Equipment	Other		Stevedoring Services	Other		
1973	4,268	2,860	1,405	889	1,119	2,705	256	133	552
1974	7,725	2,625	4,876	1,026	3,009	6,172	1,352	194	1,273
1975	14,991	1,576	2,376	674	1,255	2,581	379	230	717
1976	6,602	3,982	1,467	1,245	1,433	2,276	1,010	292	773
1977	4,415	3,182	398	679	591	2,625	450	101	336
1978	5,669	2,415	1,460	747	378	8,418	435	74	434
1979	8,744	5,412	1,818	1,147	1,044	8,106	1,126	270	787
1980	23,533	3,915	1,181	1,094	681	2,556	354	202	650
1981	10,011	5,141	2,285	984	1,423	3,014	957	239	800
1982	14,483	2,691	487	512	782	670		85	396
1983	3,240	3,390	348	186	1,269	489		42	249
1984	3,543	3,286	327	387	427	346		94	246

Notes: 1. Excluding agricultural etc., and private households employing staff.
2. Method of estimating number of employees changed after 1979 because the series, *Civilian Employees*, Australia, was suspended from that date.

Sources: Australian Bureau of Statistics, *Labour Statistics: Australia 1983*; Australian Bureau of Statistics, *Labour Statistics: Australia, 1984.*

Table 3.6: Stoppages of Work in Australia, by Cause 1913–1982

	Number of Stoppages Caused by				
	Wages, Hours & Leave	*Physical Working Conditions and Managerial Policy*	*Trade Unionism*	*Other*	*Total*
	%	%	%	%	%
1913–15	39.8	44.5	9.5	6.2	100.0
1916–20	42.2	39.0	12.7	6.1	100.0
1921–25	31.0	50.0	8.0	11.0	100.0
1926–30	26.1	47.3	10.1	16.5	100.0
1931–35	31.8	50.4	7.7	10.1	100.0
1936–40	26.2	45.3	12.2	16.3	100.0
1941–45	20.9	49.7	8.5	20.9	100.0
1946–50	17.5	50.8	8.2	23.5	100.0
1951–55	10.2	60.8	11.8	17.2	100.0
1956–60	10.6	61.3	8.7	19.4	100.0
1961–65	23.5	59.1	8.6	8.8	100.0
1966–70	32.3	52.4	9.3	6.0	100.0
1971–75	40.5	43.4	10.8	5.3	100.0
1976–80	28.4	58.2	9.5	3.9	100.0
1981–82	31.0	56.3	8.1	4.6	100.0

Notes: 1. 1913–1971 stoppages beginning in year. 1972 onwards stoppages in progress.
2. 1982 onwards leave, pensions, compensations, provisions is in 'other'.

Sources: Commonwealth Bureau of Census and Statistics, *Labour Report;* Australian Bureau of Statistics, *Industrial Disputes.*

accounted for by this category exceeded 60 per cent and while there were marked variations in the total for the period as a whole it only once dipped below 40 per cent (in that case to 39 per cent for 1916–20). Wages, hours and leave are seen to have been a less important cause of stoppages over the whole period covered by the table. The decline in this total in the post-Second World War years is particularly noticeable and has excited comment;[11] although the total started to rise from the 1960s it has remained less important as a recorded cause than physical working conditions and managerial policy. The position is somewhat different in terms of the number of working days lost

Table 3.7: Number of Working Days Lost through Stoppages in Australia, by Cause 1913–1982

| | Number of Working Days Lost through Stoppages Caused by: | | | | |
| | Wages, Hours & Leave | Physical Working Conditions and Managerial Policy | Trade Unionism | Other | Total |
	%	%	%	%	%
1913–15	39.0	46.8	12.8	1.4	100.0
1916–20	46.0	9.0	43.8	1.2	100.0
1921–25	37.1	35.2	8.1	19.6	100.0
1926–30	74.4	15.3	6.2	4.1	100.0
1931–35	52.1	35.3	4.5	8.1	100.0
1936–40	18.2	41.0	5.6	35.2	100.0
1941–45	23.7	42.0	12.5	21.8	100.0
1946–50	58.2	25.5	6.1	10.2	100.0
1951–55	33.4	45.4	11.6	9.6	100.0
1956–60	33.7	46.0	5.8	14.5	100.0
1961–65	50.5	38.8	4.0	6.7	100.0
1966–70	52.7	36.8	3.9	6.6	100.0
1971–75	75.5	15.2	4.4	5.4	100.0
1976–80	47.3	24.1	3.4	25.2	100.0
1981–82	73.5	21.5	2.8	2.2	100.0

Notes: 1. 1913–1921 working days lost in stoppages beginning in year. 1922 onwards working days lost in stoppages in progress in year.
2. 1982 onwards leave, pensions, compensations, provisions is in 'other' category.

Sources: Commonwealth of Australia. *Labour Report*; Australian Bureau of Statistics, *Industrial Disputes*.

through stoppages (see Table 3.7). Frequently 'wages, hours and leave' has been the most important category. Nevertheless there have been significant variations over the whole period. The decline in the 1930s and again in the 1950s was marked, but so was the rise from the 1960s onwards (to 75 per cent in 1971–5). The category 'physical working conditions and managerial policy' has not dominated this measure of the causes of stoppages to the same extent as it did in the case of the number of stoppages. However, for parts of the period it has been a more important cause than the 'wages, hours and leave' category, particularly in the 1930s and the 1950s.

Generally trade unionism has been relatively unimportant as a cause of stoppages in terms of both the number of stoppages and the number of working days lost. However, there have been exceptions to this general rule. The outstanding one was the 1916–20 period when it accounted for 43.8 per cent of all working days lost through stoppages. There have also been important variations in this matter by industry, for in particular instances trade union matters have been far more important than would be suggested by an analysis of the general position. Wright has examined the position for the second half of the 1970s and has highlighted those industries reacting to technological and other changes as those most affected by disputes over trade union matters.[12]

The residual category, 'other causes' was of some importance in the late 1930s and early 1940s. Since the 1950s it appears to have been less important. In 1976–80 it accounted for over a quarter of all working days lost through stoppages, though in fact the five-year average was distorted by the figures for just one year, 1976, when over 50 per cent of days lost were accounted for by the 'other' category. In that year the Australian Council of Trade Unions held its first national 24-hour strike over the government's changes to the Medibank (national health insurance).

The pattern of stoppages has varied considerably between individual states in Australia. Table 3.8 shows the number of working days lost, by state, per 1,000 employees, between 1973 and 1984. In general, New South Wales and Victoria have lost a relatively high number of working days through stoppages, whereas South Australia has lost relatively few. However, there have been significant changes in rank order between states from one year to the next. Victoria had next to the lowest number of working days lost through stoppages in 1982 to 1984 whereas in 1974, 1975, 1976 and 1979 it recorded more working days lost through stoppages than any other state; similarly whereas Western Australia lost fewer working days through stoppages than any other state in 1974 and 1975, it was at the opposite end of the rankings in 1977 and 1983.

Table 3.8: *Number of Working Days Lost through Stoppages in Australia, by State, per 1,000 Employees, 1973–1984*

	New South Wales	Victoria	Queensland	South Australia	Western Australia	Tasmania	Australia
1973	622	590	509	296	313	1,089	552
1974	1,462	1,757	807	686	656	672	1,273
1975	831	910	718	277	253	305	717
1976	847	1,051	638	323	623	464	773
1977	308	433	359	65	532	197	336
1978	555	346	536	172	473	261	434
1979	744	1,090	680	395	832	439	787
1980	660	792	866	132	445	659	650
1981	1,028	865	624	320	552	456	800
1982	481	260	672	102	352	432	396
1983	288	163	178	114	581	471	149
1984	355	131	301	56	251	352	242

Notes: 1. Australian figures include Northern Territory and the Australian Capital Territory.
2. Method of estimating number of employees changed after 1979 because the series, *Civilian Employees, Australia* was suspended from that date.

Sources: Australian Bureau of Statistics, *Labour Statistics: Australia, 1983*; Australian Bureau of Statistics, *Labour Statistics: Australia, 1984.*

In part, the variation in stoppage activity between states is a reflection of differences in the industrial structure. However, this is not entirely the case. Gordon, in an analysis of industrial disputes between 1968 and 1973, showed that there were important variations in stoppage incidence between states within the same industry.[13] A more recent analysis by Creigh, Robertson and Wooden, using techniques similar to those used by the Department of Employment in Britain to examine regional variations, showed that for the period 1978 to 1981 major differences remained once allowance had been made for industrial structure. Thus they concluded:

Differences in industrial structure between states clearly account for part of these stoppage incidents rate variations. However, substantial differences in the stoppage incidence ratio of individual states relative to the Australian average persist even after adjustment for such 'industrial structure' effects. Thus on the basis of the most detailed industrial structure adjustment procedure, Victoria lost 19 per cent more working days per 1,000 wage and salary earners than the Australian average for the period. On this adjusted basis New South Wales had an incidence rate marginally below the national average. The small states all had adjusted stoppage incidence ratios below unity with South Australia's rate running at only 35 per cent of the national average.[14]

Creigh and Wooden have also noted differences between strikes in terms of the size and duration of stoppages. For example, 'Victoria has been characterized by the largest strikes particularly in the late 1940s and in the 1970s and early 1980s'.[15] Since 1971 Tasmania has recorded longer than average strikes: in the immediate post-Second World War years (1946–59) strikes averaged 15-30 days in Queensland and 14.36 in Victoria, compared to 4.95 for Australia as a whole, but while both states have returned higher than average duration figures since then, they have not done so consistently.

One of the distinctive features of industrial relations in Australia is the dominance of arbitration. It is worthwhile looking then, at the available statistics on methods of dispute settlement to see whether this is reflected in them. Table 3.9 shows the position for 1913 to 1946 while Table 3.10 shows the detail for the later period. Oxnam noted that arbitration played a very minor role in the settlement of disputes in the pre-Second World War years, when most stoppages were settled as the result of direct negotiations between the parties concerned. However, he also pointed to an increase in the use of arbitration over time as well as an increase in settlement by 'other' methods (he said that it appeared that this increase in the incidence of 'other' methods was 'largely a reflection of the growing incidence of short-lived strikes'[16] and highlighted the large number of one-day stoppages in the coal fields, in the metal trades and on the waterfront which were concluded simply by workers returning to work the next day).

Table 3.9: Methods of Settlement of Stoppages in Australia, 1913–1950
Number of Stoppages Settled by:

Years	Negotiation	Industrial Acts	Substi-tution	Closing Down	Other Methods	Total
1913–18	69.4	8.3	5.5	1.1	15.7	100.0
1919–22	72.9	7.2	3.1	0.9	15.9	100.0
1923–26	53.6	5.9	1.4	0.2	38.9	100.0
1927–30	58.1	8.1	2.7	1.5	29.6	100.0
1931–34	66.5	11.4	2.6	1.6	17.9	100.0
1935–39	74.5	4.8	1.2	0.5	19.0	100.0
1940–45	56.4	12.0	0.1	0.0	31.5	100.0
1946–50	35.9	11.5	0.1	0.0	52.5	100.0
1913–50	55.7	9.6	1.5	0.4	32.8	100.0

Source: D. Oxnam, 'Strikes in Australia', *The Economic Record,* Vol. 29 (May 1953), p. 84.

It is clear from Table 3.10 that the trend towards the increasing use of arbitration to settle disputes noted by Oxnam in the pre-Second World War years has not been consistent in more recent years. There was a further rise in the number of stoppages settled by arbitration and under industrial legislation in the immediate post-Second World War years but this trend was reversed in the late 1970s. Wooden and Creigh note that resumption of work 'without negotiation was the major mode of dispute termination' in the post-Second World War years 'and indeed seems to have increased in relative importance

Table 3.10: Methods of Settlement of Stoppages in Australia, 1946–1982

Years	Private Negotiations & Mediation	State Legislation	Federal & Joint Federal-State Negotiation	Resump-Without Nego-tiation	Other
		Number of Stoppages			
1946–50	37.0	6.8	4.9	————51.4————	
1951–55	20.2	4.5	10.3	64.9	0.1
1956–60	19.0	7.0	15.6	58.2	0.2
1961–65	17.9	9.6	23.3	49.3	—
1966–70	25.0	11.2	14.3	49.9	*
1971–75	27.9	9.7	8.6	53.6	0.1
1976–80	23.0	8.2	8.1	60.5	0.4
1981–82	22.8	6.9	7.0	62.9	0.4
		Number of Working Days Lost			
1946–50	21.0	14.2	41.6	———— 3.2————	
1951–55	19.0	15.6	15.5	49.8	0.2
1956–60	18.7	11.0	16.4	53.8	0.1
1961–65	16.5	17.5	18.6	47.4	—
1966–70	17.6	9.1	15.9	57.4	*
1971–75	20.8	13.8	29.0	36.3	0.1
1976–80	18.3	9.1	14.0	58.6	0.2
1981–82	16.9	6.9	30.6	44.8	0.8

Source: M. Wooden and S. Creigh, *Strikes in Post War Australia: A Review of Research and Statistics*, National Institute of Labour Studies Inc., The Flinders University of South Australia, Working Paper Series, No. 60 (November 1983), p. 36.

(especially in terms of the number of stoppages) since the 1960s.'[17] In general, strikes settled through legislation are longer than the average (thus they tend to account for a higher proportion of days lost than the number of strikes) while strikes resumed without negotiation tend to be shorter.

The limited use of arbitration to settle disputes at first sight seems curious given the importance of arbitration in descriptions of the industrial relations system. However, some writers have argued that while arbitration may not dominate methods of dispute settlement it nevertheless has influenced the course of disputes.[18] In particular, recognition of the legal framework and of the legal view of stoppages of work might have influenced the duration of such action.

UNITED STATES OF AMERICA

Although the USA records a relatively large number of strikes compared to other industralised nations, surprisingly few attempts have been made to analyse trends over a long period. Of course, there are numerous studies of particular strikes or limited trends but Edwards' study of strikes in the USA between 1881 and 1974 is one of the few to look at the topic over such a time span.[19] Edwards referred in his book to Griffin's work of 1939 and argued that no 'adequate treatment of American strike patterns [had] been made since its publication.'[20]

Edwards' study, as has been indicated, looked at trends from 1881. However, the official series of strike statistics is far from complete from that date: there is a gap in the statistics between 1906 and 1914 and the publication of figures for days lost through strikes did not commence until 1927. Other changes have taken place subsequently to the basis of particular classifications which make it difficult to present a lengthy series of statistics. However, the change that was made in 1981 was the most important. Since that date the range of statistics published has been reduced: but more importantly, only those stoppages which involve 1,000 workers (compared to the previous minimum figure of 6 workers) have been counted. This has led one commentator to argue that the statistics are now so limited that they are of little analytical value.[21]

The impact of the change of definition introduced in 1981 is shown in Table 3.11. The effect is greatest when one considers the number of strikes. About 94 per cent of stoppages recorded between 1960 and 1980 would not have been covered if the new definition had applied. Although the effect is much less in the case of the number of workers involved in strikes and the number of days lost, it is still noticeable: only about two thirds of workers involved and days lost counted on the old basis would have been counted on the new basis if the 1960–80 period is considered. It is also important to recognise that the proportion of workers involved and days lost not covered by the new definition varied considerably from year to year between 1960 and 1980: thus in 1963 only 54.4 per cent of workers involved would have been counted under the new definition whereas the comparable proportion for 1971 was 76.7 per cent.

Table 3.11: Strike Indices on New Definition as Percentage of Indices on Old Definition, 1960–1980, USA

		Strikes	Workers Involved	Days Lost
	1960	6.7	67.8	69.4
	1961	5.8	71.1	62.2
	1962	5.8	64.5	63.2
	1963	5.4	54.4	62.2
	1964	6.7	72.1	70.9
	1965	6.8	64.5	65.0
	1966	7.3	66.3	63.0
	1967	8.3	76.4	74.4
	1968	7.8	70.0	72.6
	1969	7.2	63.5	68.6
	1970	6.7	74.7	79.4
	1971	5.8	76.7	74.7
	1972	5.0	56.9	61.8
	1973	5.9	62.2	58.2
	1974	7.0	64.7	66.3
	1975	4.7	55.3	56.2
	1976	4.1	62.8	63.3
	1977	5.4	59.4	59.4
	1978	5.2	62.0	64.4
	1979	4.9	59.1	58.7
	1980	4.8	56.9	61.6
Average	1960–80	6.1	66.2	66.9

Source: P.K. Edwards, 'The End of American Strike Statistics', *British Journal of Industrial Relations,* Vol. 21, No. 3, (1983), p. 393.

Estimates which try to convert the new to old count, therefore, necessarily will be very rough indeed, particularly for individual years.

Table 3.12 presents basic information on stoppages of work in the USA between 1927 and 1981. The period covered is limited to these years because of the considerations outlined above. From Table 3.12 it can be seen that the number of stoppages rose during the inter-war years and through the wartime period: thus, whereas between 1927 and 1931 the number of stoppages averaged 736 per year, between 1942 and 1946 the average was 4,282. The average fell back a little in the

Table 3.12: Stoppages of Work in USA 1927–1981, by Five-yearly Periods

Period	Number of Stoppages	Workers Involved (000s)	Days Idle (000s)
1927–31	736	292	10,872
1932–36	716	975	15,280
1937–41	3,384	1,331	17,010
1942–46	4,282	2,602	36,080
1947–51	4,040	2,358	36,180
1952–56	4,365	2,404	34,260
1957–61	3,555	1,620	28,960
1962–66	3,800	1,464	21,260
1967–71	5,239	2,917	49,598
1972–76	5,423	2,182	34,420
1977–81	4,203	1,567	33,103

Source: US Bureau of Labor Statistics, *Analysis of Work Stoppages.*

late 1950s though it started to rise again from the mid-1960s to a high point of 5,423 between 1972 and 1976.

The increase in the number of strikes from the mid-1960s is in line with similar developments in many other countries. However, there is some doubt whether 'wildcat strikes' were a major cause of the increase, as has been suggested elsewhere. Flanagan, Strauss and Ulmann note that 'wildcat stoppages accounted for just under 24 per cent of the total stoppages in manufacturing in 1970—about the same proportion registered in the early sixties and down from the 1966 peak of 29.1 per cent'.[22]

The trend of the number of workers involved in strikes shows some similarity to that noted for the number of strikes. The early post-Second World War years saw an average for workers involved that was almost ten times greater than it had been at the end of the 1920s: in fact this rise, while it followed that for the number of strikes, was considerably steeper. The total dipped in the late 1950s and early 1960s but again, as with the number of strikes, the upward trend was regained in the mid-1960s, though it was shorter lived and there was a fairly steep decline in the average in the 1970s: the total for 1981 was less than a third of that for 1970 and the average for the 1977 to 1981 period was not much more than half of what it had been for 1967–71.

The yearly totals for the number of days lost through stoppages are very erratic: in the twenty years from 1927, for example, they range from just over 3 million in 1930 to 116 million in 1946. In fact, if one takes the whole of the time period rather than just those twenty years, Burtt notes that the total number of days lost has only reached just half of the 1946 figure in three other years.[23] In each of those years the totals were particularly affected by one major strike: in 1959, 69 million days were lost (40 per cent as the result of the long steel strike), in 1952, 59.1 million days were lost (20.4 per cent as the result of the steel strike in that year), and in 1970 66.4 million days were lost (26.9 per cent as a result of a strike at General Motors).

When examined in terms of five-year averages, these variations are evened out and the fairly steady increase in the totals is noticeable up until the early 1950s. Along with the other measures there was a decline in the averages from the 1950s until the mid-1960s: the average of 21,260,000 for the period 1962 to 1966 can be compared to that of 36,180,000 for the period 1947 to 1951. Again, like the other measures, the decline in the average number of days lost was reversed in the mid-1960s though the total started to decline again in the 1970s.

The change in the basis of the USA strike statistics means that if direct comparisons are to be made between the most recent and earlier years then the figures have to be shown on a different basis. Table 3.13 shows trends for the same three strike measures covered in Table 3.12 but does so on the basis of the 'new' definition and brings the information up to 1985. It can be seen from Table 3.13 that there was a decline in all strike measures between 1981 and 1985: in two cases the 1985 total was less than a half of the comparable 1981 figure.

One of the most interesting and distinctive aspects of USA strike statistics has been the absence of any marked long-term change in duration. Table 3.14 shows the mean and median duration of stoppages between 1927 and 1981. Both figures have varied from year to year but the mean has generally been about 20 days while the median has been about 10 days. There are only two periods that might be excluded from this general statement. The first is during the Second World War when the mean

Table 3.13: Work Stoppages Involving 1,000 Workers or more, 1947–1985

Year	Number of Stoppages Beginning in Year	Workers Involved Beginning in Year (000s)	Days Idle (000s)
1947	270	1,629	25,720
1948	245	1,435	26,127
1949	62	2,537	43,420
1950	424	1,698	30,390
1951	415	1,462	15,070
1952	470	2,746	48,820
1953	437	1,623	18,130
1954	265	1,075	16,630
1955	363	2,055	21,180
1956	287	1,370	26,840
1957	279	887	10,340
1958	332	1,587	17,900
1959	245	1,381	60,850
1960	222	986	13,260
1961	195	1,031	10,140
1962	211	793	11,760
1963	181	512	10,020
1964	246	1,183	16,220
1965	268	999	15,140
1966	321	1,300	16,000
1967	381	2,192	31,320
1968	392	1,855	35,567
1969	412	1,576	29,397
1970	381	2,468	52,761
1971	298	2,516	35,538
1972	250	975	16,764
1973	317	1,400	16,260
1974	424	1,796	31,809
1975	235	965	17,563
1976	231	1,519	23,962
1977	298	1,212	21,258
1978	219	1,006	23,774
1979	235	1,021	20,409
1980	187	795	20,844
1981	145	729	16,908
1982	96	656	9,061
1983	81	909	17,461
1984	62	376	8,499
1985	61	584	7,079

Source: US Bureau of Labor Statistics. *Current Wage Developments.*

Table 3.14: Mean and Median Duration of Stoppages of Work in USA, 1927–1980

Year	Average Mean	Duration Median	Year	Average Mean	Duration Median
1927	26.5	3	1954	22.5	8
1928	27.6	—	1955	18.5	8
1929	22.6	—	1956	18.9	7
1930	22.3	—	1957	19.2	8
1931	18.8	—	1958	19.7	8
1932	19.6	—	1959	24.6	10
1933	16.9	—	1960	23.4	10
1934	19.5	—	1961	23.7	9
1935	23.8	—	1962	24.6	9
1936	23.3	—	1963	23.0	8
1937	20.3	—	1964	22.9	8
1938	23.6	—	1965	25.0	9
1939	23.4	—	1966	22.2	9
1940	20.9	—	1967	22.8	9
1941	18.3	—	1968	24.5	10
1942	11.7	—	1969	22.5	10
1943	5.0	—	1970	25.0	11
1944	5.6	—	1971	27.0	11
1945	9.9	—	1972	24.0	8
1946	24.2	—	1973	24.0	9
1947	25.6	—	1974	27.1	14
1948	21.8	—	1975	26.8	11
1949	22.5	8	1976	28.0	11
1950	19.2	7	1977	29.3	14
1951	17.4	7	1978	33.2	17
1952	19.6	9	1979	32.1	16
1953	20.3	9	1980	35.4	18

Note: Mean is the simple average: each stoppage is given equal weight regardless of size.

Source: US Bureau of Labor Statistics, *Analysis of Work Stoppages.*

duration declined significantly. Edwards argues that this was the result of the efforts of government and union leaders to prevent strikes during the war years (he notes, though, that the same trend was not observable during the First World War despite the fact that 'no strike' pledges were made during this period as well, and he suggests that one possible answer is that the unions were less willing to work with the government than during the Second

Table 3.15: Duration of Stoppages of Work in USA, 1961–1981

Period	Duration								
	1 days	2–3 days	4–6 days	7–14 days	15–29 days	30–59 days	60–89 days	90 days & over
	Number of Stoppages %								
1961–65	11.3	15.4	14.6	21.0	15.5	11.9	4.6	5.7
1966–70	12.3	13.9	13.8	20.0	16.3	13.2	5.4	5.2
1971–75	15.2	13.8	11.6	17.2	15.5	14.3	5.9	6.6
1976–80	12.5	10.1	10.0	17.9	18.3	16.1	6.9	8.3
1981	7.0	9.1	9.3	18.9	17.7	18.3	7.5	12.3
	Number of Days Lost %								
1961–65	0.8	1.8	2.6	9.0	17.9	29.6	14.9	23.4
1966–70	0.8	1.6	2.5	6.7	11.0	26.6	18.2	32.6
1971–75	0.5	1.7	2.0	7.5	13.6	23.8	12.3	38.5
1976–80	0.5	2.2	3.8	7.2	10.4	19.9	14.9	41.2
1981	0.4	0.5	1.0	3.1	7.0	21.2	36.5	30.3

Source: US Bureau of Labor Statistics. *Analysis of Work Stoppages.*

World War).[24] The other period which moved away from the general trend was the late 1970s when strike duration increased to a mean of around 30 days and a median of around 15 days, though because of changes in the basis of the statistics it is difficult to see how long-term a trend this has become.

Another measure of strike duration is given in Table 3.15. This shows the percentages of stoppages and working days lost between 1961 and 1981 that occurred in different time bands. Again there are some changes from one period to the next but the pattern is not markedly disturbed. The percentage of stoppages and days lost accounted for by strikes of less than a week has remained small: under 50 per cent in the case of stoppages and under 10 per cent in the case of days lost. Longer stoppages have dominated, and if anything increasingly so: in 1981 stoppages lasting for 60 days or over accounted for almost 20 per cent of all strikes and over two thirds of all days lost. The period covered by Table 3.15 is shorter than that covered by Table 3.14: it would not have been possible to cover the same time period with comparable information because of difficulties with the statistics. However, it is clear from other data that can be obtained that the trends have not changed markedly over time. For example, in the 1930s only 40 per cent or less of strikes were accounted for by those that lasted for less than 7 days and with the exception of the wartime years the proportion did not rise to 50 per cent over any five-year period. Similarly in the case of days lost the proportion accounted for by strikes lasting less than a week only rose above 10 per cent during the Second World War.

Table 3.16 offers information on the size of stoppages. This shows the percentage of stoppages that involved at least 10,000 workers. The percentage is tiny throughout the 1927–80 period: more importantly, though, there have only been relatively minor variations and no discernible long-term trend. If we had considered this issue in terms of the number of days lost then the totals would have been different: on average between 40 and 50 per cent of days lost have been accounted for by large strike (so defined). However, while there have been variations in the totals (particularly during the late 1930s and the early 1960s when the proportion fell to less then 30 per cent) again there has been no discernible long-term trend.

Table 3.16: Large Stoppages of Work in USA, 1927–1980

Period	Percentage of Stoppages that involved at least 10,000 Workers
1927–29	0.3
1930–33	0.8
1934–37	0.6
1938–41	0.4
1942–45	0.5
1946–49	0.5
1950–53	0.5
1954–57	0.5
1958–61	0.5
1962–65	0.4
1966–69	0.6
1970–73	0.5
1974–77	0.4
1978–80	0.3

Sources: 1927–1969: P.K. Edwards, *Strikes in the United States*, Blackwell, Oxford, 1981; 1970 onwards: US Bureau of Labor Statistics, *Analysis of Work Stoppages.*

Statistics have been produced in the USA for many years on the reasons given for striking. A consistent series is not available from 1927 to 1981 because of changes in the nature of the classification but it is possible to summarise the statistics in two tables: this is attempted in Tables 3.17 and 3.18. Both tables show that disputes over wages have dominated throughout the periods covered. Edwards examines data going back beyond 1927 and argues that there has been some decline in the importance of wage disputes since the end of the nineteenth century (he speculates that the decline might go further back).[25] However, in terms of the number of stoppages, wages seem to have recovered from this decline in the 1970s, and in 1981 accounted for over two thirds of all stoppages. Wages have usually accounted for the largest proportion of days lost and in 1981 accounted for nearly 85 per cent.

The other categories to figure strongly in the reasons given for striking in the USA are union recognition and security and

Table 3.17: Causes of Stoppages of Work in USA, 1927–1960

Period	Wages & Hours		Wages, Hours & Union Recognition		Union Recognition & Security		Other Work Conditions		Inter/Intra-Union		Other	
	% Strikes	Days Lost	% Strikes	Days Lost	% Strikes	Days Lost	% Strikes	Days Lost	% Strikes	Days Lost	% Strikes	Days Lost
1927–29	39.3	84.2	8.2	4.5	30.2	5.3	—	—	3.1	1.1	19.2	4.8
1930–33	55.8	51.9	9.2	25.3	19.1	14.5	—	—	2.8	2.8	13.1	5.4
1934–37	34.1	25.6	28.8	42.1	23.5	22.8	—	—	2.7	2.3	10.9	7.2
1938–41	30.8	34.9	22.0	15.0	28.6	38.6	—	—	6.0	5.3	12.5	6.2
1942–45	45.5	52.6	8.4	8.0	11.7	14.5	30.0	18.7	4.4	6.1	—	—
1946–49	47.2	74.7	12.9	15.3	14.6	2.6	20.6	5.9	4.8	1.4	—	—
1950–53	51.0	61.7	4.7	21.5	12.7	3.6	25.4	11.1	6.1	2.2	—	—
1954–57	50.5	70.5	7.1	12.1	12.0	5.4	22.7	10.4	7.8	1.7	—	—
1958–60	50.6	80.5	8.4	7.0	8.6	2.7	23.1	9.2	9.3	0.5	—	—

Note: Before 1942, work-conditions strikes were not separated from the 'other' category. 'Wages and hours' includes all wages and hours and supplementary-benefit issues and also the category 'othe contractual matters'.

Source: P. K. Edwards, Strikes in the United States 1881–1974, Blackwell, Oxford, 1981.

Table 3.18: Causes of Stoppages of Work in USA, 1961–1981

Period	Major Issue: General Wage Changes %	Supple-mentary Benefits %	Wage Adjust-ments %	Hours of Work %	Other Contrac-tual Matters %	Union Organisa-tion & Security %	Job Security %	Plant Admini-stration %	Other Working Condi-tions %	Inter-Union or Intra-Matters %	Not Reported %
Number of stoppages:											
1961–65	40.2	3.0	4.5	0.3	1.2	15.5	6.1	15.1	1.5	11.2	1.1
1966–70	48.1	1.4	5.0	0.1	1.5	11.3	3.7	15.4	2.9	9.9	0.7
1971–75	60.6	1.3	3.2	0.1	1.8	7.7	4.6	20.9	2.8	6.2	0.9
1976–80	60.5	1.2	2.4	0.2	4.6	5.4	4.3	15.8	2.0	3.2	0.5
1981	66.6	2.1	1.3	0.3	4.7	6.6	5.1	10.8	1.1	1.2	0.2
Number of working days lost											
1961–65	52.0	3.0	3.0	0.7	0.7	10.9	9.3	17.5	1.1	1.7	0.1
1966–70	64.2	1.0	2.5	0.1	8.8	12.1	3.0	5.6	0.8	1.8	0.1
1971–75	69.7	3.2	1.2	0.3	4.6	6.8	5.2	7.6	0.6	0.8	0.1
1976	63.1	1.0	3.6	0.2	2.3	3.3	10.6	14.8	0.5	0.5	0.1
1981	84.8	2.0	0.6	0.0	1.2	1.6	6.9	2.4	0.3	0.2	0.0

Source: US Bureau of Labor Statistics, *Analysis of Work Stoppages*.

working conditions. The first of these categories was particularly important during the 1930s (the average for the number of stoppages approached 30 per cent and the number of days lost approached 40 per cent towards the end of the 1930s). The most obvious explanation for the importance of this category during this period centres on the impact of the 'Wagner' Act and the stimulus it gave to union organisation and demands for recognition.

The other category is 'other working conditions'. A consistent series is not available for this category and the terms used in Tables 3.17 and 3.18 cannot be equated. Between 1942 and 1960 they accounted for around a quarter of all stoppages. Since 1961 the category has been split and it is worthwhile centring on one of its components, 'plant administration', rather than the residual 'other working conditions'. Plant administration was a particularly important cause of disputes especially in the 1970s. Between 1971 and 1975 it accounted for 20 per cent of all stoppages and between 1976 and 1980 it accounted for almost 15 per cent of all days lost.

The discussion of strike trends in the USA so far has been at the aggregate level but it must be expected that there will be considerable variations, for example between industries and between different parts of the country. Ross noted how strike activity in the USA was dominated by a restricted number of industries: he found that between 1927 and 1960 eight industries accounted for about 60 per cent of working days lost although they employed less than 18 per cent of non-agricultural wage and salary earners.[26] Kaufman similarly found that between 1960 and 1979 the top eight industries accounted for 66 per cent of all days idle but only 20 per cent of total non-agricultural employment.[27]

The discussion of inter-industry variations in strike propensity can be looked at in more detail and brought up to date by reference to Tables 3.19 to 3.22. Tables 3.19 and 3.20 show the proportion of stoppages, workers involved in stoppages and days lost through stoppages in different industries between 1927 and 1940 (Table 3.19) and 1950 and 1972 (Table 3.20). The basis of the industrial classification is different in the two tables so direct comparisons cannot be made. Nevertheless, some general comments might be noted.

Table 3.19: Stoppages by Industry, USA, 1927–1940

Proportion of all stoppages accounted for by following industries:	Number of Strikes	% of Workers Involved	Days Lost
Boot and shoe	1.9	2.2	2.2
Building	12.4	5.8	5.2
Clothing	13.1	12.1	8.3
Coal	4.1	21.1	31.3
Food	5.3	2.6	2.2
Machinery: non-electrical	2.6	1.9	2.0
electrical	0.8	0.6	0.7
Metals: basic metal	0.6	2.2	2.2
other iron and steel	2.8	3.7	2.1
other	1.6	1.1	1.2
Printing and publishing	1.2	0.2	0.3
Stone, clay and glass	1.8	1.1	1.4
Textiles	7.0	9.9	12.1
Tobacco	0.5	0.5	0.5
Transport: railroad	0.1	0.1	—
other	7.0	6.3	5.3
Transport equipment: locos, cars and ships	0.5	0.8	1.1
other	1.6	6.9	4.5
ALL ABOVE INDUSTRIES	64.8	79.2	82.7
Chemicals	1.0	1.1	0.7
Lumber	6.1	3.3	4.4
Rubber	0.8	1.9	0.9
Domestic and personal service	5.7	3.5	2.8
Trade	7.9	3.0	2.2
ALL ABOVE INDUSTRIES	86.4	92.0	93.7
ALL INDUSTRIES	100.0	100.0	100.0

Source: P.K. Edwards, *Strikes in the United States 1881–1974,* Blackwell, Oxford, 1981, p. 152.

The importance of the building industry is particularly noticeable and generally consistent throughout the periods examined. On the other hand the clothing industry, which accounted for the highest proportion of strikes in 1927–40, was

Table 3.20: Proportion of all Stoppages Accounted For By Each Industry, USA, 1950–1972

	1950–61 % of			1962–72 % of		
	Number of Stoppages	Workers Involved	Days Lost	Number of Stoppages	Workers Involved	Days Lost
Building	19.1	15.0	12.8	19.8	17.5	19.4
Clothing	3.6	1.5	0.9	2.0	0.8	0.7
Coal and mining	8.2	7.4	7.0	8.2	7.4	4.4
Food	4.4	3.6	2.8	4.5	3.1	2.8
Leather	1.2	0.7	0.4	0.6	0.4	0.3
Machinery:						
non-electrical	5.8	6.3	8.5	6.1	5.6	7.3
electrical	2.9	4.4	4.6	3.7	5.7	6.3
Metals:						
basic steel	2.3	10.5	19.1	2.4	2.5	2.6
other primary	3.4	3.0	3.6	2.1	2.2	3.2
fabricated	6.0	4.4	4.6	6.3	3.6	4.6
Printing and						
publishing	1.0	0.6	0.6	1.4	1.1	2.1
Stone, clay, glass	3.0	1.8	2.0	3.1	1.7	2.0
Textiles	1.9	1.7	2.3	0.9	0.6	0.5
Tobacco	0.1	—	—	0.1	0.2	0.2
Transport	7.2	10.7	7.4	6.1	20.5	13.2
Transport equip.:						
motor vehicles	2.4	8.9	5.2	1.9	7.1	9.0
other	1.4	3.5	3.6	1.5	2.7	2.5
ALL ABOVE INDUSTRIES	73.9	84.0	85.4	70.7	83.7	81.1
Chemicals	2.2	1.3	1.5	2.7	1.4	2.4
Lumber	2.0	1.2	2.2	1.4	0.6	1.0
Rubber	2.2	4.4	2.2	1.9	1.9	2.6
Services	3.5	0.8	0.8	3.9	1.4	1.5
Trade	8.4	2.8	2.9	8.7	3.1	3.1
Government	0.6	0.3	0.1	4.5	5.5	2.5
ALL ABOVE INDUSTRIES	92.9	94.9	95.2	93.7	96.4	94.3
ALL INDUSTRIES	100 0	100	100	100	100	100

Source: P.K. Edwards, *Strikes in the United States 1881–1974*, Blackwell, Oxford, 1981.

Table 3.21: Proportion of Strikes in Selected Industries, USA, 1971–1981

	Number of Stoppages			Number of Working Days Lost		
	1971–75 %	1976–80 %	1981 %	1971–75 %	1976–80 %	1981 %
All Industries						
Manufacturing	43.0	45.7	46.4	46.0	53.5	24.8
Ordinance & accessories products	0.1	0.0	0.0	0.5	0.2	0.0
Food & kindred products	3.8	3.9	4.2	3.0	3.2	1.3
Tobacco manufacture	0.0	0.0	0.0	0.2	0.1	0.0
Textile mill products	0.7	0.7	0.6	0.7	0.5	0.2
Apparel & other finished products	1.2	1.0	1.0	1.5	0.5	0.3
Lumber, wood products (excluding furniture)	1.3	1.4	1.1	0.7	1.0	0.4
Furniture & fixtures	1.4	1.5	1.8	0.8	0.8	0.4
Paper & allied products	1.8	1.9	1.8	1.6	2.8	1.2
Printing, publishing & allied industries	1.3	0.9	1.0	1.2	0.9	0.6
Chemicals & allied products	2.4	2.4	2.3	2.3	2.3	1.8
Petroleum & related industries	0.4	0.5	0.5	0.8	2.4	0.5
Rubber & miscellaneous plastic products	1.9	1.9	1.4	2.0	4.4	0.4
Leather & leather products	0.2	0.3	0.4	0.2	0.3	0.0
Stone, clay & glass products	2.9	2.9	2.8	1.7	1.7	1.1
Primary metal industries	3.6	4.1	4.4	4.1	4.5	3.6
Fabricated metal products	6.2	6.9	7.9	4.5	4.6	2.9
Machinery (except electrical)	6.0	6.8	7.0	7.1	9.3	3.6
Electrical machinery, equipment & supplies	3.2	3.8	4.1	4.4	4.1	2.3
Transportation equipment	3.0	3.0	2.6	7.2	8.9	3.8
Instruments & related products	0.6	0.6	0.6	0.7	0.6	0.3
Miscellaneous manufacturing industries	0.9	1.0	0.7	0.5	0.7	0.1
Non-manufacturing	57.0	54.3	53.6	54.0	46.5	75.2
Agriculture, forestry & fisheries	0.2	0.3	0.4	0.6	0.4	0.1
Mining	18.6	14.2	7.6	6.7	12.4	35.9
Contract construction	12.3	8.0.	9.5	21.1	8.5	18.0
Transportation, communication, etc.	5.6	6.4	7.0	14.5	9.8	2.6
Wholesale & retail trade	8.7	9.6	9.6	4.7	4.4	2.7
Finance, insurance & real estate	0.4	0.5	0.6	0.2	0.4	0.5
Services—personal business	3.9	5.3	7.5	1.8	4.7	4.9
Government	7.3	9.9	11.3	4.4	5.9	10.5

Source: US Bureau of Labor Statistics, *Analysis of Work Stoppages.*

less noticeable in the later period. The coal mining industry accounted for more workers involved and days lost than any other industry in 1927–1940, but not in the later period. The transport category held a relatively high proportion of stoppages, workers involved and days lost throughout the periods covered. Table 3.21 shows the percentage of stoppages and working days lost in the USA which can be accounted for by strikes in particular industries between 1971 and 1981. During this period certain industries seem to dominate the scene: these including mining, construction, transport and communications and government. A number of other industries also account for a significant proportion of stoppages, and days lost, including the wholesale and retail trade, fabricated metal products, machinery, and transportation equipment. Of course, there are considerable variations from year to year, period to period and measure to measure. Mining, for example, accounted for less than 7 per cent of days lost in 1971–5 but for over 35 per cent in 1981. Similarly, the wholesale and retail trade accounted for over 9 per cent of stoppages between 1976 and 1980 but less than 3 per cent of days lost in 1981. Such variations over a short period of time have echoes if one takes earlier periods.

Some comment has already been made about trends in particular industries. Possibly the most interesting development, though, has not yet been mentioned: the growth of strike activity in the public sector. Stoppages in the 'government sector' accounted for a tiny proportion of all strikes and days lost in the immediate post-Second World War years and up until the 1960s (less than 1 per cent), but by the early 1980s they were accounting for about 10 per cent of all stoppages. In part this growth in strike activity might be linked to some relaxation on the restrictions imposed on government employees taking strike action. However, this does not seem to be the whole of the story because such relaxation has been conditional (Chamberlain, Cullen and Lewis provide details of the kind of conditions still imposed by individual states[28]), and there is evidence that anyway the restrictions have not been effective (Burton and Krider,[29] in a study of strikes between 1968 and 1971, argued that the statutory prohibition of strikes seemed to have little impact, and Becker[30] noted that although strikes by Federal employees have been prohibited, in the case of most of the 39 stoppages recorded between 1962 and 1981 either no penalty was enforced or the only penalty was loss of pay). Other factors to take into account in explaining the rise in public-sector strike activity include increasing union activity in some areas and the changing approach of some professional groups.

Table 3.22: Stoppages of Work by Industry in USA, 1970–1981:
Standardised by Number of Employees

	Stoppages of Work (per 100,000 employees)		Days Lost (per 1,000 employees)	
	1970–75	1976–81	1970–75	1976–81
Mining	1,371	685	3,265	5,861
Construction	200	88	2,424	796
Manufacture	120	101	1,045	845
Transport & communications	68	59	1,216	618
Wholesale & retail	29	22	106	74
Finance, insurance & real estate	6	5	30	27
Services	16	15	51	99
Government	29	29	122	123
Agriculture, forestry & fishing	4	4	63	38

Note: Number of employees in industry, used for the calculations except in agriculture, forestry and fisheries when employment by industry has been used.

Source: U.S. Bureau of Labor Statistics, *Analysis of Work Stoppages.*

Table 3.21 allows comments to be made, primarily about the relative importance of an industry in terms of overall strike figures. However, this does not relate the number of strikes and days lost in the industry to the size of the workforce in that industry. Such an exercise has been attempted and is shown in Table 3.22. The importance of certain industries is merely confirmed by that table. Throughout the 1970s mining, for example, had stoppages markedly in excess of other major industrial groups. Other industries that were highlighted from earlier tables as accounting for a large proportion of stoppages and days lost also had relatively high figures on the basis of calculations used in Table 3.22 (such as construction for 1970–5). However, some industries appear differently when considered by the criteria used for Table 3.22. In particular, wholesale and retail trades and government seem far less strike-prone; in fact they are well below the USA average. The relatively large number of employees in these industries, compared to say mining or construction, puts the totals recorded in earlier tables into a different context. Table 3.22 also allows us to highlight other industries where there have been relatively few strikes or days lost if account is taken of the number of employees: in particular, agriculture, forestry and fishing, plus finance, insurance and real estate.

Of course, one could go beyond these measures of strike activity when looking at variations between industries. There are major variations in patterns of strike activity between industries in, for example, the duration of strikes, the number of workers involved and the issues over which strikes have occurred. Some of these issues were discussed by Britt and Gallie when they attempted to go beyond merely looking at variations in terms of working days lost.[31] However, they developed their measures looking at a very short time period and there are obvious difficulties in dealing with such matters over a prolonged period (and in a short space). In this instance probably the best that can be done is to point to an illustration of variations in the patterns of strike activity. For example, if one looks at the proportion of strikes and days lost accounted for by wages and related matters, the number recorded in some industries was double what it was in others.

Table 3.23: Stoppages by Region in USA, 1974–1979:

Region	Stoppages (per 100,000 workers)	Days Lost (per 1,000 workers)
New England	4.8	296
Mid-Atlantic	8.0	398
East North Central	8.3	606
West North Central	4.8	394
South Atlantic	5.7	296
East South Central	6.9	542
West South Central	2.3	235
Mountain	3.8	248
Pacific	4.4	405

Note: Employment 16 years and over.

Source: US Bureau of Labor Statistics, *Analysis of Work Stoppages.*

The distribution of stoppages by region in the USA is shown in Table 3.23. Again, in this case, some attempt has been made to relate the regional distribution of stoppages and days lost to the number of employees in each region. On this basis three regions score particularly highly in terms of the number of stoppages— East North Central, Mid-Atlantic and East South Central: two of these regions, East North Central and East South Central, also score highly in terms of days lost. At the other end of the spectrum, West South Central and the Mountain Region score lowly on both strike measures. One part of the explanation for the variations between the regions relate to the industrial complexion. For example, if one compares the most highly strike-prone region (East North Central) with the most lowly strike-prone region (West South Central) the former has a higher proportion of employees in the manufacturing sector (the comparison is approximately 25 per cent to 15 per cent) and a higher proportion of employees in the construction sector (the comparison is about 3 per cent to 0.6 per cent). On the other hand there is evidence that regional variations in industrial complexion do not by themselves offer a satisfactory explanation for strike proneness.

In Palomba's study of variations of strike activity between states the issue of the extent to which such variations in strike activity can be explained by differences in manufacturing employment was specifically addressed. Palomba found 'that the level of manufacturing activity in a state has no effect on the level of strike activity'.[32] He also looked at the explanatory power of two other variables, union membership and the hourly earnings of production workers. He concluded, though, that the issue was too complex to be explained by any simple hypothesis.

Some researchers have taken the analysis of geographical variations further by looking below the regional level. Stern did so by looking at strikes in 243 US Standard Metropolitan Statistical Areas. There are some problems working at this level of analysis: Stern notes, for example, that the US Bureau of Labor Statistics only published statistics for a city with five or more strikes in a given year. Nevertheless, some further work can be undertaken to try to identify explanations for variations in strike activity between different areas. One of the issues that Stern was able to comment on was the extent of the 'industry effect': that is, are variations between areas simply a reflection of the differences in industrial structure? Stern argued that once this effect had been allowed for there were still major variations to be explained. He said that 'the mix of industries seem to be somewhat less important on the community level than might have been expected.'[33] Other variables which were particularly important were city size and the economic position of workers. The first of these was the most important. City size apparently showed a negative relationship to strike activity. Stern explained the relationship by referring to a 'probability of success' model:

Large cities have diversified economic bases and as a result are not as dependent as small or moderate cities on a given plant or industry. Therefore workers in all but a few crucial occupations are unable to exert the economic pressure available to a group of workers in a smaller city that might be central to the economic functioning of the community.[34]

UNITED KINGDOM

There have been a number of major studies of strikes in the UK. The best known is undoubtedly that by Knowles.[35] He looked at trends from 1911 to 1947 and produced a piece of work which has been widely recognised as a classic. The study of Durcan, McCarthy and Redman[36] is also an impressive and detailed analysis of strikes in the UK. They dealt with the period after the end of the Second World War, up to 1973. The latter part of this period is also covered by research for the Department of Employment reported by Smith.[37] This offered a comprehensive analysis of the 1966 to 1973 years drawing on some statistics not widely available. It contained a wealth of descriptive material as well as sections on explanations of aspects of strike activity. There are a host of other studies of particular periods and particular industries.

The coverage of strike statistics in the UK is adequate for most purposes. There are no major gaps in the statistics over particular periods, as there are in the case of the USA. However, there are some problems with the published statistics, particularly with the frequent changes in categorisation. This affects, for example, duration, cause and industrial distribution.

Table 3.24: Stoppages of Work due to Industrial Disputes in UK, 1911–1985

Period	Number of Stoppages	Number of Workers Involved in Stoppages 000s	Working Days Lost Through Stoppages 000s
1911–15	962	795	14,736
1916–20	1,077	1,357	15,101
1921–25	656	762	26,554
1926–30	357	445	12,497
1931–35	438	282	3,492
1936–40	937	365	1,774
1941–45	1,765	545	2,408
1946–50	1,690	461	1,946
1951–55	1,917	658	2,382
1956–60	2,612	771	4,450
1961–65	2,416	1,511	3,160
1966–70	2,691	1,398	5,531
1971–75	2,559	1,369	13,045
1976–80	2,120	1,663	12,854
1981–85	1,255	1,268	9,188

Source: Department of Employment, *Gazette.*

Table 3.24 shows the basic strike statistics over the 1911 to 1984 period, by five-yearly groupings. Such groupings allow general trends to be identified more easily than if the individual yearly totals were examined. However, one of the costs is that significant variations from one year to the next cannot be spotted. If one considers the broad trends, though, then a number of patterns can be identified. As far as the number of stoppages is concerned the very much higher level in the post-than in the pre-Second World War period is evident: before the Second World War the number of stoppages averaged less than 1,000 (only 357 between 1926 and 1930, though 1,077 between 1916 and 1920) whereas following a decline in the late 1940s the average rose to over 2,000 from the mid-1950s onwards, only falling below this total in 1981 to 1985. The trend as far as the number of workers involved in strikes shows some similarities. The average number of workers involved before the Second World War was frequently between 300,000 and 500,000, though on occasions it rose much higher (between 1916 and 1920 it rose to over 1,300,000). After the Second World War the total dipped but then the average started to rise from the early 1950s, though it did not reach the 1 million level until the 1960s (the highest average was over 1.6 million for the period 1976 to 1980). The trend in the case of the number of working days lost through stoppages has been rather different. The highest averages were recorded in the immediate post-First World War years, with a peak of over 26 million between 1921 and 1925. In the years following the Second World War the averages were lower, at around 2 million. The average increased somewhat from the early 1950s, though it was the 1970s before the major increase occurred (between 1971 and 1975 over 13 million working days were lost and the average for the following five years was much the same). This increase in days lost was in large measure a result of lengthy public-sector strikes. In his discussion of the 1970–4 period Clegg notes that the 'main contribution to the totals came from a wholly unprecedented series of major public sector strikes which arose from conflicts between the unions concerned and the Heath administration over the application of successive incomes policies to them'.[38] The same is true to some extent in later years: the 'winter of discontent' of 1978–9 was a reaction against the policy of the Labour government of that time, and in the early 1980s a number of lengthy public-sector strikes were a reaction against the consequences for pay of the application of cash limits by the Conservative government.

Some care needs to be taken, though, in interpreting these figures. In part, this is because of the point noted earlier about the way that averages mask significant variations between years. This is particularly the case when considering the number of working days lost. For example the 1921–5 average masks the fact that the total for 1921 was over 86 million, almost four times greater than the preceding year and more than four times greater than the succeeding year. Again the 1976–80 average masks the fact that the 1979 total was over 29 million, about three times greater than the totals for the preceding and succeeding years. The yearly totals for working days lost are particularly likely to be affected by major national strikes, even one major national strike: in the case of the 1979 total that was affected not by one major strike but by a series of strikes in the public sector referred to above as the 'winter of discontent'. If the years 1960 to 1979 are taken then 46 per cent of all days lost were a result of 64 large strikes.[39]

Care also needs to be taken in interpreting these figures because of the impact of trends in particular industries on the national figures. The obvious example is provided by the coal-mining industry. This will be discussed in more detail later but for the moment it is important to recall that in some years that industry accounted for over 80 per cent of all days lost through strikes in the UK (in 1926 and 1984, both years when crucial national strikes occurred in the industry) and for one fifteen-year period coal mining never accounted for less than half of all strikes. If one excluded the coal-mining industry from consideration then changes in strike trends that occurred between say 1961 and 1980 would look very different. Over that period the number of strikes including coal mining rose in the late 1960s but fell back in the late 1970s so that by 1976–80 the

Table 3.25: Stoppages of Work due to Industrial Disputes in UK, 1911–1985: Average number of workers involved in and average duration of each strike

Period	Average Number of Workers Involved in Each Strike	Average Duration of Each Strike (days)
1911–15	826	19
1916–20	1,260	11
1921–25	1,161	35
1926–30	1,247	28
1931–35	644	14
1936–40	390	5
1941–45	309	4
1946–50	273	4
1951–55	343	4
1956–60	295	6
1961–65	625	2
1966–70	520	4
1971–75	535	10
1976–80	784	8
1981–85	1,010	7

Source: Department of Employment, *Gazette.*

yearly average was about 12 per cent lower than it had been in 1961–5. However, if coal mining is excluded then the yearly average was approaching 50 per cent higher in 1976–80 than it had been in 1961–5.

The differences noted in the trends of strikes in the UK between different measures is in part a reflection of changes that occurred in the size and duration of stoppages. Table 3.25 presents the simplest measures of size and duration by the same five-year periods used for the previous table. This information suggests that both the average number of workers involved in stoppages and the average duration of stoppages declined after the inter-war years. Between 1921 and 1930 on average over 1,000 workers were involved in each stoppage, and stoppages lasted for around 30 days. Each average fell in the 1930s and continued at a relatively low level in the post-Second World War years: between 1946 and 1960 on average around 300 workers were involved in each stoppage, and stoppages lasted for 4-6 days. The average number of workers involved in each stoppage rose in the 1960s, continuing into the 1970s, and the average duration rose in the 1970s, though neither average has reached the heights of the 1920s (the average number of workers involved in stoppages came closest with a figure of over 1,000 in 1981–4).

Further information on the duration of stoppages is given in tables 3.26 and 3.27. These give a more detailed breakdown of the spread and duration of stoppages. Unfortunately such information suffers from changes in categorisation. Nevertheless, broad trends can be identified. It is clear, for example, that over most of the periods covered the short stoppage has dominated. Between 1935 and 1951 over half of the workers involved in stoppages took part in strikes that lasted under one week: between 1946 and 1971 over half of the totals were accounted for by stoppages of six days or less: and between 1972 and 1975 over half of the totals were accounted for by stoppages lasting five days or less. The position changed somewhat in the mid-1970s: between 1976 and 1980 on average less than 30 per cent of the total was accounted for by stoppages that lasted for five days or less and the average for the same duration did not reach 50 per cent in 1981. The second half of the 1970s also saw an increase in the proportion of relatively long

Table 3.26: Analysis of Stoppages by Duration of Dispute, UK, 1935–81

Analysis of Duration by Dispute,
Workpeople Directly and Indirectly Involved

Duration of dispute	1935	1936–40	1941–45	1946–50	1951
under 1 week	51.7	70.6	63.2	60.6	53.8
1 week & under 2	34.3	12.2	15.9	20.3	29.3
2 weeks & under 4	6.6	13.4	16.6	14.6	6.9
4 weeks & under 6	3.7	2.0	1.2	4.0	7.6
6 weeks & under 10	0.4	1.0	2.9	0.5	1.6
10 weeks & under 20	2.6	0.6	0.2	0.1	0.3
20 weeks & over	0.7	0.2	0.0	0.0	0.5
TOTAL	100.0	100.0	100.0	100.0	100.0

Duration of dispute	1946–50	1951–55	1956–60	1961–65	1966–70	1971
not more than 6 days	69.8	79.1	60.0	90.2	75.1	59.9
over 6 days – 12 days	15.3	8.6	24.2	4.7	7.4	10.8
over 12 days – 24 days	11.8	6.6	8.8	3.1	8.9	5.5
over 24 days – 36 days	2.5	3.3	4.6	1.3	5.9	2.3
over 35 days – 60 days	0.5	1.6	2.3	0.5	1.9	20.8
over 60 days	0.1	0.8	0.1	0.2	0.8	0.7
TOTAL	100.0	100.0	100.0	100.0	100.0	100.0

Duration of dispute	1972–75	1976–80	1981
not more than 5 days	53.6	29.1	47.7
over 5 days – 10 days	11.8	10.1	7.1
over 10 days – 20 days	16.3	26.0	8.1
over 20 days – 30 days	10.9	3.7	2.8
over 30 days – 50 days	3.1	9.2	1.2
over 50 days	4.3	21.9	33.1
TOTAL	100.0	100.0	100.0

Note: The time bands used for duration changed three times over the period covered.
Figures are available which allow some overlap of information for 1946–1951.

Source: Department of Employment, *Gazette.*

stoppages: stoppages lasting over fifty days accounted for over
20 per cent of the total between 1976 and 1980 and for over 30
per cent of the total in 1981 (in earlier periods the proportion of
the totals accounted for by such lengthy stoppages was far less).
Table 3.27 shows more detailed information on the most recent
time period. It covers the three main measures of stoppages in
terms of duration, not just (as with Table 3.26) the number of
workers involved. The position as far as the number of
stoppages is concerned has been relatively consistent since 1979.

Table 3.27: Stoppages of Work by Duration, UK, 1979–1985

				Percentages			
Number of stoppages	*1979*	*1980*	*1981*	*1982*	*1983*	*1984*	*1985*
Not more than 1 day	19.8	26.8	31.0	37.0	34.5	29.6	36.3
Over 1 day, not more than 2	12.3	14.2	14.7	14.3	13.8	13.6	13.8
Over 2 days, not more than 3	9.9	10.4	9.7	8.8	7.3	8.5	6.8
Over 3 days, not more than 4	7.6	7.4	6.3	5.9	6.5	7.9	5.8
Over 4 days, not more than 5	7.2	6.8	6.3	4.5	5.9	6.1	6.2
Over 5 days, not more than 10	17.4	14.5	13.9	13.7	14.1	15.0	12.7
Over 10 days, not more than 15	9.5	7.1	5.7	7.1	6.1	6.5	7.0
Over 15 days, not more than 20	4.2	3.5	4.1	2.7	3.6	3.7	3.3
Over 20 days, not more than 30	5.6	4.0	3.7	3.0	3.3	3.2	3.9
Over 30 days, not more than 50	4.1	3.4	2.4	1.9	2.8	2.6	2.4
Over 50 days	2.4	1.9	2.2	1.1	2.1	2.3	1.8
Workers involved in stoppages							
Not more than 1 day	3.7	18.5	30.0	21.2	16.7	22.0	25.5
Over 1 day, not more than 2	2.9	7.4	8.4	6.3	12.6	6.1	10.6
Over 2 days, not more than 3	1.3	7.8	4.5	2.0	6.8	4.9	2.2
Over 3 days, not more than 4	3.1	4.1	1.8	1.7	4.3	2.0	2.3
Over 4 days, not more than 5	1.6	2.8	5.3	1.7	5.4	14.1	1.5
Over 5 days, not more than 10	4.2	18.2	4.8	4.3	11.1	8.9	8.4
Over 10 days, not more than 15	35.3	4.9	6.6	3.1	7.4	7.4	3.0
Over 15 days, not more than 20	0.9	7.1	2.2	3.6	4.7	1.9	2.0
Over 20 days, not more than 30	2.8	2.3	4.1	1.7	6.0	2.4	21.5
Over 30 days, not more than 50	10.1	2.0	0.5	0.6	10.9	15.3	1.7
Over 50 days	34.1	24.9	31.8	53.8	14.1	15.0	21.1
Number of days lost							
Not more than 1 day	0.5	1.1	6.5	7.7	2.1	0.7	2.7
Over 1 day, not more than 2	0.6	0.8	4.7	4.1	2.3	0.4	1.4
Over 2 days, not more than 3	0.4	1.3	3.2	1.7	2.0	0.4	0.6
Over 3 days, not more than 4	1.2	0.8	2.0	2.4	2.1	0.2	0.7
Over 4 days, not more than 5	1.0	0.8	6.1	2.7	2.2	0.7	0.8
Over 5 days, not more than 10	3.5	4.1	9.0	9.6	8.9	2.0	4.7
Over 10 days, not more than 15	57.7	3.2	15.0	10.4	11.5	2.2	3.0
Over 15 days, not more than 20	1.5	2.6	9.5	17.5	7.7	1.1	2.6
Over 20 days, not more than 30	6.0	2.0	8.9	10.2	16.7	1.7	68.3
Over 30 days, not more than 50	8.2	3.5	5.8	4.3	31.0	3.4	4.3
Over 50 days	19.4	79.8	29.3	29.4	13.5	87.2	10.8

Source: Department of Employment, *Gazette.*

Between 1980 and 1984 (inclusive) over 65 per cent of all stoppages lasted five days or less, and in 1982 that total reached its height, over 70 per cent. At the same time only a very small proportion of stoppages lasted more than fifty days. The position as far as workers involved in stoppages is concerned is more volatile. If one takes short stoppages as being those lasting five days or less, then such stoppages accounted for only about 12 per cent of the total in 1979 but about 50 per cent in 1981. In fact the 1981 total was closer to the average for the 1980s which was in excess of 40 per cent for the years 1980 to 1984 (inclusive). The volatility can also be seen in the number of longer stoppages: those lasting for more than 50 days accounted for over 50 per cent of the total in 1982 but only about 14 per cent the following year. If the number of days lost are considered then this volatility persists. For example, in 1980 almost 80 per cent and in 1984 over 87 per cent of all days lost resulted from strikes lasting for over 50 days but in 1983 that total was only just over 13 per cent. The proportion of days lost accounted for by short stoppages has always been small, though in 1981 16 per cent were lost as the result of strikes lasting 3 days or less and in 1982 over 13 per cent, compared to less than 2 per cent for 1984.

The volatility of the figures and the somewhat different impressions given by changes from one year to the next by different measures makes it difficult to identify major trends and developments. However, in the post-Second World War years two major developments are worth highlighting. The first is that in the early 1960s there was an absence of large strikes, and a decline in the duration of strikes. This latter point is visible in the sets of figures presented in Table 3.26. Both developments have been extensively discussed. Durcan, McCarthy and Redman suggest that the large, official strike made a comeback in the 1950s after an absence of twenty years: 'the macro-strike made a reappearance in 1953 and continued to command the stage until 1959. Most of these stoppages occurred in the private sector, although the government's fumbling attempts at wage restraint were a significant influence'. After 1959, though, Durcan, McCarthy and Redman note a major change. 'Between 1960 and 1970 the macro-strike virtually disappeared again—apart from the single event of the seamen's strike in 1966.'[40] The growing importance of the short strike was one of the main features of the analysis of the Donovan Commission.[41] In this case the explanation offered was the breakdown of the formal system of industrial relations, though others have placed emphasis on other factors like changed economic conditions, and expectations of workers. The number of short strikes reached its peak in the first half of the 1960s and fell back from 1965: consequently by the time the Donovan Commission reported (in 1968) the trends seemed to have changed, though it is likely that this apparent change was largely if not entirely a reflection of the reduction in the number of strikes in the coal-mining industry, and it is at least arguable (though the data are not available to permit a precise examination of the thesis) that the proportion of short strikes continued to rise outside coal mining throughout the 1960s.[42].

The second development that might be highlighted is the increase in the number of large strikes and the increase in the average length of strikes in the 1970s. Again this latter trend is noticeable from the data presented in Tables 3.26 and 3.27, though the details differ according to the information under consideration. In their review Durcan, McCarthy and Redman note that between 1969 and 1973 strike activity 'in volume and especially in duration was higher than at any other time in the post-war years'.[43] This review did not look beyond 1973 though in fact the trends they identified can be seen in later years. Many of the large strikes occurred in the public sector when governments tried to restrict pay increases in line with incomes policy guidelines and as an example to the private sector. Some, though, occurred in the private sector, like the national engineering stoppage of 1979. This trend continued into the 1980s and was best exemplified by the national strike in the coal-mining industry, though in fact this was only one of a number in the public sector. There is little doubt that government pay policy, particularly towards its own employees, was an important explanatory factor, though other aspects of government policy were important as well, as were worsening economic conditions.

However, Edwards offers a word of caution on this interpretation. He accepts that a significant change took place in the 1970s but argues that short strikes nevertheless still predominate in Britain. This is particularly so, he argues, if one includes those strikes that escape inclusion in the national figures.

The typical British strike is, thus, extremely short. Any tendency for strikes to have grown longer must be seen in this context. It is possible to point to certain tendencies in the economic and industrial relations climates which may have led to longer strikes. With the growing importance of very large disputes it is easy to give the impression that the whole strike picture has dramatically altered. In a way this is true, and it would be wrong to ignore the upsurge of the large national strike. But most strikes remain extremely short and limited affairs, of significance only in the workplaces in which they occur.[44]

Considerable attention has been focussed in the UK on the reasons given for strikes. In his analysis of strikes between 1911 and 1947 Knowles regrouped the then official classification to try to determine trends. The regrouping left him with a threefold classification:

1. *Basic issues*— including wage increase questions,
   wage decrease question,
   other wages questions,
   hours of labour.
2. *Frictional issues*— including employment of certain classes of person, other working arrangements, rules and discipline.
3. *Solidarity issues*— including trade union principles,
   sympathetic action,
   miscellaneous causes.

Knowles distinguished between two periods, with the break being made in 1926, the year of the General Strike. The results of his examination are shown in Table 3.28. The very general trend he highlighted was a decline in strikes over basic issues and an increase in strikes over frictional issues. Knowles made an initial assessment of the reasons for these trends. First, he argued that the reduction in the importance of basic issues was largely accounted for by the reduction in one of its sub-categories, wage-increase strikes, which in turn might be linked to the realisation by unions that the strike 'is not an instrument by which the wages problem can be solved.'[45] Second, he suggested that the relative increase in frictional issues was largely accounted for by the increase in the sub-category, working arrangements, which in turn might be linked to workers' demands to be consulted by management over a wide range of matters. Third, the position of solidarity issues, which showed a

Table 3.28: Strike Causes Before and After 1926

Number of Strikes (per year)	Basic	Frictional	Solidarity	All
1911–25	617 (69%)	198 (22%)	83 (9%)	898 (100%)
1927–47	543 (54%)	395 (39%)	66 (7%)	1,004 (100%)

Thousands of workers directly involved (per year)	Basic	Frictional	Solidarity	All
1911–25	618 (76%)	114 (13%)	89 (11%)	821 (100%
1927–47	188 (60%)	86 (27%)	41 (13%)	315 (100%

Workers directly involved per strike (per year)	Basic	Frictional	Solidarity	All
1911–25	1,050	580	1,070	950
1927–47	350	220	630	316

Source: K.G.J.C. Knowles, *Strikes—A Study in Industrial Conflict,* Blackwell, Oxford, 1952, p. 234.

decrease in terms of the number of strikes but an increase in terms of the number of workers involved, might be accounted for by changes in the sub-category of trade union principle, which in turn might be linked to the fact that such strikes were no longer about the right to organise or about recognition but were concerned with the closed shop.

Table 3.29: Stoppages of Work over Pay, UK, 1915–1984

Period	Percentage of Stoppages over Pay	Percentage of Days Lost over Pay
1915–24	66.9	—
1925–34	53.1	87.5
1935–44	52.7	60.2
1945–54	44.4	49.7
1955–64	47.1	70.9
1965–74	56.1	82.3
1975–84	50.4	81.0

Source: Department of Employment. *Gazette.*

In fact, the trends identified by Knowles started to change after the period covered by his study. In particular the decline in stoppages accounted for by wage disputes was halted and reversed. Table 3.29 shows that the percentage of stoppages accounted for by wage disputes rose steadily from the mid-1950s until the mid-1970s, and although the average for the following decade fell back a little it remained at over 50 per cent for the number of stoppages and over 80 per cent for the number of days lost. If the effect of the changing pattern of strikes in the coal-mining industry is excluded (relatively few strikes in coal mining were over wages and the number of strikes in that industry declined dramatically from the 1960s) then the trend is in the same direction but less erratic.

The position with respect to all the categories of causes of stoppages between 1966 and 1985 is summarised in Table 3.30. The dominance of wage disputes is again noticeable though in

Table 3.30: *Percentage Distribution of Stoppages and Working Days Lost, by Cause, in the UK, 1966–1985*

	Number of Stoppages (%)			Number of Working Days Lost (%)		
	1966–74	1975–80	1981–85	1966–74	1975–80	1981–85
Pay—wage rates and earnings levels	54	52	41	82	83	24
Pay—extra wage and fringe benefits	3	3	2	2	2	1
All pay	57	55	43	84	85	25
Duration and pattern of hours worked	2	2	4	2	1	2
Redundancy questions	4	4	11	2	2	65
Trade union matters	8	6	6	4	3	2
Working conditions and supervision						
Manning and work allocation	29	33	36	8	9	6
Dismissal and other disciplinary matters						
Miscellaneous	*	—	—	*	—	—
Total	100	100	100	100	100	100

*—less than 0.5 per cent.

Source: Department of Employment, *Gazette,* various issues.

the latest period, 1981–5, the proportion of both stoppages and days lost accounted for in this way was much lower than in previous years. The other interesting aspect of the recorded causes of stoppages shown in Table 3.30 is the importance of factors like working conditions and supervision, manning and work allocation and dismissal and other disciplinary measures. They were the recorded cause of over 30 per cent of all stoppages and 9 per cent of all working days lost through stoppages between 1966 and 1985; at the end of this period, 1981–5, the totals for this category of causes were 36 per cent for stoppages and 6 per cent for days lost. The dramatic increase in the proportion of days lost accounted for by redundancy questions is a result of the 1984–5 miners' strike.

Inter-union disputes (which have been recorded primarily under the heading of trade union matters, though this category covers other issues as well) generally have not been recorded as a major cause of stoppages in the UK in recent years. From Table 3.30 it can be seen that between 1966 and 1985 only around 7 per cent of stoppages and 4 per cent of days lost were accounted for by 'trade union matters' and in fact less than a third of these were inter-union disputes.

UK governments have only published statistics relating to the distinction between official and unofficial stoppages since the 1960s. The available information is shown in Table 3.31. Prior to the publication of such information it was normally assumed that in the post-Second World War years up to 95 per cent of all strikes and 80 per cent of all days lost through strikes were the result of unofficial stoppages of work.[46] The information in Table 3.31 shows that while these estimates might have been in the right region, there were major fluctuations from year to year. For example, in 1980 nearly 85 per cent of working days were lost through official strikes compared to about 33 per cent during the 1960s. Trends are difficult to discern in this matter. While in particular years the number of working days lost through official stoppages was significant, in the 1970s and early 1980s the percentages fluctuated widely from year to year. The figures were particularly influenced by a number of large official stoppages and this can give a misleading impression of general developments. The use of the national official strike was an important feature of the 1970s and early 1980s but the unofficial

Table 3.31: Stoppages of Work in the UK Known to Have Been Official, 1960–1980

Number of Stoppages

	Beginning in Year			
	Total	of which known official	Col. (2) as % of col. (1)	in progress in year
	(1)	(2)	(3)	(4)
1960	2,832	68	2.4	2,849
1961	2,686	60	2.2	2,701
1962	2,449	78	3.2	2,465
1963	2,068	49	2.4	2,081
1964	1,524	70	2.8	2,535
1965	2,354	97	4.1	2,365
1966	1,937	60	3.1	1,951
1967	2,116	108	5.1	2,133
1968	2,378	91	3.8	2,390
1969	3,116	98	3.1	3,146
1970	3,906	162	4.1	3,943
1971	2,228	161	7.2	2,263
1972	2,497	160	6.4	2,530
1973	2,873	132	4.6	2,902
1974	2,922	125	4.3	2,946
1975	2,282	139	6.1	2,332
1976	2,016	69	3.4	2,034
1977	2,703	79	2.9	2,737
1978	2,471	90	3.6	2,498
1979	2,080	82	3.9	2,125
1980	1,330	67	5.0	1,348

Number of Workers Involved in Stoppages

	Beginning in Year		
	Total	of which known official	in progress in year
	(5) 000s	(6) 000s	(7) 000s
1960	814	24	819
1961	771	80	779
1962	4,420	3,809	4,423
1963	590	80	593
1964	872	161	883
1965	868	94	876
1966	530	50	544
1967	731	36	734
1968	2,255	1,565	2,258

Table 3.31 continued

1969	1,654	283	1,665
1970	1,793	296	1,801
1971	1,171	376	1,178
1972	1,722	635	1,734
1973	1,513	396	1,528
1974	1,622	467	1,626
1975	789	80	809
1976	666	46	668
1977	1,155	205	1,166
1978	1,001	123	1,041
1979	4,583	3,648	4,608
1980	830	404	834

Working days Lost in All Stoppages in Progress in Year
All industries and services

	Total (8) (000s)	of which known official (9) (000s)	Col. (9) as % of col. (8) (10)
1960	3,024	497	16.4
1961	3,046	861	28.3
1962	5,798	4,109	70.9
1963	1,755	527	30.0
1964	2,277	690	30.3
1965	2,925	607	20.8
1966	2,398	1,172	48.9
1967	2,787	394	14.1
1968	4,690	2,199	46.9
1969	6,846	1,613	23.6
1970	10,980	3,320	30.2
1971	13,551	10,050	74.2
1972	23,909	18,228	76.2
1973	7,197	2,009	27.9
1974	14,750	7,040	47.7
1975	6,012	1,148	19.1
1976	3,284	472	14.4
1977	10,142	2,512	24.8
1978	9,405	4,052	43.1
1979	29,474	23,512	79.8
1980	11,964	10,081	84.3

Sources: Yearbook of Labour Statistics, HMSO, London, 1975; *Employment Gazette,* July 1981.

strike still dominated. It is necessary, anyway, to exercise caution, in interpreting such statistics, for as has been stressed by a number of authors, the term 'unofficial strike' covers a variety of different kinds of action.[47] It is clear, for instance, that while some unofficial strikes may be disapproved of by union national executives not all will be viewed in that way.

Table 3.32: Stoppages of Work in Coal Mining in the UK, 1926–1985

Year	Number of Stoppages	Percentage of UK Total	Number of Days Lost (000s)	Percentage of UK Total
1926	1	0.3	145,209	89.5
1927	110	35.7	688	58.6
1928	97	32.1	452	32.6
1929	153	34.5	576	7.0
1930	150	35.5	663	15.1
1931	147	35.0	2,848	40.8
1932	111	28.5	287	4.4
1933	112	31.4	446	41.6
1934	143	30.4	365	38.0
1935	217	39.2	1,368	70.0
1936	270	33.0	852	46.6
1937	457	40.5	1,496	43.8
1938	363	41.5	697	42.2
1939	404	43.0	565	41.7
1940	381	41.3	505	53.7
1941	463	37.0	334	31.0
1942	526	40.4	840	55.0
1943	835	46.8	890	49.2
1944	1,253	57.1	2,480	66.9
1945	1,295	56.5	640	22.6
1946	1,329	60.3	422	19.6
1947	1,049	61.0	912	37.5
1948	1,116	63.5	464	23.9
1949	87	61.2	754	41.7
1950	863	54.5	431	31.0
1951	1,058	61.6	350	20.7
1952	1,221	71.2	660	36.8
1953	1,307	74.9	393	18.0
1954	1,464	73.6	468	19.1
1955	1,783	73.7	1,112	29.4
1956	2,067	78.1	502	24.1
1957	2,224	77.8	514	6.1

Table 3.32 continued

Year	Number of Stoppages	Percentage of UK Total	Number of Days Lost (000s)	Percentage of UK Total
1958	1,963	74.7	450	13.0
1959	1,307	62.4	363	6.9
1960	1,666	58.8	494	16.3
1961	1,458	54.3	737	24.2
1962	1,203	49.1	308	5.3
1963	987	47.7	326	18.6
1964	1,059	42.0	302	13.3
1965	731	31.1	412	14.1
1966	553	5.1	118	4.9
1967	394	18.6	105	3.8
1968	215	9.0	53	1.1
1969	193	6.2	1,041	15.3
1970	165	4.2	1,092	10.0
1971	135	6.1	63	0.5
1972	218	8.7	10,797	45.3
1973	301	10.5	90	1.3
1974	183	6.3	5,625	38.1
1975	212	9.3	52	0.9
1976	271	13.4	70	2.1
1977	262	9.7	88	0.9
1978	338	13.7	195	2.1
1979	295	14.2	112	0.4
1980	302	22.7	152	1.3
1981	302	22.6	235	5.5
1982	403	26.4	374	7.0
1983	355	26.3	484	12.9
1984	78	6.8	22,483	84.6
1985	160	17.7	4,142	68.6

Source: Department of Employment, *Gazette.*

It was noted earlier that consideration of strike trends in the UK has to be undertaken with a recognition that for a substantial period the influence of one industry, coal mining, was considerable. This issue can be taken further now by reference to Table 3.32. From this table it can be seen that from the General Strike until the 1960s the coal-mining industry dominated stoppage activity in the UK. 1926 was clearly an atypical year, yet from 1937 to 1964 coal mining never accounted for less than 35 per cent of all stoppages and between 1931 and 1945 it only accounted for less than 40 per cent of all days lost on four occasions. The domination of the coal-mining industry started to fade, as far as days lost are concerned, in the 1950s and as far as the number of stoppages are concerned in the 1960s. The reduction in the number of stoppages in coal mining from about 2,000 in the mid-1950s to around 250 in the mid-1970s, and in the number of working days lost from about 0.5 million in the mid-1950s to around 75,000 in the mid-1970s, had important implications for overall strike trends in the UK. It is worthwhile noting, though, that despite the general reduction in the proportion of stoppages in the UK occurring in the coal-mining industry, in particular years this general trend has been reversed. In 1972, 1974 and 1984–5 a very large proportion of days lost through stoppages in the UK were accounted for by strikes in the coal-mining industry. The same is not the case if the number of stoppages rather than the number of working days lost is looked at because in each of these years the coal-mining industry was the scene for a major national strike. An additional consideration is put forward by Winterton. He argues that the proportion of stoppages qualifying for inclusion in the published statistics declined over the 1960–78 period. 'This accounts', he says 'for a significant amount of the apparent decline in coal mining strike proneness since 1960.'[48].

A broader view of strike activity in the UK by industry is offered in Tables 3.33 and 3.34. Information is given per 1,000 employees in each industry list for the period 1971 to 1981 and then for the period 1982 to 1985 (different industrial groupings are used for the two time periods). The dominance of certain industries over this period is clear from these tables, although there are some variations from year to year. Again the importance of the coal-mining industry can be seen, although between 1976 and 1980 its average was less than that for all industries and services. Ship-building, motor vehicles and port transport have also been heavily strike-prone: between 1971 and 1981 when all three industries are easily identifiable they regularly showed totals far higher than the all-industries average. In fact these industries, along with coal mining, have long been recognised in the UK as being particularly highly strike-prone. For example, they were highlighted by the

Table 3.33: Stoppages of Work due to Industrial Disputes, UK, 1971–1981, by industry

Industry Group	Working Days Lost (per 1,000 employees)		
	1971–75	1976–80	1981
Agriculture, forestry, fishing	11	4	0
Coal mining	10,429	423	856
All other mining and quarrying	44	188	28
Grain milling	87	1,042	120
Bread and flour confectionery, biscuits	401	1,106	75
All other food industries	209	467	337
Drink	559	1,008	448
Tobacco	725	718	18
Coal and petroleum products	637	317	13
Chemicals, dyestuffs, plastics, fertilisers etc.	312	420	499
Pharmaceutical and toilet preparations	121	147	4
Paints, soap and other chemical industries	112	430	198
Iron (incl. castings) and steel (incl. tubes)	1,138	6,953	85
All other metal manufacture	854	1,304	97
Mechanical engineering	841	2,133	143
Instrument engineering	405	828	55
Electrical engineering	1,188	1,931	157
Shipbuilding and marine engineering	3,031	1,018	799
Motor vehicles	3,670	4,467	1,067
Aerospace equipment	1,569	1,978	506
All other vehicles	1,405	2,236	3
Metal goods not elsewhere specified	370	655	65
Cotton flax and man-made fibres	518	256	13
Woollen and worsted	63	72	5
Hosiery and other knitted goods	575	185	14
All other textile industries	109	215	64
Clothing other than footwear	107	79	37
Footwear	73	147	1
Bricks, fireclay and refractory goods	581	365	296
Pottery	72	132	13
Glass	364	594	260
Cement, abrasives and building materials not elsewhere specified	158	234	134
Furniture, bedding, upholstery	75	67	57
Timber, other manufacturers of wood and cork	129	81	53

Table 3.33 continued

Industry Group	Working Days Lost (per 1,000 employees)		
	1971−75	1976−80	1981
Paper and board, cartons etc.	277	187	27
Printing, publishing etc.	160	775	65
Other manufacturing industries	631	407	93
Construction	781	374	38
Gas, electricity, water	231	148	29
Railways	1,111	128	13
Road passenger transport	417	353	147
Road haulage contracting	229	966	32
Sea transport	50	81	585
Port and inland water transport	3,599	1,449	1,115
Other transport and communications	2,009	100	41
Distributive trades	18	20	14
Insurance, banking, finance and business services	2	5	6
Professional and scientific services	45	91	12
Miscellaneous services	14	66	4
Public administration and defence	70	513	341
Total, all industries and services	587	565	101

Source: Department of Employment, *Gazette.*

Donovan Commission[49] in its report in 1968 (using data referring to 1964−6) and they have all been the subject of extensive analysis and discussion.[50]

This is not the place to attempt a full review of the literature on the explanation for strike propensities in particular industries: the causes of strikes and industrial conflict will be dealt with in the next two chapters. The extent to which changes in employment policy and practices have affected strike records, though, has been one focus of interest. The introduction of the Power Leading Agreement in the coal-mining industry in 1966 reduced fragmented bargaining and the fluctuation of earnings in the industry[51], and this is widely held to be one of the most important factors explaining the subsequent decline in strike activity in that industry. However, in other industries the same

Table 3.34: Stoppages of Work due to Industrial Dispute, UK, 1982–1985, by industry

Industry Group	Working Days Lost (per 1,000 employees)			
	1982	1983	1984	1985
Agriculture, forestry, fishing	—	2	3	—
Coal extraction	1,395	1,901	97,849	19,248
Extraction and processing of coke, mineral oil and natural gas	49	1,854	21	23
Electricity, gas, other energy and water	148	2,252	102	167
Metal processing and manufacture	406	637	94	285
Mineral processing and manufacture	110	131	126	225
Chemicals and man-made fibres	61	62	187	14
Metal goods not elsewhere specified	237	91	185	125
Mechanical engineering	316	406	228	107
Electrical engineering and equipment	276	236	284	93
Instrument engineering	670	150	348	18
Motor vehicles	1,710	1,775	3,575	245
Other transport equipment	480	573	1,634	866
Food, drink and tobacco	255	127	372	201
Textiles	113	61	74	85
Footwear and clothing	97	58	167	36
Timber and wooden furniture	35	20	129	147
Paper, printing and publishing	200	180	277	143
Other manufacturing industries	242	342	169	16
Construction	39	67	340	52
Distribution, hotels and catering, repairs	6	5	4	2
Railways	6,641	20	127	140
Other inland transport	393	137	377	149
Sea transport	462	224	800	865
Other transport and communications	541	248	141	147
Supporting and misc., transport services	451	448	1,641	62
Banking, finance, insurance business services and leasing	2	6	11	3
Public administration, sanitary services and education	109	32	214	265
Medical and health services	618	4	17	24
Other services	14	74	107	29
All industries and services	249	178	1,283	298

Source: Department of Employment, *Gazette*.

result is not apparent. The decasualisation of dock labour in 1967[52] was not accompanied by a decline in strike activity of the same order, though it can be argued that decasualisation in itself, as a change in working practices, caused additional strike activity, and any benefits might take some time to work through, especially given the debate over containerisation in progress at the same time.

One of the most interesting developments in strike activity in recent years has occurred outside the major strike-prone industries. In the public sector a number of groups, like health-service workers, civil servants, teachers and local-authority workers, who historically have not readily engaged in strike activity, have started to do so. A study by Terry of thirty British local authorities in 1979 sugggested that 60 per cent had experienced a strike of one day or longer, and some form of industrial action (not necessarily a one-day strike) seemed to have occurred in every authority over a two-year period.[53] Although in general local authorities experience less strike action than industry as a whole (Smith suggested that the incidence of strikes in local authorities was less than that for all industries[54]) this does not detract from the increasing use of strike activity amongst some workers in local authorities. Teachers, for example, until recently would not have been expected to engage in strike activity. Although one of the 'teachers' unions', the Professional Association of Teachers, still refuses to undertake such action, the rest of the teachers' unions do not take such a stance and in 1984 and 1985 engaged in a series of strikes (bolstered by other forms of industrial action) throughout Britain. The same kind of picture emerges if one looks outside the local authorities but still within the public sector. One of the nurses' representative organisations, the Royal College of Nursing, still refuses to engage in strike activity, but other organisations representing more nurses do not share that view. In the early 1980s nurses, along with other health-service workers, engaged in a prolonged series of strikes, which was controversial, but nevertheless gained support from large sections of the profession. In part, the growing militancy of the public sector can be linked to the growth in unionisation: however, it can also be linked to a change of tactics by trade unions and a recognition by groups of workers, who would not have seen strike activity as appropriate, that it may be necessary to achieve their objectives.

Discussion of the strike record of different industries is to some extent complicated by the recognition that most strikes occur in a relatively small number of workplaces rather than in the whole of an industry. Smith noted, for example, that in manufacturing industry in Britain only 2 per cent of workplaces had a recorded strike in any one year.[55] Of course, over a longer period of time a higher proportion of workplaces will experience recorded strikes and others will experience industrial action that is never recorded. Creigh and Makeham noted that although a small number of plants may be affected in any one year, this is a changing set and they may thus reflect the general characteristics of an industry.[56] Nevertheless suggestions have been made that highly strike-prone workplaces frequently differ from others in the same industry (for example, they tend to be larger) and this issue clearly makes the whole discussion of strike activity within industries more complex.

Regional variations in strike propensity have been identified in analyses of the strike records of most industrial nations, and

Table 3.35: Regional Distribution of Strike Activity, 1946–1973

Region	Percentage of Employees in Employment	Average Number of Workers Involved (000s)	Workers Involved as percentage of Employees in Employment	Average Number of Working Days (000s)	Working Days Lost per 1,000 Employees in Employment
South East	35.8	238.6	2.9	1,207	149
South West	5.6	44.8	3.5	199	157
Midlands, Yorkshire and Humberside	24.7	389.6	6.9	1,689	301
North West	12.8	198.1	6.4	982	337
North	5.6	79.1	6.2	473	372
Scotland	9.2	182.5	8.7	802	384
Wales	4.2	90.1	9.4	522	545
Northern Ireland	2.0	28.7	6.2	136	297
UK	100.0	1,238.5	5.5	6,010	265

Source: J.W. Durcan, W.E.J. McCarthy and G.P. Redman, *Strikes in Post-War Britain*, Allen and Unwin, London, 1983, p. 186.

the UK is no exception to the general rule. They have received considerable attention: the earliest study, by Bevan, dates back to 1880,[57] the matter was examined by Knowles in his book published in 1952[58], and more recently a number of projects have sought to examine matters further. Table 3.35 looks at the position between 1946 and 1973. This table is taken from Durcan, McCarthy and Redman's study of strikes in Britain over that period.[59] They note that two regions appear to have been most strike-prone in terms of worker involvement: Wales and Scotland. Four regions appeared to have been moderately strike-prone, the Midlands, Yorkshire and Humberside, the North West, the North, and Northern Ireland. The least strike-prone regions were the South West and South East. If time lost per 1,000 employees is considered then the pattern is similar. The most strike-prone regions were Wales and Scotland, followed in rank order by the North, North West, Midlands, Yorkshire and Humberside, Northern Ireland, the South West and South East. Durcan, McCarthy and Redman offer a word of caution, though, about examining these variations, which echoes that made when considering strikes by industry: 'the regions themselves are far from homogenous and . . . only a small minority of employees in each region was involved in stoppages e.g. even in Wales 90 per cent of employees were not, on average, involved in stoppages at any time in the course of the year.'[60]

The most comprehensive study is that by Smith, in which part of the time period examined by Durcan, McCarthy and Redman was considered. Smith's study of regional variations beteen 1968 and 1973 went below the major regional units to look at 61 subdivisions. A procedure was adopted to allow for account to be taken of the most obvious explanation for regional variations, differences in industrial structure. It was found that even after variations in industrial structure had been allowed for, substantial differences remained in strike incidence between different parts of the country. The analysis suggested that two factors were particularly strongly associated with high strike-proneness: higher than average plant size and a rapid rate of earnings growth. Nevertheless, problems still remain. A considerable amount of the variation still has to be explained (if differences in industrial structure are discounted). Smith accepts that his study may have failed to find such explanations either because the range of economic variables employed was inadequate or because social-cultural factors (which were not looked at in this study) are important. The problems with the statistics being affected by strikes in a small number of plants also recurs yet again. Smith reported that in the analysis of manufacturing industry in Britain it was found that variations between areas were due to the better or worse performance of a small minority of plants.

Table 3.36: Stoppages of Work in the UK, by region, 1982–1985

Region	Working Days Lost (per 1,000 workers)			
	1982	*1983*	*1984*	*1985*
South East	174	138	212	67
East Anglia	163	86	126	60
South West	113	58	258	56
West Midlands	243	152	713	142
East Midlands	222	140	2,061	333
Yorkshire and Humberside	322	236	5,339	1,179
North West	414	331	587	169
North	407	232	4,065	859
Wales	314	395	3,914	1,035
Scotland	328	162	1,210	348
Northern Ireland	216	170	112	87
United Kingdom	252	180	1,283	298

Source: Department of Employment, *Gazette.*

The position as far as regional variations are concerned is updated by Table 3.36. This looks at four years: 1982–1985. The breakdown of regions is different to that used by Durcan, McCarthy and Redman. Nevertheless, some similarities with the earlier period can be pointed to. For example, Wales lost many more days per 1,000 workers than the UK average over this period while the South East and South West both lost markedly fewer than the UK average. However, there are some differences, including the markedly lower strike figures for

Scotland (in two of the three years the Scottish totals were lower than the UK average).

SIMILARITIES AND DIFFERENCES

The examination of strike trend in Australia, USA and the UK shows some broad similarities. For example, in each country there was a rise in the number of strikes recorded in the post-Second World War years, which reached a height in the late 1960s and early 1970s, and in each country there was a rise in the number of days lost through disputes in the 1970s. Similarly, in each country a comparable range of industries were recorded as being highly strike prone, like mining and dock work, while a comparable range of industries were recorded as being lowly strike-prone. Again, in each country significant variations in the level of strike activity were recorded between different regions and these differences could not be explained simply by reference to differences in industrial structure.

While such broad similarities are important, they need to be tempered by a recognition of significant differences in experience between the three countries. Probably the most important difference is in the area of duration. In the UK and Australia the average duration of strikes declined after the Second World War: no such general trend can be discerned for the USA. In the UK and Australia the duration of strikes increased in the early 1970s: in the USA the duration increased at the end of the 1970s. The longer duration of stoppages in the USA and the absence of any long-term trend towards a reduction in duration has been an important part of what some writers have referred to as American 'exceptionalism'. It has been an important distinguishing feature of industrial relations in the USA and an important comparison with other countries.

Other differences are also important. In the USA and the UK wages have dominated the recorded causes of stoppages. There have been variations from period to period but the domination of wages has endured. In the UK pay was the recorded cause of more than half of all stoppages and days lost except for the period 1945–64. The position was different in detail in the USA, but in most years wages have accounted for more than 50 per cent of stoppages and days lost. In Australia working conditions and managerial policy have been the most important cause as far as the number of stoppages are concerned and in a number of periods the same has also been true as far as the number of days lost is concerned.

Similarly, while the distribution of stoppages by industry shows comparable patterns in all three countries, there are some differences. The dominance of mining in the pre-1960 period in the UK and Australia was more noticeable than in the USA as was the subsequent decline in strike activity in that industry. In Australia stoppages in mining accounted for two thirds of all strikes and over half of all days lost. In the UK, stoppages in coal mining accounted for around 40 per cent of all strikes in the 1930s, approaching 60 per cent in the 1940s and about 70 per cent in the 1950s. In the USA coal mining has never accounted for more than about 10 per cent of stoppages for more than short periods (the percentage of working days lost has been higher but not so high as in Australia and the UK). The three countries also occupy different positions in the strike 'league table'. The differences are most noticeable in terms of the number of stoppages (Australia has a far higher frequency of stoppages, taking account of the number of employees in the country: in the 1970s more than four times as many as the UK and about eight times as many as the USA). Differences on other measures are also noticeable. Some of these differences can be explained in part by recording and classification practices but significant variations remain in the experience of strike activity.

The comparison of strike trends in these three countries reinforces the message from the border analysis of strike patterns in the last chapter. The challenge for explanation of strike activity is to examine both important similarities in experience and significant differences. The challenge is a formidable one and has attracted the attention of different disciplines and a multitude of researchers and writers.

NOTES

1. D. Oxnam, 'Strikes in Australia', *Economic Record,* May 1953, pp. 73–89.

2. See, for example, M. Waters, *Strikes in Australia,* Allen and Unwin, Sydney, 1982.
3. M. Wooden and S. Creigh, *Strikes in Post-War Australia: A Review of Research and Statistics,* National Institute of Labour Studies, Flinders University, Working Paper No. 60, 1983.
4. D. Oxnam, *loc. cit.;* P. Bently and B. Hughes, 'Cyclical Influences on Strike Activity: The Australian Record 1952–1968', Australian Economic Papers, Vol. 9 (December 1970), pp. 149–70.
5. *Op cit.*
6. *Loc. cit.,* pp. 79–80.
7. P. Bentley, 'Recent Strike Behaviour in Australia: Causes and Responses', in G.W. Ford, J.M. Hearn and P. Landsbury (eds) *Australian Labour Relations: Readings,* Sun Books, Melbourne, 1980. p. 25.
8. *Op. cit.,* pp. 59–60.
9. See for example D. Oxnam, *loc. cit.*
10. T. Sweet, *Australia Strike Statistics 1913–1976,* University of Aston Management Centre, Working Paper No. 89, 1978.
11. See D. Oxnam, *loc. cit.,* and D. Oxnam, 'Issues in Industrial Conflict: Australian Experience 1913–1963', *Journal of Industrial Relations,* Vol. 9 (1967), pp. 11–24.
12. K. Wright, *Demarcation and Jurisictional Disputes in Australia, 1975–79,* Industrial Relations Research Centre, University of New South Wales, 1983.
13. B. Gordon, 'A Ninety-Sector Analysis of Industrial Disputes in Australia 1968–73', *Journal of Industrial Relations,* Vol. 17 (1975) pp. 240–54.
14. S.W. Creigh, F. Robertson and M. Wooden, 'Research Note: Inter-State Variations in Strike Proneness', *Australian Bulletin of Labour,* Vol. 9 (1983), p. 214.
15. S. Creigh and M. Wooden, 'Strikes in Post War Australia: A Review', *Journal of Industrial Relations,* Vol. 27 (June 1985), p. 144.
16. *Ibid.,* p. 85.
17. *Op. cit.,* p. 35.
18. See T. Sweet, *Op. cit.*
19. P.K. Edwards, *Strikes in the United States 1881–1974,* Blackwell, Oxford, 1981.
20. *Ibid.,* p. 31.
21. P.K. Edwards, 'The End of American Strike Statistics', *British Journal of Industrial Relations,* Vol. 21, No. 3 (1983), p. 392.
22. R.T. Flanagan, G. Strauss and L. Ulman, 'Worker Discontent and Work Place Behaviour', *Industrial Relations,* Vol. 13 (1974), p. 111.
23. E.J. Burtt, *Labour in the American Economy,* Macmillan, London, 1979.
24. P.K. Edwards (1981), *op. cit.*
25. *Ibid.*
26. A.M. Ross, 'The Prospects for Industrial Conflict', *Industrial Relations,* Vol. 1 (October 1961), pp. 57–74.
27. B.E. Kaufman, 'Interindustry Trends in Strike Activity', *Industrial Relations,* Vol. 22 (Winter 1983), pp. 45–57.

28. N.W. Chamberlain, D.E. Cullen and D. Lewis, *The Labour Sector,* McGraw-Hill, New York, 1980.
29. J.F. Burton and C.E. Krider, 'The Incidence of Strikes in Public Employment', in D. Hammermesh (ed.) *Labour in the Public and Non Profit Sectors,* Princeton, 1975.
30. E.H. Becker, 'Analysis of Work Stoppages in the Federal Sector 1962–81', *Monthly Labor Review,* Vol. 105, No. 8, (August 1982), pp. 49–53.
31. D. Britt and O. Gallie, 'Industrial Conflict and Unionisation', *American Sociological Review,* Vol. 39 (October 1974), pp. 642–51.
32. See Kaufman, *op. cit.*
33. R.N. Stern, 'Intermetropolitan Patterns of Strike Frequency', *Industrial and Labour Relations,* Vol. 29, No. 2, (January 1976), pp. 218–35.
34. *Ibid.,* p. 229.
35. K.G.J.C. Knowles, *Strikes—A Study of Industrial Conflict,* Blackwell, Oxford, 1952.
36. J.W. Durcan, W.E.J. McCarthy and G.P. Redman, *Strikes in Post War Britain,* Allen and Unwin, London, 1983.
37. C.T.B. Smith *et al., Strikes in Britain,* Department of Employment, Manpower Paper 15, HMSO, London, 1978.
38. H.A. Clegg, *The Changing System of Industrial Relations in Great Britain,* Blackwell, Oxford, 1979.
39. 'Large Industrial Stoppages, 1960–1979', *Employment Gazette,* Vol. 88 (1980), pp. 994–9.
40. *Op. cit.,* p. 403.
41. Royal Commission on Trade Unions and Employers Associations, 1965–68, *Report,* HMSO London, 1968.
42. P.K. Edwards, 'Britain's Changing Strike Problems?', *Industrial Relations Journal,* Vol. 13, No. 2, (Summer 1982), pp. 5–20.
43. *Op. cit.,* p. 401.
44. *Op. cit.*
45. *Op. cit.,* p. 235.
46. See Royal Commission on Employers Associations and Trade Unions, *op. cit.*
47. See for example, G.C. Cameron and J.E.T. Eldridge, 'Unofficial Strikes', in J.E.T. Eldridge, *Industrial Disputes,* Routledge and Kegan Paul, London, 1968, pp. 68–90.
48. J. Winterton, 'The Trend of Strikes in Coal Mining 1949–1979', *Industrial Relations Journal,* Vol. 12, No. 6 (November/December 1981), p. 16.
49. *Op. cit.*
50. See for example, H.A. Turner, G. Clack and G. Roberts, *Labour Relations in the Motor Industry,* Allen and Unwin, London, 1967.
51. See H.A. Clegg, *op. cit.*
52. See M.P. Jackson, *Labour Relations in the Docks,* Saxon House, Farnborough, 1973.
53. See M. Terry 'Organising a Fragmented Workforce: Shop Stewards in Local Government', *British Journal of Industrial Relations,* Vol. 20, No.

1 (March 1982) pp. 1–19, for a discussion of 1979 survey and related research.
54. *Op. cit.*
55. *Ibid.*
56. S. Creigh and P. Makeham, 'Variations in Strike Activity Within UK Manufacturing Industry', *Industrial Relations Journal,* Vol. 11, No. 5, (November/December 1980), pp. 32–7.
57. G.P. Bevan, 'On Strikes of the Past Ten Years', *Journal of the Statistical Society,* Vol. 12, No. 1, 1880.
58. *Op. cit.*
59. *Op. cit.*
60. *Ibid.,* p. 187.

4 Explanations for Variations in Strike Patterns and Trends

The variations in strike patterns and trends that have been noted have excited researchers over a long period and led to the search for explanations. Many have taken variations between countries as a starting point though some have concentrated on variations in one country over a period of time. The studies can be classified into three broad categories and will be discussed in such a fashion in this chapter. However, this raises some problems as some researchers have looked at factors which span more than one category and some have changed their emphasis over time. These problems will be noted in the course of the review.

INSTITUTIONAL FACTORS

The Work of Ross and Hartman
One of the first major attempts to provide an explanation for strike activity came from Ross and Hartman.[1] They built on work undertaken by Ross with a number of other collaborators in the previous decade (for example a study by Ross and Irwin examined strike trends in five countries for the 1927 to 1947 period.[2]) Ross and Hartman concentrated on analysing two measures of strike activity, the membership involvement ratio (the sum of all workers involved in strikes in a year divided by the average number of union members in that year) and the strike duration ratio (the number of workers involved in strikes divided by the number of working days lost through strikes). Data were collected for fifteen countries between 1900 and 1956.

Two main themes can be discerned from this study. The first is the general reduction in strike activity over the period concerned: what Ross and Hartman referred to as the 'withering away of the strike'. Three main reasons were put forward to explain the trend identified. First it was argued that employees had developed more sophisticated policies and more effective organisations. Second, the state had become more prominent as an employer, in economic affairs, in the provision of benefits and in the supervision of industrial relations. Third, in most countries (though not in the USA) it was said that the labour movement was forsaking the use of the strike in favour of broader political activity.

The second main theme in Ross and Hartman's study was the identification of distinctive patterns of industrial conflict and the linking of them to different industrial relations systems. They argued that it was possible to classify the fifteen countries they had looked at into 'several distinct patterns of industrial conflict'. The four groups they isolated were termed, the North European pattern first variant (Denmark, Netherlands and West Germany with the UK on the borderline), the North European pattern second variant (Norway and Sweden), the Mediterranean/Asian pattern (France, Italy, Japan and India) and the North American pattern (Canada and USA). They argued that the North European pattern first variant was characterised by a nominal propensity to strike and a low or moderate duration of strikes; the North European pattern second variant was characterised by infrequent but long stoppages; the Mediterranean/Asian pattern was characterised by high participation in strikes but short duration; and the North American pattern was characterised by a moderately high propensity to strike as well as a relatively long duration. Three of the original countries—Australia, Finland and South Africa—were excluded from this classification because they were 'special cases'.

Ross and Hartman argued that the distinctive strike patterns they had identified were associated with particular kinds of industrial relations systems. Five key characteristics of such systems were identified and are shown in Table 4.1. In the North European pattern first variant the countries were said to have mature labour movements with firm and stable memberships;

leadership conflicts were subdued; there was a widespread acceptance of the role of trade unions in industry with centralised collective bargaining; there was an important labour party; and governments rarely intervened to regulate the terms of employment though they frequently intervened in collective bargaining. The North European pattern second variant

Table 4.1: Principal Features of an Industrial Relations System Used For Comparison

1.	*Organisational Stability*
(a)	Age of labour movement
(b)	Stability of membership in recent years
2.	*Leadership Conflicts in the Labour Movement*
(a)	Factionalism, rival unionism and rival federations
(b)	Strength of communism in labour unions
3.	*States of Union-management Relations*
(a)	Degree of acceptance by employers
(b)	Consolidation of bargaining structure
4.	*Labour Political Activity*
(a)	Existence of Labour Party as a leading political party
(b)	Labour Party governments
5.	*Role of the State*
(a)	Extent of government activity in defining terms of employment
(b)	Dispute settlement policies and procedures

Source: A.M. Ross, 'Changing Patterns of Industrial Conflict', in G.G. Sommers (ed.), *Proceedings of the 12th Annual Meeting of the Industrial Relations Research Association,* 1959.

showed many of the characteristics of the first variant but there was less active intervention in labour-management relations. The Mediterranean/Asian pattern countries were said to have relatively young labour movements (either they had just become mass organisations or were reorganised after 1945); union membership was often an 'ephemeral phenomenon'; and internal leadership conflicts were endemic; labour-management relations were weak and unstable with unions too weak to conduct long strikes; left-wing parties were divided; and there was considerable state direct intervention in industry. In the last of the four patterns, the North American, Ross and Hartman argued that while labour movements were older than in the Mediterranean/Asian pattern they were younger than in the other patterns; union density had become more stable in recent years and inter-union rivalry had subsided; unions were increasingly accepted by employers; bargaining structures were decentralised; terms and conditions of employment were largely determined privately; and there was not a successful labour party.

Ross and Hartman, in their discussion, put forward particular arguments. However, it is the more general themes, rather than the detail of the argument that are worth looking at further. The first theme can be discussed under the heading of the institutionalisation of industrial conflict; the second theme can be discussed under the heading of the impact of particular institutions of industrial relations on strike records.

The 'Withering Away' of the Strike and the Institutionalisation of Industrial Conflict

The two themes developed by Ross and Hartman have been taken up by a number of other writers. The first theme can be seen, for example, in the work of Kerr and associates.[3] In their discussion of the 'logic of industrialism' they sought to highlight the consequences of industralisation. In this context they argued that there was a link between industrialisation and industrial conflict. The earlier stages of industrialisation would lead to conflict connected to adjustment to new methods of production, but as industrialisation proceeded conflict would lessen. Union organisation would develop, eventually becoming accommodated within the system, and mechanisms such as collective bargaining would be established to bring order into industrial relations. Kerr argued that the influence of industrialisation would be so strong and pervasive that all industrial countries would move in the same direction and come to discover similar ways of dealing with problems. The 'convergence' of industrial societies to which Kerr referred, despite differences in the social, political and economic backgrounds of the countries, has been widely debated. Nevertheless, the issue raised in this context, the effect of industrialisation on industrial conflict, has found echoes in the work of many.

There is a widespread discussion in the literature about what is sometimes termed the institutionalisation of industrial conflict. This assumes that as mechanisms are developed to institutionalise industrial conflict it will become less violent and less intense. Two agents are frequently seem to be crucial in this development: trade unions and collective bargaining. Wright Mills commenting specifically on US unions, has shown how trade unions can help to institutionalise conflict.[4] He has done so by tracing the development of unions and analysing their role during different periods of time; he highlighted four stages. First, he argued, labour unions arose as a counterforce to the corporate form of business enterprise. The unions were 'economic attempts to equalise the bargaining power of the workers and the corporations'.[5] As a result the typical businessman saw labour unions as a threat; they challenged his freedom of action and his economic position. The second stage of development, therefore, saw the business community forming trade associations of their own, to counter 'union power'. This drove unions to bargain and take action on a national basis; it also incidentally increased the pressure on small businessmen because they were not efficient enough to meet the demands of industry-wide agreements. The end product was growing centralisation within both the business and labour hierarchies. The third stage of development saw the entry of the state into the arena in a major fashion. The state intervened increasingly in disputes between labour and business and on occasions took over the control of industries. This led on to the fourth stage during which political questions increasingly dominated discussion and action. However, in many ways union leaders were ill-suited to the new situation; they were used to taking short-term pragmatic economic decisions, not debating in the political arena. Therefore in the final stage of development union leaders were faced with a problem. They had to deal with a situation which was alien to them and they had to find some way to defend the gains they had made. They had no long-term political strategy; neither for that matter did most of their members. In an attempt to stabilise their position, therefore.

. . . the labor leaders allow their unions to evolve into institutions which integrate the industrial worker into a political economy that is changing from laissez-faire to monopoly and to state capitalism with many corporate features. The labor leaders become part of a machinery which keeps them as leaders but makes them the go-betweens of the rank and file workers and the class of owners and managers.[6]

The labour leader, therefore, today maintains his role by bargaining on behalf of labour. He offers to make a contract with the owners and managers; he will provide labour for a certain price. However, if he is to maintain his credibility then he must supply that labour when it is required and see that it does not rebel. As a result, he has to act as a discipliner of the labour force and a manager of discontent.

Thus Wright Mills concluded that although the union leader may be seen, and at times act, as one who 'whips up the opinion and activity of the rank and file and focuses them against the business corporation', because of 'his timidity and fear and eagerness to stay alive in a hostile environment'[7] in fact, he serves to hold back rebellion. 'He organizes discontent and then sits on it, exploiting it in order to maintain a continuous organization; the labour leader is a manager of discontent. He makes regular what might otherwise be disruptive, both within the institutional routine and within the union which he seeks to establish and maintain'.[8]

Although the comments of Wright Mills were drawn from the history of unions in the USA there is little doubt that he saw them as having a more general application. Allen, in his study of British trade unions, has painted a picture which has many similarities. Although Allen argues that militant trade unionism is possible (after a process of 'resocialisation') at the moment most British trade unions are required to fit, and succeed in fitting, neatly into the capitalist system. 'At every point of their involvement unions are accommodated comfortably within the system of distribution they are struggling against . . ... In the main they have evolved equipped to struggle in a limited short-term fashion and, though many pay lip-service to socialist aims, they accept the capitalist system largely for what it is'.[9]

Allen also comments on one other way in which the activity of unions in Britain may be seen as helping to maintain the present system. They have, he says, accepted the capitalist norms of peaceful competition, to such an extent that now 'they are competing against each other in a wasteful, resource-consuming and fruitless activity, of benefit only to employers'.[10]

Smelser, who looked at 'Anglo-American unionism', developed a similar theme.[11] He argued that such unions had only recently moved into the third stage of their development. However, this stage was characterised by the rationalisation of the conduct of strikes, a reduction in violence and unnecessary damage to industry and the gradual withdrawal from secondary action. Trade unions are now concerned with their public image. 'Peaceful collective bargaining', argued Smelser, 'has become the standard form of conflict'[12] only disturbed in the upheaval of wildcat strikes.

The second agent of the institutionalisation of industrial conflict, the development of collective bargaining, has obvious links with the growth and acceptance of trade unions. It is recognised that in most instances employers fought against trade unions as organisations and against giving them bargaining rights. Taft and Ross note that in the USA employers (often aided by governments) fought pitched battles to prevent the spread of unionism and deny bargaining rights.[13] This reaction to trade unions and bargaining changed in some cases because opposing bargaining was causing more problems than were likely to be met by accepting it. However, there were other more positive reasons for the acceptance of collective bargaining. These centre on the notion that collective bargaining can help to regularise and institutionalise industrial conflict. There are a number of elements to this belief.

First, collective bargaining is the means by which a 'normative system' is created for regulating industrial conflict and ensuring that it is kept within acceptable bounds. Collective bargaining does not prevent industrial conflict but it provides a forum for discussion and a 'means for systematic social change in the working code governing management-men relations'.[14]

Second, collective bargaining enables parties to a dispute to view the situation more dispassionately than might otherwise be the case; it allows time to pause for thought and review the consequences of possible courses of action. In particular, the costs as well as the benefits of violent conflict may come to be appreciated. Thus, Kerr has argued that collective bargaining aids 'rationality-knowledge of costs and consequences—and thus the diplomatic resolution of controversies'.[15] Similarly, Dubin has noted how collective bargaining helps to introduce a time perspective into industrial conflict, and suggests that this

time perspective can have an important tempering influence toward limiting disorder. It is significant that in the United States strike violence has been inversely related to the permanence of unionism. As collective bargaining becomes an established feature of our society both sides come to recognise that each conflict-created disorder is inevitably succeeded by a re-established order and that permanently disruptive disorder may materially impede the resolution of the conflict.[16]

Third, collective bargaining absorbs energy which might otherwise be more destructively directed. Thus, Harbison has argued that collective bargaining provides a 'drainage channel' for worker dissatisfaction.[17] In essence, if workers and their leaders devote a considerable proportion of their time to scoring bargaining points and winning concessions at the bargaining table this is likely to divert attention from questioning more fundamental aspects of industrial society.

Fourth, collective bargaining, by providing a forum for meetings between management and unions, can help to facilitate improved relations and gradual change. Thus Dahrendorf has argued that 'by collective bargaining the frozen fruits of industrial conflict are thawed. If the representatives of management and labour meet regularly for negotiations, gradual changes of social structure replace the tendency toward revolutionary explosions and civil war'.[18]

The discussion of the institutionalisation of industrial conflict, though, needs to be carefully considered, for while there is some evidence of the way in which it can operate there is also evidence of some limitations to the process. Although Dahrendorf[19] noted the changes that had taken place since the early stages of industrialisation (he discussed post-capitalist society, to indicate that significant changes had taken place since early classic capitalism, and argued that in post-capitalist society industrial conflict was institutionally isolated and robbed of its earlier influence on the rest of society) he also pointed to limits on the extent to which industrial conflict has been and can be institutionalised. He highlighted a number of specific circumstances which might militate against institutionalisation. One was the continued reluctance of some managers to accept that conflict exists, what he called 'the necessity and the reality of the conflict situation'. Conflict can be properly institutionalised only if structures are developed and used to contain it: this will not happen if the very existence of conflict is not accepted. Another limitation on the institutionalisation of industrial conflict noted by Dahrendorf relates to the co-ordination of interest-group activity. In particular, if there is fragmentation of worker representation then the ability of union leaders to 'manage' conflict will be weakened. One clear danger is that workplace organisations may distance themselves from the national union leadership, challenging its policy. Paradoxically, the success of workplace organisations may in part be a result of the success of moves to institutionalise industrial conflict. Close relationships between national union officials and representatives of employers or government and/or the acceptance of arguments on, say, wage restraint may result in a gulf opening up between national leaders and rank-and-file members.

The criticism of the institutionalisation thesis are echoed in the more general comment on the Ross and Hartman argument about the 'withering away' of the strike. In fact, the strike activity has not withered away but after the immediate post-Second World War years started to flourish. Many writers have noted that the Ross and Hartman prediction on this matter has proved inadequate:[20] in the particular context of the USA, Edwards noted the long-term consistency in strike patterns.[21] In earlier chapters it was noted that in many countries strike activity rose rather than fell in the 1960s and 1970s. It was also noted that consistent trends across countries were hard to identify. Nevertheless, it is fair to argue that no evidence was found consistent with the 'withering away' of the strike thesis.

Strikes and Industrial Relations Institutions
The second theme developed by Ross and Hartman, the importance of institutional arrangements, has similarly been

taken up by many writers and continues to be the source of controversy. It has much in common with the general approach of Dunlop.[22] In his discussion of industrial relations systems, Dunlop used the work of Parsons[23] and Smelser[24] to develop the view of industrial relations as a sub-system of the wider society. The main actors in this sub-system—managers, workers and specialised government agencies—seek to determine the rules that govern the system. In doing so they are not completely free agents; they are confronted by the environment (the significant aspects of the environment are the technological characteristics of the workplace, market or budgetary constraints and the locus and distribution of power in the wider society) and are limited by it. The emphasis on the development of rules to govern the workplace is crucial to the approach adopted.

More specifically, a number of writers have sought to explain particular aspects and patterns of industrial conflict by reference to industrial relations institutions, in particular to collective bargaining. In Britain the analysis of the Donovan Commission fits into this context.[25] The Donovan Commission sought to explain the rise in the number of strikes, particularly short workplace stoppages in the 1960s, and centred on the problems surrounding the collective bargaining machinery. Britain, it was argued, had two systems of industrial relations. One was the formal system which was embodied in the official institutions: it was based on the assumption that industry-wide organisations were capable of imposing their decisions on their members, and centred on national bargaining machinery. The other was the informal system which was created by the actual behaviour of trade unions, employers' associations, managers, shop stewards and workers. The informal system consisted largely of tacit arrangements and understandings, and of custom and practice, rather than formal machinery. The formal and the informal systems, it was argued, were in conflict: the informal undermined the formal. For example, the 'gap between industry-wide agreed rates and actual earnings continues to grow' and procedure agreements 'fail to cope adequately with disputes arising within factories'.[26]

The arguments put forward in the Donovan Commission report were broadly supported by Fox and Flanders.[27] Historically, they said, collective bargaining kept manifest conflict within socially tolerable bounds. However, in Britain and in some other European countries, it had failed to do so. The principal reason was that the machinery had not been altered to take account of changes in power relationships, and in particular the growth in the power of employees at the workplace. The inadequacy of the bargaining machinery, it was suggested, had led to a state of 'anomie': there was no adequate system for developing norms which could regulate behaviour in the field of industrial relations.

The Donovan analysis has been subject to critical review. Clegg has complained that it was not based on detailed investigation but relied on a linking of trends.[28] More recently Edwards has questioned whether the evidence of developments in British industrial relations since 1970 support the Donovan thesis. He points out that workplace bargaining has changed considerably in recent years with a rapid growth in the number of shop stewards who have played an increasingly important role in bargaining and negotiation at plant and company level:

According to the Donovan model the increasing volume of bargaining, together with the presence of more shop stewards, would be expected to be associated with more strikes. At the same time, however, the nature of bargaining has changed, with a growth in the prevalance of disputes procedures and with a formalised structure replacing the informality of the 1960s.[29]

These latter developments might be expected to reduce the number of strikes. The expectations of the developments in British industrial relations are difficult to disentangle and the evidence, at least the detailed evidence, of what has happened is far from comprehensive. Edwards, though, is clearly sceptical of whether the Donovan model provides a basis for analysis. He says that the 'relationship between strike patterns and the structures of bargaining became increasingly uncertain during the 1970s and as well as the ambiguities of the process of reform itself bargaining was far from being the only influence at work'.[30]

The discussion introduced in the Donovan report, of course, was specifically designed to highlight and explain the experience of British industrial relations in the 1960s. The broader arguments, though, of which this is just one example, have been applied in different contexts by many others. Kassalow sought to compare industrial conflict in the United States with that in Western Europe by examining the level and the scope of collective bargaining.[31] Industry-wide bargaining was noted in many Western European countries. Parties to such negotiations were seen as reluctant to allow them to break down because of the widespread effects of any conflict. In addition such bargaining was not seen as providing a major challenge to managerial prerogatives at the shop-floor level. In the United States bargaining was seen as more decentralised and likely to involve conflict over the control of the workplace. Kassalow also drew attention to the impact of reliance on international trade. The relative dependence on international trade in Western Europe was contrasted with the position in the USA. Dependence on international trade may inhibit strike action because parties will be aware of its possible effect on exports. Although Kassalow argued that Ross and Hartman paid insufficient attention to the 'political-legislative' area and that the social, economic and political substructure is critical to the understanding of unionism and labour relations, he concluded nevertheless 'by emphasising the significance of "purely industrial relations elements" as opposed to "broad social and economic forces".'[32]

Clegg's study of industrial conflict in six countries (Australia, France, West Germany, Sweden, the UK and the USA) covered the 1950–74 period.[33] It is a major study which is worth looking at in some detail. He also sought to relate strike-proneness to the structure of bargaining. In particular, he drew attention to the bargaining level and the extent of disputes procedures. His analysis of strikes was based on the number of stoppages, the size, the duration and the number of working days lost.

Clegg noted that in the United States strikes were larger than in other countries and the majority were official and constitutional. These two factors were related because, according to Clegg, official and constitutional strikes are generally longer and are likely to involve the whole of the bargaining unit. The explanation offered for the strike pattern in the United States is the predominance of plant-level bargaining. This reduces the cost to the union (for example in terms of strike benefit) as it does not have to involve the whole of the industry. However, while a higher proportion of strikes in the United States are official than in any of the other countries looked at, there is still a relatively high absolute number of unofficial strikes. Clegg relates this to the degree of factionalism in United States trade unions.

The Swedish and the West German strike patterns, Clegg claims, have much in common. There are relatively few strikes in either country. In Sweden the strikes that occur are usually unofficial and unlawful. The comprehensive disputes procedure is designed to minimise the likelihood of strikes during the currency of an agreement. Although West Germany does not have such a comprehensive disputes procedure as Sweden, the labour courts which handle grievances and interpret agreements, according to Clegg, are a 'fair substitute'. Another reason for the low strike incidence in West Germany is the system of works councils and the co-operative relations of such bodies with employers. Strikes which occur during the period of an agreement in West Germany are unlawful. Clegg notes one difference between strikes in West Germany and Sweden: strikes in Sweden are longer.

This may be explained by the greater authority and discipline of Swedish unions within the plants. Swedish unions may not always be able to prevent an unoffical strike where the workers are determined to remedy a grievance themselves because, for whatever reason, they think the disputes procedure has failed, or will fail to deal with it, but they can usually hold their members back from token or demonstration strikes.[34]

Unions in West Germany lack authority in the plant because of the dominance of works councils and are unable to prevent token strikes.

Clegg classified the Australian and French strike patterns in the same category. There are a relatively large number of strikes in both countries, though in Australia most strikes are illegal whereas in France they are not. In France collective agreements, and in Australia arbitration, fail to provide agreed disputes procedures that avoid strikes while an agreement is in force. 'Another parallel between the two countries', argued Clegg, 'is that Australian workers sometimes stop work in large numbers when their claims are before a tribunal, generally for no longer than a day or so, in order to make the arbitrators aware of their feelings. Similarly French unions quite commonly call one-day strikes during negotiations in order to call attention to the feelings and unity of the workers, without involving them in great hardship, or as political demonstrations. These practices help to account for the low average duration of strikes in the two countries.[35]

Clegg argued that the British pattern of strikes was more similar to that of Australia and France than to Sweden and West Germany: some difficulty was encountered in the discussion of unofficial, and particularly of unconstitutional, strikes, in part because of the problem of categorisation but more importantly because the ineffectiveness of many dispute procedures in private industry means that it is difficult for workers to believe that they are under a moral obligation not to strike. The British pattern of strikes was attributed by Clegg 'to the widespread practice of two-level bargaining which has led to a decline in the influence of industry procedure agreements as well as industry agreements on pay'.[36] Another feature of strikes in which British practice was said by Clegg to be closer to that in Australia and France than to that in America, Sweden and West Germany was the question of strike pay. Whereas American, Swedish and West German unions frequently give substantial amounts to workers when they call them out on strike, Australian and French unions rarely do so; in Britain unions can pay strike benefit but when they do it is often at a lower level.

Clegg concluded by drawing general lessons. He argued that plant bargaining leads to a smaller number of larger official strikes. Comprehensive and efficient disputes procedures are associated with low numbers of unofficial and unconstitutional strikes, although plant procedures are associated with a higher incidence of such strikes than are industry procedures. He then went on to add that the number of strikes is likely to be high where disputes procedures are absent or defective, and where 'the distinction between unofficial and official strikes and/or unconstitutional and constitutional strikes are blurred or non-existent'.[37] He recognised, though, that the theory does not explain the fluctuations in the number of major strikes which seem to be particularly affected by changes in economic circumstances and changing relations between unions and governments.

The case of Australia is particularly interesting when considering the influence of bargaining structures and procedures, because of its unique system of compulsory arbitration. The precise impact of the procedures is difficult to discern. Clegg argued that sometimes in Australia when their case was being considered by arbitrators workers went on strike to back up their claim. Niland argues that compulsory arbitration discourages early bargaining concessions because an arbitrator is likely to split the difference between the final position of both sides.[38] However, as Creigh, Poland and Wooden[39] point out, the arbitration systems of both Australia and New Zealand were established to avoid strikes, so that a plausible case could be made that one might expect this particular structure to be associated with a reduction of strike totals. In their own analysis they found that while stoppage incidence for countries using compulsory arbitration was lower than for those that did not, this difference was not statistically significant.

Ingham's study offers specific criticisms of the Ross and Hartman thesis.[40] Some of those relate to detailed aspects of the study. For example, Ross and Hartman conducted their analysis on the basis of averages for three different periods of time, 1900–29, 1930–42, and 1948–56. They gave no reason for the selection of the periods concerned nor for the fact that the first period covers thirty years, whereas the second period covers only twelve years and the third period only covers nine years. Ingham points out that the selection of different time spans would have produced different results. However, the main thrust of Ingham's analysis is not on the detail of Ross and Hartman's study but is concerned with an attempt to move away from the 'functionalist' towards a Marxist approach. Ingham characterises the functionalist approach as one which sees manifest variations in the levels of institutionalisation between industrial societies as a consequence of diverse 'cultural' and 'historical' factors 'which are not intrinsic to capitalism as such but are features of the pre-industrial social order which are more entrenched in some countries than others'.[41] Ingham's alternative is to 'account, in general terms, for observed variations in the levels of institutionalisation by reference to important differences in the industrial infrastructure of the societies in question'. The industrial infrastructure is taken 'to refer to those features of a society's economic and technological system which shape the organisation of and the social relationship between those groups engaged in the process of production'.[42] Three dimensions of the infrastructure are isolated as particularly important in this context: the degree of industrial concentration, the complexity of the technical and organisational structure, and product differentiation and specialisation. 'Each of these closely related dimensions sets a framework on the nature of the power relations between the respective organisations of capital and labour which, in turn, determine to a large extent a society's capacity for developing centralised institutions for the regulation of conflict'.[43]

Ingham points to the contrasting examples of Sweden and Britain. In the case of Sweden industrialisation occurred relatively late and the market has been dominated by a relatively small number of large firms, with a particular emphasis on the export market. Employers' organisations were able to establish a common front against employees and enforce regulations on the 'capital-labour' relationship. Unions, for their part, have tended to be organised on an industrial basis, essentially missing out on the impact of craft-based associations. Industrialisation occurred much earlier in Britain; in practice Britain is seen as the first industrialised economy. For a period British firms faced little external competition and had little need to rationalise to take advantage of economies of scale. There was less of a development of a common interest and less of an attempt to take a leading role in the development of the industrial relations system. British unions were also affected by the lengthy period of industrial development, which passed through a number of different phases. The emergence of a large number of occupational specialisms led to a highly differentiated trade union structure with a variety of different organisational bases. As far as industrial conflict is concerned Ingham sees regulation and centralisation, exemplified in Sweden, as reducing conflict, whereas the opposite is exemplified in Britain. He summed up his argument in the following way:

high levels of concentration, relatively simple technical, and business structures and high levels of product specialisation in the small-scale Scandinavian countries supported the growth of highly centralised employers' associations and labour movements, which, after a period of intense and widespread conflict result in their highly regulated system of industrial relations. On the other hand, the fragmented bargaining structure and low level of normative regulations in Britain [should be seen] in the context of the low levels of industrial concentration, product specialisation and infrastructural complexity which shaped its distinctive character.[44]

Criticisms of the Institutional Thesis

A number of the criticisms of writers who have tried to develop the Ross and Hartman theme of the importance of institutional arrangements have centred on the understanding of developments in particular countries. Korpi, for example, has criticised the interpretation by a number of other authors of the position in Sweden.[45] These criticisms can be applied, for instance, to the comments of both Clegg and Ingham. Korpi highlights the assumptions made about the nature of bargaining, industrial conflict and the hold of centralised arrangements. In particular he argues that the Swedish system of industrial relations has never been so tightly under the control of the central union and employers' organisations as has been claimed. In theory, workplace bargaining simply has been the third tier of a highly integrated and centralised system (the other two tiers have been the negotiations at the national level between the Swedish Confederation of Trade Unions and the Swedish Confederation of Employers' Organisations, and those between the national union and the corresponding employers' organisation in the branch of industry where the union operates). In practice, the main workplace bargaining organisation, the works club, always has operated with considerable independence: according to Korpi, workplace bargaining in Sweden has been no more under the control of the union hierarchy than it has been in Britain. Further, Korpi argues that 'Swedish workplace bargaining largely relies on informal agreements and tacit understandings'.[46]

Korpi, together with Shalev, extends the criticism of Ingham's work by arguing that political factors have been given too little attention.[47] In Sweden the real downturn in industrial conflict occurred from the 1930s onwards. This coincided with the rise of the Social Democrats and their assumption of power. The Social Democratic dominance of Swedish politics, it is claimed, gave the unions an entry to political decision-making, and meant that they were able to pursue their interests in this fashion rather than through more restricted dispute with employers. Korpi and Shalev argued that 'Swedish labour in effect renounced the strike weapon in order to more effectively pursue its . . . class interests in the political arena; what Pizzarno[48] has called a "political exchange" took place'. It is also noted that the institutional arrangements, of which much has been made by both Ingham and Clegg, date back to the beginning of the twentieth century, but it was only after the political changes that industrial conflict declined.

If one looks outside Sweden then the problems identified with Ingham's analysis, and those of others taking an institutional approach, can be exemplified. A number of writers have pointed to the relatively late development of the Canadian economy and to the concentration of industrial activity.[49] The Ingham thesis would place Canada in the same category to Sweden though in fact its strike record is very different.

Shalev, in another article, makes more general criticisms of both Clegg and Ingham.[50] In reference to Clegg he argues that his 'predisposition to equate institutional characteristics with behavioural outcomes renders his "theory" of strikes little more than a mechanical restatement of some of Ross and Hartman's "tendency statements"'.[51] Shalev goes on to criticise Clegg for making no attempt 'to trace the origins of national variations in bargaining structures and characteristics, except for throwaway lines such as "the structure and attitudes of employers' associations and managements are the main direct influences"'.[52] Shalev sees more of merit in Ingham's approach. He describes his attempt to move away from functionalist analysis as 'an innovative and constructive step forward'.[53] Shalev also argues though that Ingham erred by attributing the dominant role to employers in the formation of industrial relations institutions. 'Viewed in historical perspective, employer organisation has typically occurred in response to an actual or perceived challenge to capital by working class movements. It makes more sense, and is certainly more faithful to Marx, to conceive of the development of worker and employer organisations dialectically, that is, as an ongoing process of challenge and response'.[54]

These detailed criticisms, however, are less important than the general point that is being made. Essentially the argument is that the institutional arrangements themselves are not a satisfactory explanation for variations in the level of strike activity. Institutional arrangements cannot be seen as independent variables. This is not to deny them any importance but it is to argue that they need to be seen in a broader context, particularly in the context of the power relationships that exist and develop in a society.

Political Factors

The criticisms made of those who try to explain strike patterns by reference to institutional arrangements find concrete expression in an alternative school of thought. In essence this 'school' starts from the position that conflict is endemic in capitalist society because of the different interests of particular sections of society. The question to be addressed is how these different interests can be, or are, pursued, and in what circumstances strike action will occur.

The Work of Shorter and Tilly

Shorter and Tilly's work, initially on France, but extended to cover other countries, is one of the best known examples of this approach.[55] There are two central themes behind their work. The first is that organisation is essential for strike activity. Trade unions have a crucial role to play. They take worker dissatisfaction and translate it into strike action. The second theme is that strikes have political aims and implications. When the labour movement does not have political power strikes are a way of putting pressure on those who do.

Shorter and Tilly specifically challenge the view that strikes are to be seen simply as an expression of economic interest. Strikes and disturbances 'do not blossom forth because wages are low, living costs high (although such economic factors might widen the networks which the contending organisations control); strikes and violence do not erupt because for some reason—structural or adventitious—those who participate in them suddenly feel "alienated" "frustrated" or "aggressive"'. Major accumulations of strikes and disturbances occur 'when it becomes apparent to the working classes as a whole that a point of criticial importance for their own interests is at hand in the nation's life, *and* when the latticework of organisation suffices to transform these individual perceptions of opportunity into collective action'.[56]

In their study of France, Shorter and Tilly identify a number of 'strike waves' where action spread from one group and one region to the next. Their definition of a strike wave is that 'both the number of strikes and the number of strikers in a given year exceed the means of the previous five years by more than 50 per cent'.[57] According to Shorter and Tilly, strike waves 'march as exclamation marks in labour history' in France from late in the nineteenth century to 1968. Twelve individual years are highlighted as meeting the criteria for a strike wave: 1890, 1893, 1899, 1900, 1904, 1906, 1919, 1920, 1936, 1947, 1948 and 1968. The timing of these strike waves depends to a large extent on the timing of political crises. It is argued for example that the 1968 strike wave 'came in the immediate wake of the severest political crisis since 1947'.[58] However, in line with their main theme, Shorter and Tilly argue that 'organisation is essential to the successful launching of such forms of large-scale political action as strike waves'.[59]

In seeking to extend their analysis beyond France, Shorter and Tilly tried to explain differences in strike records by reference to the extent to which the labour movement had gained political power. In the pre-war years 'the working classes in all western countries mobilised themselves for political action, with varying degrees of effectiveness and within disparate constellations of national politics; their mobilisation generated everywhere a great wave of strike activity.[60] Strike activity before the Second World War, then, was of a similar kind, throughout the countries they looked at, and this led Shorter and Tilly to dismiss national character as a way of explaining strike differences between countries. Thus they say that the 'startling similarity in strike shapes means that it is pointless to attach great importance to stereotypes of "individual" psychological characteristics in explaining "collective" action'. The picture is frequently painted of 'the individualistic French worker, quick to explode in outburst of fury' and the 'well disciplined German'. While these sketches may have some merit 'and it may in fact be that Frenchman, taken one by one, fly off the handle more easily in confronting authority than do individual Germans', the point is made by Shorter and Tilly that 'these traits of national character are unimportant in explaining "collective" behaviour, for the aggregate is more than the sum of its parts'.[61]

After the Second World War, though, patterns started to differ. In European countries, where labour gained political power (such as Scandinavia), strike activity declined, whereas in those countries where labour did not gain political power (such as France) strikes continued at a higher level and as an expression of political aspirations.

In North America strikes in the post-war era did not differ greatly from those in the pre-war era. This was despite the fact that during the depression 'the North American working classes succeeded to political power'.[62] Strike activity did not wither away in North America as it had done in Northern Europe, according to Shorter and Tilly, because the government failed to intervene in shop-floor conflicts on the side of the working class. Eventually American labour became reconciled to a water-tight division between job action, where free collective bargaining unhindered by government intervention operated, and political action executed through 'interest-coalition political parties'. Shorter and Tilly comment that the North American case is important because it shows that 'admission to the polity need not automatically lead to the withering away of the strike; other variables such as national tradition interpose themselves'.[63]

The Importance of Political Power

The issue of political power is clearly seen by Shorter and Tilly as a crucial variable. Strikes can be used as a way of gaining political power or at least fostering political aspirations, but whether they are used in this way or not will depend on the extent of political power already held by the labour movement. Korpi and Shalev, in their criticisms of the institutional explanation of strike action, referred to the importance of political power in the Swedish case. They argued that the rise to power of the Social Democratic Party was crucial. In the same way as Shorter and Tilly, however, they have tried to use their ideas outside the context in which they were originally expressed.

The general assumption of Korpi and Shalev was that where labour can be effectively mobilised to gain political power there will be a reduction in strike activity. Labour will renounce the strike weapon because it believes it can more effectively pursue its objectives through the political arena. In order that this can happen the political power of labour has to be secure and enduring. Labour is also likely to need to be organised effectively internally with a high degree of centralisation. On the other hand where labour is fragmented and fails to gain political power, strikes will remain at a high level. Two sets of examples of countries at the opposite extremes of their continuum are cited, which seem to fit the assumptions. Austria and Norway follow the Swedish model in that labour has been effectively organised and Social Democratic parties have gained power. As a result strikes have been renounced as a method of achieving broad objectives. At the other end of the spectrum, in countries like Canada, USA and the Republic of Ireland, labour movements have been much less effective. Socialist parties enjoy little support and labour movements are not centralised or co-ordinated. Korpi and Shalev argue that in these cases 'the working class person has never played a significant role in national politics'. There has not been

any long run decline in conflict, which in addition retains a degree of intensity unknown in other countries since the war. In these instances, conflicts between buyers and sellers of labour power continue to be manifested primarily within the employment context, something which is no longer the case elsewhere. The long duration of strikes in these countries has contributed to give them very high *relative volumes* of strikes (man-days idle) in the post war period'.[64]

If one leaves the two extremes, however, then there are three other groups of countries which also have to be accounted for. In one of these groups of countries although the labour movement has been relatively strong it has not been able to gain a commensurate influence at the central political level, and strike activity has been above its pre-war level in the post-war period. Australia, Finland, France, Italy, Japan and New Zealand come into such a category. In France, Italy and Japan

working class parties enjoy significant electoral support, but are excluded from the primary locus of legitimate political power, namely the executive branch of government. In such a situation, conflict in the industrial arena becomes not only the inevitable alternative to a political conflict strategy of the Swedish type . . . it also takes on the role of an extra-parliamentary vehicle of working class political participation in the way that Shorter and Tilly argued.[65]

In Finland, Australia and New Zealand, Korpi and Shalev argued, the unfavourable relationship of vote shares to cabinet shares also results in political frustration on the left. For example, the 'Labour parties of New Zealand and Australia, although gaining close to half of the total vote in the post war period have respectively been in office for only one third and one quarter of that period'.[66]

There is another group of countries covering Belgium, Britain and Denmark where the relationship between the political role and status of the labour movement on the one hand, and strike activity on the other, is even more complex. Although the labour movement has been involved in post-war governments, this involvement has not been continuous and the level of industrial conflict has changed little between the pre and post Second World War periods. Belgium shows evidence of a frustrated or alienated working-class movement but the level of mobilisation in strikes, while it is significant, is no higher than in the pre-war period. In Britain, although the Labour party has gained power commensurate with its strength, its control of the polity has been insecure and this has limited the possibility of managing class conflict through 'political exchange' for long periods. The post-war strike record has been similar to, not greater than, what it was in the pre-war period. In Denmark, though labour has enjoyed a high degree of cabinet participation, such participation has been less stable than in the rest of Scandinavia. 'This instability may well have contributed to the continuing wave-like incidence of industrial conflict in post war Denmark, at what is nevertheless a relatively low level by international standards'.[67]

The final group of countries does not fit easily into the basic model. In this case labour movements have not been influential in national governments, and in some instances they have been weak but there has been a low (rather than the assumed high) level of conflict. West Germany, Switzerland and the Netherlands come into this category. For example in

Switzerland despite the absence of a strong labour movement overt conflict has remained low: the explanation offered is the integration of the working classes into public policy-making through extra-parliamentary action.

The line of argument followed by both Shorter and Tilly and Korpi and Shalev has centred on the extent to which the labour movement has been able to gain power at the central political level. Hibbs' work fits into this theme but offers a variation on it by arguing that it is not simply the assumption of power by the labour movement that is important: the critical factor is the policy pursued.[68] (In particular, the emphasis is placed on policy on the development of welfare provision). Hibbs argued that a high level of expenditure on the public sector, particularly on social services, will shift the centre of debate to the place where decisions on these matters are made, the central political arena. In such situations industrial conflict will subside. In other countries where parties of the 'right' or 'centre' have dominated, and where public/social expenditure has been maintained at a low level, then conflict will be concentrated on the private market and strike activity will be maintained at a high level.

Hibbs presented data to test his thesis for eleven countries and compared the number of working days lost in the inter-war and post-war periods. The proportion of the GDP spent in the public sector on non-defence matters was used as a guide to public-sector resource allocation. He found that there was a strong positive correlation between the percentage of cabinet posts held by Socialist/Labour parties and changes in public-sector allocation. He also found a strong negative correlation between changes in the public-sector allocation and the volume of strikes.

Hibbs argued that in a number of countries, like Denmark, Norway and Sweden, where the public-sector share of the GNP was about 50 per cent in 1972, where the tax rate for blue-collar workers averaged 30-35 per cent, and where the marginal tax rate was about 60 per cent, 'the political arena is the key locus of distributional outcomes and, therefore, industrial conflict stands at comparatively low levels'. In a number of other countries, like the United States, Canada and Italy, where the proportion of the GNP accounted for by the public sector was around 25-30 per cent in 1972, the tax rate for manufacture workers averaged 15 per cent or less, and where the marginal tax rate was around 23-28 per cent, 'the bulk of the national income is allocated in the private sector and, therefore, the economic marketplace remains the most important area of conflict over distributional outcomes'.[69] The result in these countries is a relatively high volume of strikes.

The crucial issue then, according to Hibbs, in explaining long-run trends in strike activity, was not the assumption of political power by social democratic parties *per se,* but rather the change in the locus of the distribution of the national income produced by the welfare state policies of social democratic regimes. Such regimes, by socialising the consumption and production of a high proportion of the national product, 'engineer a massive circumvention of the private market'. This leads to a shift in the principal locus of the distribution of national income 'from the private sector, where property and capital interest enjoy a comparative advantage, to the public sector, where the political resources of the organised working class are more telling'.[70]

In another article, which will be referred to later, Hibbs examined the importance of economic variables in explaining strike patterns.[71] In the article discussed above, Hibbs did not discount the value of economic variables in explaining short-run fluctuations in strike activity. His argument was that these were of little value in explaining longer-run fluctuations. In order to understand such fluctuations one had to look at the 'political economy of distribution'.

Snyder's Model

It would be wrong to characterise Snyder's model as one which simply demonstrated the importance of political issues and power in determining strike activity.[72] Snyder had a broader aim: a range of issues were recognised as potentially influencing strike activity. However, one of the points of his explanation was to determine when political factors would be crucial. The interest in and comment on political factors, particularly on the work of Shorter and Tilly, makes it sensible to discuss his work in this context.

Snyder distinguished two different kinds of situation. In the first, labour organisation will be relatively strong and the labour movement as a whole will be effective politically. The institutions of collective bargaining will have been well established. In this kind of situation strikes will be determined by economic factors. In the second situation trade unions are weaker, with fewer members, and they are less stable organisations. The labour movement has little influence over general political matters. In this instance the institutions of industrial relations are less well developed. Economic matters will have a less important role in strikes. The incidence of strikes will vary according to the basis of union organisation and political changes. In general, though, labour organisations will not be sufficiently strong in organisational terms to be able to take advantage of economic conditions. Strikes, in such circumstances, will have a political role, since unions will concentrate on longer-term aims rather than shorter-term economic considerations.

Snyder tested his thesis in three countries: France, Italy and the USA. Data was collected for specific time periods in each case: in France for 1876–1937 and 1946–66; in Italy for 1901–24 and 1947–70, and in the USA for 1900–48 and 1949–70. The lengthy break between the two periods in the data collected for Italy is a consequence of the absence of strike data for a good part of the inter-war years while Italy was under fascist rule.

Snyder argued that in the USA prior to the Second World War industrial relations were not institutionalised, but after the war this changed. The prediction was that before the war strikes would be sensitive to political variables, but after the war they would be sensitive to economic factors. His results showed that prior to the Second World War the political rather than economic variables were indeed important. The net effects of unemployment and changes in real wages were 'weak and not significant', but unionisation, the percentage of Democrats in Congress and the party of the President had 'strong positive effects on year-to-year fluctuations in the measures of strikes'.[73] He recognised that these 'political attitude' variables represented a different dimension than what Shorter and Tilly referred to as a 'political crisis', but argued that the party affiliation effects were 'indicative of similar underlying processes'.[74] After the war political variables ceased to be important. This was, Snyder argued, because, given 'the polity entrance of labour in the post war United States', political demands were 'routinely expressed in less public influence attempts (e.g. lobbying) than strikes'.[75] As political variables declined in importance, economic variables took their place. 'In the post war years unemployment and the expectations-achievements gap in real wage changes are both important predictors of strike fluctuations. These post war findings indicate that workers act as if they calculate short run economic costs and benefits in their strike behaviour'.[76]

When he looked at France and Italy, Snyder was forced to change some of the variables used to test his thesis. In particular, national income rather than unemployment was used as a measure of economic activity (it was argued that reliable unemployment statistics were not available) and election years along with cabinet changes were used rather than political composition. The assumption was that in both the pre- and post-Second World War periods strike activity in France and Italy would relate to organisational/political rather than to economic factors.

In the pre-Second World War period in France and Italy the economic variables, as expected, were not significant. Other variables, political and organisational, were much more important, particularly the extent of union organisation. Nevertheless there were some difficulties with the political variables. Political change and/or crises did not seem to be as important as expected and Snyder was forced to conclude that 'conclusive evaluation of the relative importance of political components of the "organisational/political" model'[77] was precluded.

In the post-Second World War period economic variables were again, as expected, unimportant in explaining variations in strike activity. In Italy organisational factors (the impact of unionisation) but not political factors were noted as important and in France none of the organisational/political variables performed well.

The difficulties with some of the findings did not prevent Snyder claiming that they broadly supported his thesis. He concluded that the nature and strength of the labour movement, the extent to which the labour movement had political channels open to it, and the degree of institutionalisation of collective bargaining were the factors likely to determine whether strike activity was primarily related to economic or political matters.

Criticisms of the Political School

There have been a number of criticisms of specific aspects of Snyder's work. For example, it has been argued that the use of cabinet changes as an indicator of the political position of labour is unsatisfactory, and the use of variables in Italy and France different to those used in the USA makes comparisons difficult. The statistical results need to be treated with caution and the difficulties posed by the results for Italy and France given more weight. Other studies have questioned the conclusion that Snyder reached. For example, Kaufman has questioned Snyder's argument that the institutionalisation of industrial relations in the United States after the Second World War means that economic factors will be more, and political factors less, important in explaining strike trends.[78] On the issue of the institutionalisation of bargaining, Kaufman argued that

a formal bargaining process is largely irrelevant to the basic question of whether strikes will fluctuate with economic variables. A good argument can be made, in fact, that one form of institutional change—the growth in the average duration of union contracts from one year to three years—may actually have reduced the sensitivity of strike activity to the business cycle.[79]

In the case of political variables Kaufman argued that the growing role of organised labour in the political process could conceivably cause strikes to be more sensitive than in the pre-war period to changes in political power. This would be the case, for example, if organised labour attempted to achieve its demands primarily through the political process under pro-labour administration and through the bargaining process under unfriendly administrations.[80] In this last matter Kaufman was echoing the comments of Shalev.[81] Other aspects of Snyder's findings were challenged by Skeels.[82] He argued that in the USA 'both economic and union organisation factors were important in determining the level of strike activity in the 1900–48 period'. He went on to claim that 'economic factors were surprisingly vigorous in the light of Snyder's claim to the contrary. Unemployment and price changes were always significant and performed in a manner consistent with the findings of studies of post-1948 strike activity.'[83]

Similarly detailed criticisms have been made of other pieces of research referred to in this section. For example, Hibbs' findings do not seem to fit easily with another piece of research examining similar issues. Gifford looked at fifteen countries, between 1956 and 1965, to examine whether there was a link between the number of days lost through strikes and the socialist policies adopted by governments.[84] The measures used to determine socialist policies were not unlike those used by Hibbs (the ratio of public expenditure to GDP, the percentage of tangible wealth owned by the state and whether a socialist party was in power) but the results were very different. No significant relationship was found between any of these variables and strike activity.

Shorter and Tilly's work is also open to criticism on specific points. For example, the interpretation of the motivation of strike activity has been questioned. Bean has referred to the interpretation put on the finding that after 1945 strikes in France became shorter, but larger in terms of the number of workers involved.[85] The explanation of Shorter and Tilly is that politicised unions are able to interest a wider range of workers in limited commitments of time and energy to make a political point. Bean argues, however, 'that somewhat different interpretations of the frequency of short strikes as a dominant characteristic of industrial conflict in France are possible, such as relating this type of stoppage to features of the prevailing system of collective bargaining, together with an inability on the part of the unions to finance lengthy strikes'.[86]

More general criticisms have been made which apply to a number, not just one, of the studies reviewed. For example, one of the themes developed by a number of writers is the importance of a strong and co-ordinated labour movement. This can be a determinant of ability to take action and gain political power. However, the direction of such links can be questioned. While it may be the case that a strong labour movement is able to take advantage of favourable conditions, whether to pursue political power or to take industrial action, in practice strength may also be the consequence of such action. If a union is able to show that it can take effective action either against an employer or in the political arena then it may help that union, or the union movement, to recruit members, co-ordinate activities, and organise more effectively.

At a similar level of generality it can be argued that care needs to be taken about interpreting the implications of a labour or socialist party gaining power. There are examples where it has resulted in more not fewer strikes. Creigh, Poland and Wooden point out that 'in Australia the highest levels of strike activity in the post war era were recorded under the Labour Governments of the late 1940s and early 1970s.'[87] Similar examples might be quoted from the British experience. The 'winter of discontent' (1978–9) saw an explosion in strike activity in direct opposition to the policy of the Labour government. In many cases left-wing governments, when they gain power, are forced to take actions which are opposed by the trade unions: this may be because their election to office in itself drives the financial institutions to adopt postures which threaten stability, or it may be because after long periods in office a left-wing government has ceased to pursue the ideals it espoused before it gained power. In this context it is interesting to record that a study by Paldam and Pederson, which will be reviewed in more detail later, found that one of the 'political' variables included in their analysis, the political orientation of the government, showed a significant and negative relationship with strike activity.[88] This suggested that there were more strikes under left-wing than right-wing governments. In particular significant negative correlations were found for Australia, Canada, the Republic of Ireland, Finland and Norway.

The kind of criticisms made of those who adopted the approach that the 'institutions' determined strike action can also be made of those who would argue that political and organisational factors would do so. At their extreme either position would seem to be placing too much emphasis on simply one factor. It is not necessary to argue that such a factor has no role to play in explanation: simply that it does not by itself provide an explanation. In fact, as has been noted, a number of writers have suggested that one factor alone has not been adequate to explain strike trends. Some have recognised the importance of a combination, including institutional arrangements, political, and economic factors.

ECONOMIC FACTORS

The discussion of economic factors as a way of explaining strike trends is the most extensive of the approaches considered. There is a wealth of material, much of it attempting to explain variations in strike trends in one country over time, but some of it also attempting comparative analysis.

Strikes and the Business Cycle

The first major study within this approach was undertaken by Hansen in the early 1920s. He attempted to link strikes to the business cycle in the USA between 1881 and 1919 though because no general strike statistics were available for the USA for the 1906–14 period the Canadian statistics were used instead to indicate the general movement of strikes. He suggested that analysis might be aided by splitting the period looked at into two: the first part would then cover 1881 to 1897 during which there was a long-run trend towards falling prices, while the second would cover 1898 to 1919 during which there was a long-run trend towards rising prices. Such a split would be useful, he argued, because the explanation for strike trends might be different during a period of falling than during a period of rising prices.

In the period of long-run falling prices, Hansen argued, labour is on the defensive. 'A disproportionate part of the struggle of labour is directed against the reduction of wages, the lengthening of hours and the worsening of conditions generally. With regard to wages, especially, labour is battling to hold on to what it has already gained'. This means that the greatest pressure for the reduction of wages will occur in periods of business depression. It therefore follows that 'in a period in which the secular trend of prices is downward the struggle between labour and capital may be expected to become most severe and the number of strikes greatest in the years of depression'.

On the other hand in a period when the general trend is for prices to rise one should expect, Hansen argued, labour to be particularly aggressive. 'Employers are no longer trying to reduce wages; they are endeavouring to prevent wage increases. When the general trend of prices is upward and the cost of living is mounting labour cannot afford to be satisfied with a defensive struggle to retain what it has already secured'. Labour must be expected to take the offensive. 'The struggle between labour and capital now becomes most bitter in the years of prosperity. There are two reasons for this: first, it is in the prosperous years that prices and living costs rise; and second, 'the large profits accruing in years of prosperity give rise to a contest over its distribution'.[89]

The analysis undertaken, Hansen claimed, supported the hypotheses. 'Strikes correlate inversely with the business cycle in periods of long-run falling prices, while they correlate directly with the business cycle in periods of long-run rising prices'.[90]

Although in this formulation the attitude of employers is recognised as having a role to play, most writers saw strikes in the main as the result of union action and therefore concentrated on the ability and willingness of workers to take such action. For example, Hiller discussed the tactical advantage to workers of undertaking strike action during a period of economic prosperity.[91] When such conditions prevailed, workers' pressure on employers was particularly likely to be successful because employers were unwilling to put at risk the greater profits that could be earned. Despite questions about the applicability of this model after the Second World War when prosperity might be seen as putting pressure on workers not to strike (because of the commitments that went with it, for example, through the use of credit), the view that strike action was related to the business cycle held sway for many years.

It would be a mistake, however, to portray the position at this time as one where economists simply had one consistent view about the causes of strikes. There were differences, even between those who held that the relationship between strikes and the business cycle was crucial. Rees pointed out that there was disagreement between such writers 'on the nature of the relation between strikes and business fluctuation'.[92] He exemplified the point by comparing the work of Hansen to that of Griffen,[93] Yoder,[94] Burns and Mitchell[95] and Jurkat and Jurkat.[96]

Rees himself introduced another dimension to this debate by suggesting that the strike peak consistently preceded the peak in the business cycle. His explanations centred on the differing expectations of employers and unions. Unions, he said, 'pay close attention to employment which generally does not lead at the peak'. They are also influenced by matters like the wage increases gained by other unions and by cost-of-living increases. On the other hand employers' attention 'is likely to be focussed on some of the activities which do lead at the peak, and they will thus resist demands for which unions are still willing to fight'.[97] Among the matters employers will look at will be business failures, orders and investments. 'As the cyclical peak is reached, the more pessimistic expectations may be shared by some union leaders, and strikes fall off'.[98]

Ashenfelter and Johnson and Subsequent Studies
The economic analysis of strikes was given new impetus in the late 1960s through the publication of the work of Ashenfelter and Johnson.[99] They did not discard the idea that the business cycle had a role to play but introduced a new element by looking centrally at the relationship between union members and leaders. The study was based on USA strike statistics for the 1952–67 period. Their argument was that in many instances member expectations of a wage demand may be greater than the union leaders are able to deliver from an initial negotiation with employers. Union leaders can try to lower expectations during the negotiations and thus be able to propose an agreement which is acceptable to members and employers. If they are unable to do so then they may be forced either to try to conclude an agreement even though they know that it will not be acceptable to members, or to organise a strike. One of the functions of the strike may be to lower the aspirations of their members so that eventually an agreement may be signed.

Rank and file expectations it is argued, will be influenced by economic factors, like the level of demand for labour and the level of profits. The aggregate level of strike activity will be related to the degree of tightness of the labour market and previous rates of change of real wages. They found that a decline of one percentage point in the current unemployment rate was associated with an increase of around 123 strikes per quarter, and a steady-state decline of one percentage point in the rate of real wages was associated with an increase of about 62 strikes per quarter. However, the introduction of discussion about relationships between union leaders and rank and file members was an important extension of earlier work, and they returned to the policy implications of this matter in their conclusion. Thus, they argued that policies which are geared to induce labour leaders to convince their constituencies to be satisfied with 'more reasonable' wage settlements are likely to result eventually in political turmoil in trade unions. It does not, therefore, seem likely that such a policy can continue for long without encouraging the growth and power of more militant leadership and a subsequent decline in the effectiveness of the original policy.[100] In this respect the comments by Ashenfelter and Johnson seem to have much in common with those reported earlier about the limits to the institutionalisation of industrial conflict.

The Ashenfelter and Johnson approach was followed by a number of studies which further explored the relationship between strikes and economic variables in a variety of countries. Pencavel, for example, examined strikes in the United Kingdom, outside mining, between 1950 and 1967.[101] Although he recognised that differences between the systems of industrial relations in the United Kingdom and the United States meant that the Ashenfelter-Johnson model would need adapting, the basic approach was retained. The specific adaptation proposed arose from the high proportion of unofficial strikes in the United Kingdom, which meant that leadership positions had to be seen as resting with the branch official or shop steward. 'In short . . . officials lower down in the echelon of authority take on much of that function of trade unionism which relates to the welfare of the member at his place of work, and in this capacity they operate much like the union leadership described by Ashenfelter and Johnson'.[102] Pencavel's conclusion was that the Ashenfelter-Johnson type of approach operated quite successfully in the British context. There were some 'cautionary notes' but despite these reservations the findings were said to 'suggest that this framework for analysing the frequency of strike activity is not fruitless, and further refinement of the model should enhance our understanding of the relations involved'.[103]

Pencavel's attempt to adapt the Ashenfelter-Johnson model, though, raises questions. Mayhew has argued that the assumption that the relationship between the shop steward and the workgroup is similar to that between a potential union leader and union members is not supported by the available evidence: 'The implicit assumption would have to be that there was a well-defined consistent relationship between the shop steward and his members, in the sense that there is an implication either that the shop steward is privy to information not available to his membership, or that he is more realistic or rational'. He points to the study by Batstone, Boraston and Frenkel which defined four different types of shop steward, each implying a different relationship to the rank and file member. 'Add to this the doubt that union leaders would wish to behave in the Machiavellian way suggested, coldly using a strike to knock sense into their members, or that they could for long get away with behaving in this way, and we can conclude that the conceptual foundations of Pencavel's model are weak'.[104] Pencavel's approach has also been criticised by Knight, who argued that the predominance of unofficial strikes in Britain meant that a model which sought to explain the actions of groups of workers rather than trade unions should be developed.[105] Knight's analysis of strikes in the British manufacturing industry between 1950 and 1968 concluded that the most important source of short-run variation in strike incidence was the response to past money wage increases (although past changes in output per man hour and profit seemed also to play some part).

The Ashenfelter and Johnson model assumptions were specifically but more generally examined by Mauro.[106] He argued that the views that two parties to negotiations, union and management, are perfectly informed, but that strikes occur because of the overblown expectations of the rank and file, is wrong.[107] Mauro suggests that strikes are likely to occur when one party incorrectly perceives its opponent's position. Strikes from this point of view can be a way of correcting misconceptions and, crucially, a less costly way of doing so than other methods. 'It is usually difficult for a negotiator to obtain an accurate reading of his opponent's stance, and it is even more difficult for other members of the negotiator's organisation to obtain such a reading, especially when each side's stance is determined by different factors'.[108] Striking, then, can be viewed as a search for information. Mauro, then, is re-opening the issue of the extent to which strikes should be seen as the result of 'mistakes'.

Paldam and Pederson's study is attractive because not only is it comparative (it covered seventeen OECD countries) but it also (unlike many other studies) looks at post-1960s strike trends: their analysis covered 1948–75.[109] The study is also interesting because it raises questions about the general applicability of the Ashenfelter and Johnson model. Three of their conclusions seemed to refute the Ashenfelter and Johnson model. First, they argued that nominal wage changes 'have a superior overall explanatory power compared to real wage changes'.[110] (Ashenfelter and Johnson had placed emphasis on the importance of real wage changes). Second, they argued that the dominating signs on both nominal and real wage changes are positive (Ashenfelter and Johnson argued that a decline in real wages was associated with an increase in strikes). Third, they argued that the relationship between unemployment and strikes was unstable. The relationship between unemployment and strikes was only significant in one third of the cases. Further, the direction of the influence varied between countries. Ashenfelter and Johnson had suggested that a decrease in unemployment was associated with an increase in strikes.

In their discussion of the results of their study of economic variables Paldam and Pederson considered a number of possible explanations for the variations between their results and those from earlier literature. One that they suggested was that the results reported by Ashenfelter and Johnson for the United States for 1952–67 which dominated subsequent empirical research, were an exception rather than the rule. Another possibility is that the superiority of the nominal wage relationship (over the real wage relationship) which they identified, did not exist before the data from the big strike wave starting in the late 1960s could be used in analysis. They also considered that the positive signs for the nominal wage increases might reflect a causality that was the reverse of what they had suggested: nominal wage increases might reflect the impact of strikes rather than the other way round.

In their overall conclusion, though, Paldam and Pederson returned to their attack on the Ashenfelter and Johnson model. They argued that the main problem with that model was the 'aggregate assumption, which rules out all effects from the wage structures'. They went on to say that it is quite likely that *'change in the wage structure is a dominating force behind change in conflict intensities.* Conflicts may thus be generated by tensions between individuals' actual positions in the wage structure and their desired positions—as formed by tradition, conceptions of justice and reason, and so forth'. There are two elements to the macro-implications of this theory.

First, tensions are likely to increase when the wage structure changes since the relative position of different groups will then change. Second, there is likely to be a positive correlation between changes in the wage structure and the rate of wage increases in the sense that an acceleration in average wages is correlated with a narrowing of the wage structure.[111]

This latter element might help to explain why Paldam and Pederson found a strong relationship between conflict intensity and the rate of increase in nominal wages.

The issue of the link between wage rises and industrial conflict is taken up by Paldam in another article.[112] Again the strength of the connection between conflicts and nominal wage rises is stressed. Paldam also points to interconnections between these two variables as well as to a positive relationship between real wage rises and conflicts. He goes on to suggest that, taken together

the results explain how a large conflict wave, such as we have witnessed in the last decade, may occur. It is due to the fact that conflicts and wage inflation are mutually reinforcing phenomena: conflicts induce wage inflation which induces more conflict, etc. Thanks to the lags the process may go on for some time once it has taken off. The existence of conflict waves (sometimes known as strike movements) is one of the reasons why the basic correlations between conflicts and nominal wage rises have to be positive both ways.[113]

A study of strikes in Britain by Davies allows discussion of the relationship between inflation and strikes to be taken a stage further.[114] Davies suggests that the effect of inflation on strikes will be dependent on the extent to which the evaluations of unions and employers differ on this matter.

During periods when inflation is fairly constant the actual inflation rate and the expected inflation rate are likely to converge, making incorporation into current wage agreements less problematical. However, during periods when the inflation rate is accelerating, the expected inflation rate and the actual inflation rate are likely to diverge, resulting in the emergence of 'unanticipated' inflation. In addition to increasing the degree of uncertainty surrounding collective negotiations and thereby providing more room for disagreement, unanticipated inflation is also likely to cause increased rank and file dissatisfaction with existing wage agreements, and therefore produce increased pressure on the union leadership to reopen negotiations. Under such circumstances the probability of a strike will almost certainly be increased.[115]

The study by Davies is also interesting because of the comments made about the impact of incomes policy on strike activity. He argued, using evidence from Britain for the 1966–75 period, that while incomes policy seems to reduce strike activity over pay issues, it leads to an increase in such activity over non-pay issues. The net effect then will be minimal. On the other hand Davies argued that the breakdown of an incomes policy can be associated with a rise in the number of strikes.

The attempt by Davies to distinguish different phases of incomes policy is an advance on a number of other studies in the same area. However, even so there are problems with the kind of classification used. The distinction between 'hard, soft and re-entry phases, together with that between pay and non-pay strikes' may be 'insufficient to capture the complexities of incomes policies'.[116] How, for example, is the UK social contract of the mid-1970s to be interpreted? In the early stages (1975–6) it was associated with low levels of strike activity which could be seen as the result of official trade union acceptance of the policy and the ability of union leaders to persuade their members to accept it.

Are these events to be summed up as examples of 'hard' policy, in that the government was fairly firmly committed to it and the union leaders were willing to try to impose it on the rank and file, or a 'soft' policy, in that there was none of the rigid statutory enforcement which characterised earlier policy? If it is accepted that the social contract policy was a very different animal from earlier incomes policies then trying to find relationships which are the same for all norms, guidelines and understanding which come under the rubric of incomes policies becomes futile.[117]

Strikes and Unemployment

Most of the studies referred to above are based on the number of strikes. It has been argued, however, that the number of strikes is not the most reliable measure, particularly for international comparisons. In a colourful commentary Evans draws attention to the limitations of the use of the number of stoppages: a 'measuring rod not composed of comparable units can never be of more than limited value, and strike frequency figures, which give the same weight to one national coal strike losing ten months as to a three day stoppage at the local grocer's shop fall into this category'.[118] While this view is open to challenge itself because the measure of days lost (the alternative suggested by Evans) is likely to be significantly affected by, say, just one major national strike (Stern[119] pointed out that a number of analyses of strikes in the USA which used days lost as the basis of their analysis were distorted because of the impact of the long steel strike in 1959) the view has gained some support. There is special interest, then, in the study by Creigh and Makeham, for not only did they use recent strike data (they looked at the period 1975–9 for fifteen OECD countries) but they also used the number of working days lost through strikes.[120] In their discussion they suggested that there was a relationship between price inflation and stoppage incidence: larger rates of price inflation can increase the incidence of stoppages because of the way in which they threaten the level of real income. Creigh and Makeham also suggested a positive relationship between unemployment and strike activity. The argument was that during periods of high unemployment employers may be less willing than they would be in more buoyant conditions to take what action was necessary to avoid the disruption likely to be caused by strike action. Consequently, if strikes occurred during periods of high unemployment they would be likely to last longer.

This latter finding is interesting because it contrasts with the argument in much earlier work. The argument had been that unemployment would be negatively related to strike action.

Emphasis was placed on the lack of willingness of workers to strike during periods of high unemployment. Creigh and Makeham, however, by turning to look at employer attitudes, have suggested that there are other factors to take into account which might reverse the expected relationship. This approach has echoes in the explanation of Edwards for the pattern of strikes in the UK in the 1970s.[121] This period, he notes, was characterised by both rising unemployment and rising inflation:

On the former, it is often argued that recession will be associated with long strikes because employers can afford to take a long stoppage and because they will try to recoup the concessions made to workers during the previous boom: strikes then become bitter battles . . . .. On the latter, inflation in the context of slow economic growth meant that workers faced substantial problems of maintaining real wages while employers suffered a squeeze on profits.

The result, according to Edwards, was that in contrast to the 1960s 'strikes became lengthier battles, with employers feeling that they could not afford to give way and with workers having to fight hard even to maintain their living standards'.[122]

The findings of Creigh and Makeham on the relationship between strikes and unemployment contrast though with those of Hibbs.[123] He also looked at working days lost rather than the number of strikes and yet he found a negative relationship between unemployment and strike activity. He argued that the inverse relationship between the volume of industrial conflict and the rate of unemployment demonstrates considerable sophistication in the use of the strike weapon. It shows that 'on the whole strikes are times to capitalise on the strategic advantages of a tight labour market. What Hobsbawm has called "the common sense of demanding concessions when conditions are favourable" indeed seems to prevail'. He also went on to argue that labour is sophisticated in another respect: it does not appear to be misled by 'money illusion'. 'Industrial conflict, therefore, responds to movements in real wages rather than money wages, which is further and rather persuasive evidence that rational behaviour underlies observed strike fluctuations'.[124] When comparing the work of Hibbs with that of Creigh and Makeham it is important to note that there are differences in the sets of data used in the two studies. Whereas

Creigh and Makeham looked at data for fifteen countries between 1975 and 1979, Hibbs looked at data for ten countries between 1950 and 1969. Similar comments can be made when comparing the findings of Hibbs on real wages to those of Paldam and Pederson (which emphasised the importance of nominal wages). Hibbs' study covered an earlier period and Paldam and Pederson explicitly considered the possibility that the relationship they found might not have been visible using data from before the late 1960s.

In another study, this time with Poland and Wooden, Creigh took an even wider spread of countries (twenty OECD countries, though evidence was not available on all variables for all countries) and a longer time period (1962–81).[125] A large number of possible explanations for stoppage incidence (number of working days lost) were tested, but standardised unemployment rates were found to be the most important single explanatory factor. 'The variable accounted statistically for 18 per cent of total stoppage incidence variation, with a percentage point higher unemployment rate being associated with an increase of over 91 days lost in the stoppage incidence rate'. Critically, they also added that the 'result supports the argument that higher unemployment rates raise stoppage incidence since those stoppages which do occur tend to be of long duration'.[126]

This issue is clearly a difficult one on which to reach a conclusion. It is not just that unemployment has been found by some writers to have a positive association while it has been found by others to have a negative association with strikes; a third group of writers have concluded that there is no relationship at all. For example, one study that looked at strike trends in the UK in considerable detail concluded that unemployment was not helpful in explaining patterns or variations.

Given the general level of success of the econometric models tested it is of some interest to note that there does not appear to be any general relationship between strike measures and unemployment rates, either at the level of industries or at the level of subdivisions of regions.[127]

This conclusion was echoed by others, like Shorey[128] and Knight,[129] who also looked at strikes in post-war UK.

Inter-Industry Variations

The studies looked at so far have concentrated on explaining economy-wide strike trends. It has long been recognised though that there are major variations in strike incidence between industries. Kerr and Siegel sought to examine variations between industries across countries. They argued that a league table could be constructed of strike propensity by industry which held across countries. This league table (reproduced as Table 4.2) was based on an analysis of strikes in eleven different countries. They found that certain industries (notably mining and maritime and longshore) were highly strike-prone in all of the countries looked at, whereas others (notably railroad and agriculture) were lowly strike-prone in every country. From this basis, they looked in more detail at the industries concerned to see if they could discover any reason for the different strike propensities.

Their explanation centred on two theories. The first was that the location of the worker in society determines his propensity to strike, and that his location is heavily influenced by his industrial

Table 4.2: General Pattern of Strike Propensities

Propensity to Strike	Industry
High	Mining
	Maritime and longshore
Medium High	Lumber
	Textile
Medium	Chemical
	Printing
	Leather
	Manufacturing (general)
	Construction
	Food and kindred products
Medium Low	Clothing
	Gas, water and electricity
	Services (hotels, restaurants, etc.)
Low	Railroad
	Agriculture
	Trade

Source: C. Kerr and A. Siegel, 'The Interindustry Propensity to Strike—an International Comparison', in A. Kornhauser, R. Dubin and A. Ross (eds.), *Industrial Conflict*, McGraw-Hill, New York, 1954.

environment. In summary this theory stated that industries will be highly strike-prone when workers form a relatively homogeneous group which is usually isolated from the general community and which is capable of cohesion; on the other hand, industries will be relatively strike-free when their workers are individually integrated into the larger society, are members of trade groups which are coerced by government or the market to avoid strikes, or are so individually isolated that strike action is impossible. On this basis the high strike-proneness of groups like miners, sailors, dock workers, and to a lesser extent textile workers, would be explained by reference to the type of communities they live in. They all live apart in their separate communities and these communities have their own codes, myths, heroes and social standards. There are few neutrals in such a community and all members are subject to the same grievances. The union plays a crucial role; not only is it an industrial organisation but it is also a kind of working-class solidarity which is reinforced by the support of the community.

The second theory looked at by Kerr and Siegel was that the character of the job and the worker influenced the strike propensity. Stated briefly it argued that the nature of the job determines, by selection and conditioning, the kind of workers employed and their attributes, and these workers in turn cause conflict or peace. Thus, if a job is physically difficult and unpleasant, unskilled, casual and fosters an independent spirit, it will attract tough, inconsistent and combative workers who will be inclined to strike. On the other hand, if the job is physically easy, skilled, performed in pleasant surroundings and subject to close supervision, it will attract women or the more submissive type of men, who are unlikely to strike.

Kerr and Siegel argued that the most satisfactory explanation could be gained by an amalgamation of the two theories. This led them to outline two polar opposites as far as strikes are concerned: the isolated mass of workers undertaking unpleasant work who will be highly strike-prone, and the dispersed workforce engaged in more attractive work who will be less strike-prone.

Kerr and Siegel's work has attracted criticism as a study in its own right. For example, they have been criticised for the way they left certain industries out of their final analysis. Thus, the steel industry was initially examined by Kerr and Siegel but was omitted from their final league tables; in fact, the steel industry is difficult to fit into the Kerr and Siegel pattern because its strike record is not consistent in different countries. It has also been argued that while the Kerr and Siegel thesis may be persuasive in explaining the exceptional strike records in a small number of industries (like mining and dock work) it is less persuasive as a general explanation of strike proneness. Nevertheless, these criticisms do not detract from a fairly general acceptance that there are important variations between the strike records of different industries which seem to endure across many if not all countries.

In recent years the issue of inter-industry strike variations has been taken up by economists. In some cases the studies have concentrated on variations within a particular group of industries. Thus, McLean examined variations in strike activity across USA manufacturing industries. He argued that two factors were particularly important in explaining the variations found. The first was what he called a 'relative deprivation' hypothesis. This suggests that the higher the previous increases in wage rates for the workers in a given bargaining unit have been the greater will be the relative deprivation (and, therefore, the dissatisfaction) for those workers associated with any wage increase. On the other hand, workers who are 'unaccustomed to large wage increases will experience less deprivation from any current wage increase and will, therefore, be less likely to demand high wage increases in the current period'.[130] The second factor was geographical location. McLean expressed himself as puzzled by the emergence of the finding that a Southern location was a significant determinant of strike activity, especially as the direction of the relationship was different to that expected (he concluded that the larger the proportion of establishments in an industry located in the South, the greater the propensity to strike in that industry). It may be, he said, 'that firms in industries which are especially strike prone in other parts of the country locate new establishments in the South in order to escape strike costs', or it may be 'that the bargaining relationships in the South are newly formed and thus more conflict prone than are mature bargaining relationships'.[131]

A similar concentration on manufacturing industries can be found in two UK studies. Shorey examined thirty-three manufacturing industries over the period 1963–7.[132] In putting forward an explanation for the variations discovered Shorey recognised some limitations, in particular the concentration on economic variables (it was noted that 'non-economic factors must be brought into the picture if a full explanation is intended'.)[133] Nevertheless it was argued that the tested equation explained about 90 per cent of the variation in inter-industry frequency statistics. On this basis, then, Shorey argued that 'maintaining a high national level of economic activity, especially if it is spread unevenly across industry, will mean high levels of strike frequency. Increasingly rapid technical change and further increases in plant size are both likely to increase still further the number of stoppages'.[134]

The other UK study that concentrated on manufacturing industry was undertaken by Creigh and Makeham.[135] This was based on data at a highly disaggregated level (120 minimum list headings were used) and covered the period 1971 to 1975. The analysis dealt with stoppage frequency (the number of stoppages per 100,000 employees) and stoppage incidence (the number of working days lost per 1,000 employees). The model that was tested was that negotiations are more likely to break down 'the greater the number of bargaining occasions that exist and the more remote contact is between the sides in the bargaining process; commonly, management and the shop floor'.[136] The variable used to test the model included the proportion that wages and salaries form of net output, the level of active working, the percentage of workers on a payment by results system (indicators of the number of occasions on which bargaining is likely to take place), the plant-size structure of an industry and the extent to which an industry's output is controlled by a small number of firms (indicators of the remoteness of communications). Although they found that the overall explanatory power of the regression was less for stoppage incidence than for stoppage frequency, and they recognised that the relationships may be more complex than the model suggests, Creigh and Makeham argued nevertheless that 'there seems to be an empirical basis for considering that those hypotheses have some force'.[137]

Other studies have looked beyond manufacturing industry. For example, Kaufman's study sought to examine strike trends among all major industries in the United States.[138] The data covered the years 1960 to 1979. For the purposes of his exercise he grouped the industries into four categories. In the majority of cases he found that factors like unemployment change and inflation accounted for the patterns highlighted. However, in other cases they were affected by unique industry-specific developments:

These include the creation of the Construction Industry Stabilization Committee by President Nixon in 1971, the adoption of the Experimental Negotiating Agreement in Basic Steel in 1972, the breakdown of contact administration machinery in coal and the political turmoil in the United Mine Workers Union, and in apparel, the movement of firms to the non union South and the growing threat from foreign competition.[139]

One of the most detailed examinations of inter-industry variations in strike activity, across the whole range of industries, has been attempted on UK data for the years 1966 to 1973. The study was published as part of a Department of Employment research paper.[140]

Twelve different possible explanations for variations between industries were examined. These ranged from the proportion of white-collar employees (white-collar workers have been less well organised and less forceful in bargaining and generally are less strike-prone than manual workers), to trade union density (it is assumed that unorganised workers are less likely to take collective action), to the state of the labour market (the bargaining power of labour will be high in industries with low unemployment and, assuming that employers do not simply respond with higher wage offers, there will tend to be more strikes). At the end of the analysis it was claimed that four variables appeared to be particularly important and consistent as explanations. These were:

1. *Earnings levels.* Industries with relatively high earnings levels also tended to be those with high strike-proneness. One explanation might be that 'workers in industries which pay relatively high wages will be likely to strike, according to a "probability-of-success" theory, because they have the economic resources to endure a stoppage. They also have a

greater interest in developing the earnings potential of their jobs since they are less likely to find financial improvement by seeking jobs in other industries'.[141]

2. *Labour intensity*. Industries where labour costs account for a high proportion of total costs appeared to be more strike-prone. It might be that in such industries employers' costs levels are more sensitive to wage costs, and other things being equal, a given wage claim will be more likely to meet with employer resistance.

3. *Establishment size*. Industries with above-average establishment size appeared to be subject to more strike activity. One explanation may be that large plants or establishments appear to experience more industrial conflict because of the increased problems of communication and control.

4. *Female workers*. A high proportion of female workers was negatively correlated with strike incidence. This is consistent with the view that, for a number of reasons, female workers are less likely to engage in strike activity than male workers.

Two other factors, the extent of trade union membership and the state of the labour market, appeared to work as explanations in certain, but not all, circumstances.

One of the arguments put forward in the Department of Employment research paper which has found support in a number of other studies of inter-industry variations is that size might be an important issue. Shorey, for example, argued explicitly for economists to pay more attention to this issue, while supporting the thesis that there is a causal link between size and the quality of working relationships which is reflected to some extent in the level of industrial conflict.[142]

There is quite a widespread literature (though by no means all of it from economists) which has discussed the relationship between size (of the plant or the establishment or sometimes both) and industrial conflict.[143] One view is that the effect of size on industrial conflict may not be direct: it might operate through what are referred to as 'structural intermediaries'. For example, an increase in organisational size may lead to an increase in impersonal rules, which in turn may lead to increased industrial conflict (including, but not just, strikes). If this is the case then it will complicate matters, for the 'structural intermediaries' can be affected by factors other than size with the result that attempts to isolate and measure a size effect may not always be accurate. Ingham too argued that a number of the studies of the effect of size have been too restrictive because they have not looked at all the different measures of discontent.[144] Some writers have argued that the size effect need not necessarily operate through structural intermediaries like bureaucratisation. Prais,[145] Edwards[146] and Marginson[147] all take this view. Marginson also argues that company rather than plant size may be particularly important. Other studies, like that referred to earlier by Mayhew, used both plant and company size as an explanation for strike trends over time.[148]

A Review of Economic Theories
A substantial number of studies have been reviewed in this section: many more could have been considered. However, the number of studies using economic variables to explain variations in strike activity is not an indication that this approach, as yet at least, has been able to provide anything more than a partial answer. One recent review of this literature has noted that many of the individual studies have produced conflicting results: often, as has been argued, this has been because different time periods or countries have been covered and there is some evidence that explanations which appear persuasive in one context are not as persuasive in another. This issue was taken up at one level, of course, by Snyder who tried to identify the conditions under which economic variables in general could be influential in determining strike patterns. The point that can be made, though, can be applied in more detail and to more limited time periods than proposed by Snyder. Edwards has argued that 'all the relationships considered by the models relate only to the specific periods under investigation'.[149] In this context it can be said that a relationship which was found in a study in one country, say in the 1950s or 1960s, would not necessarily hold, even in the same country, in the 1970s and 1980s. As an example it might be noted that when Pencavel's explanation for strikes in Britain between 1950 and 1967 was examined by Hunter for a later time period, 1967 to 1972, it seemed less convincing.[150]

Another explanation for the different results may lie in the strike measures examined. It has been noted, for instance, that 'almost all the time-series studies which reveal a negative relationship between unemployment rates and strike activity have focussed exclusively on stoppage numbers',[151] whereas a number of more recent studies which have argued a different relationship between the two variables have used the number of working days lost as their strike measure (though Hibbs' study is an exception).

Many studies are also open to question because of the assumptions that are incorporated. Two such assumptions might be highlighted. First, the emphasis in earlier studies in particular, was almost exclusively on employee behaviour. Sapsford, in a review of such studies, has noted that they

tend to treat one party (invariably workers) as the 'aggressor' during negotiations and the other as a 'passive respondent', meaning that they give inadequate consideration to the influence of economic variables upon the behaviour and/or reactions of the threatened party. In short, work to date has given little or no recognition to the basic feature that strike activity is the product not only of (say) workers' action during bargaining but also of employers' resistance and reaction.[152]

Such a concentration is clearly unhelpful and has been remedied in some later studies, though not in all. The second assumption has been that strikes are essentially concerned with wages and related issues. In his study Davies said that his model was developed on the assumption that 'all disputes occur over wages or wage related issues'.[153] The contrast with the assumptions made by some of the studies reviewed under the political/organisational heading, where in certain circumstances strikes were viewed as having a primary political objective, highlights the contentious nature of such assumptions.

A question also needs to be raised about whether studies using aggregated data are the most valuable. Most economic studies of strikes have sought to explain trends in overall strike figures by reference to economy-wide variables. In most cases, though, the majority of firms and plants are not affected by strikes. Even if one accepts that more firms are affected than indicated by the official figures (because of the inadequacy of such figures) the problem being analysed is one that is concentrated in particular industries and in particular plants. This might suggest that concentrating attention on smaller-scale studies, on say the most strike-prone firms and industries, would be more appropriate.

Conclusion

The vast amount of literature on the causes of strikes, and particularly on explanations for strike patterns, can be ordered around a number of themes. One theme suggests that strikes are related to the nature of the institutions or industrial relations. For example, certain kinds of bargaining machinery will be associated with certain levels and types of strike activity. A second theme sees strikes much more in a political context. They are an expression of the endemic conflict in capitalist societies, and the level of strike activity may be related to factors like the extent to which labour has been able to gain influence through the central political arena. A third theme views strikes in an economic context: attention is centred on the relationship between certain kinds of economic conditions and particular levels of strike activity.

The identification of just three such themes, of course, is an oversimplification. Any categorisation, to a degree, is artificial and a number of writers looked at in this chapter have straddled boundaries. Perhaps the best example can be seen in Snyder's work which was examined in the context of political theories, though Snyder clearly also recognised the importance of industrial relations institutions and economic conditions.

No attempt has been made in this chapter specifically to explain the strike records of individual countries. In some instances, the work reviewed has been based on examples from a particular country or a small group of countries (some of these countries were looked at in some detail in the last chapter). Other pieces of work reviewed have been of a broader comparative nature. The intention, though, in all cases has been to try to see whether one can learn lessons about strikes which can be valuable generally, and ultimately could be used to understand strike behaviour in whatever country one may particularly be interested in.

In many ways, though, the most important conclusion must be that despite the enormous amount of work that has been undertaken in this area there is still nothing like a comprehensive or general theory. In some instances the more work that is completed the more questions and doubts seem to be produced. This is not to denigrate the research that has been reviewed in this chapter. Many of the studies have produced interesting and valuable results. The knowledge, for example, that over a certain period of time particular economic conditions seem to have been associated with high strike-proneness may help one to better understand strike patterns over that period. Nevertheless, this is different to a general theory, for as was pointed out when the 'economic theories' were being reviewed, relationships that seem to have explanatory value in one time period may have much less value in a different time period. In practice, it may be that the idea that a general theory could be produced is mistaken. Strikes are enormously complex and are themselves a classification of a variety of different kinds of activity under one head. Such activity is undertaken for different reasons at different times and has a different meaning for different participants. This does not mean that lessons cannot be learnt from one strike, or one strike wave, or strikes over one period, that can be useful in a different context: it suggests though that explanations cannot simply be transferred, and that one all-embracing explanation, however complex, will be inadequate.

NOTES

1. A.M. Ross and P.T. Hartman, *Changing Patterns of Industrial Conflict,* Wiley, New York, 1960.
2. A.M. Ross and I. Irwin, 'Strike Experience in Five Countries 1927–47: An Interpretation', *Industrial and Labor Relations Review,* Vol. 4, No. 3 (1951) pp. 323–42.
3. C. Kerr, *et al., Industrialism and Industrial Man,* Heinemann, London, 1962.
4. C. Wright Mills, *New Men of Power: America's Labor Leaders,* Harcourt, New York, 1948.
5. *Ibid.,* p. 233.
6. *Ibid.,* p. 234.
7. *Ibid.,* p. 8.
8. *Ibid.,* p. 9.
9. V.L. Allen, *Militant Trade unionism,* Merlin, London, 1966, p. 165.
10. *Ibid.*
11. N.J. Smelser, *The Sociology of Economic Life,* Prentice Hall, Englewood Cliffs, N.J., 1963.

12. *Ibid.,* p. 50.
13. P. Taff and P. Ross, 'American Labor Violence: Its Courses, Character and Outcome', in H.D. Graham and T.R. Gurr (eds.) *Violence in America,* Bantam, New York, 1969.
14. R. Dubin, 'Constructive Aspects of Industrial Conflict', in A. Kornhauser, R. Dubin and A.M. Ross (eds) *Industrial Conflict,* McGraw-Hill, New York, 1954, p. 46.
15. C. Kerr, 'Industrial Conflict and its Mediation', *American Journal of Sociology,* Vol. 60 (1954) p. 199.
16. Dubin, *loc. cit.,* p. 45.
17. F.H. Harbison, 'Collective Bargaining and American Capitalism', in A. Kornhauser, R. Dubin and A.M. Ross (eds.) *op. cit.*
18. R. Dahrendorf, *Class and Class Conflict in Industrial Society,* Routledge and Kegan Paul, London, 1959, p. 260.
19. *Ibid.*
20. R.O. Clarke, Labour-Management Disputes: A Perspective', *British Journal of Industrial Relations,* Vol. 18, No. 1 (1980) pp. 14–25. J.E.T. Eldridge, *Industrial Disputes: Essays in the Sociology of Industrial Relations,* Routledge and Kegan Paul, London, 1968.
21. P.K. Edwards, *Strikes in the United States, 1881–1974,* Blackwell, Oxford, 1981.
22. J.T. Dunlop, *Industrial Relations Systems,* Holt, New York, 1955.
23. T. Parsons and N.J. Smelser, *Economy and Society: A Study in the Integration of Economic and Social Theory,* Routledge and Kegan Paul, London, 1956.
24. N.J. Smelser, *Social Change in the Industrial Revolution,* Routledge and Kegan Paul, London, 1959, presents a case study of social change in the Lancashire textile industry using the systems theory perspective.
25. Royal Commission on Trade Unions and Employers Associations 1965–1968, *Report,* Cmnd 3623, HMSO, London, 1968.
26. *Ibid.,* p. 36.
27. A. Fox and A. Flanders, 'The Reform of Collective Bargaining: From Donovan to Durkheim', *British Journal of Industrial Relations,* Vol. 7, No. 2 (1969) pp. 151–80.
28. H.A. Clegg, *The Changing System of Industrial Relations in Great Britain,* Blackwell, Oxford, 1979.
29. P.K. Edwards, 'The Pattern of Collective Industrial Action', in G.S. Bain (ed.) *Industrial Relations in Britain,* Blackwell, Oxford, 1983, pp. 209–36.
30. *Ibid.,* p. 214.
31. E.M. Kassalow, *Trade Unions and Industrial Relations: An International Comparison,* Random House, New York, 1969.
32. M. Shalev, 'Industrial Relations Theory and the Comparative Study of Industrial Relations and Industrial Conflict', *British Journal of Industrial Relations,* Vol. 18, No. 1, 1980, p. 28.
33. H.A. Clegg, *Trade Unionism Under Collective Bargaining.* Blackwell, Oxford, 1976.
34. *Ibid.,* p. 77.

35. *Ibid.*
36. *Ibid.,* p. 78.
37. *Ibid.,* p. 82.
38. J. Niland, *Collective Bargaining and Compulsory Arbitration in Australia,* New South Wales University Press, Kensington, New South Wales, 1978.
39. S. Creigh, A. Poland and M. Wooden, *The Reasons for International Differences in Strike Activity,* National Institute of Labour Studies, Flinders University of South Australia, Working Paper No. 61, 1984.
40. G.K. Ingham, *Strikes and Industrial Conflict,* Macmillan, London, 1974.
41. *Ibid.,* p. 9.
42. *Ibid.,* p. 10.
43. *Ibid.,* p. 42.
44. *Ibid.,* p. 44.
45. W. Korpi, 'Unofficial Strikes in Sweden', *British Journal of Industrial Relations,* Vol. 19, No. 1 (1981) pp. 66–86.
46. W. Korpi, 'Workplace Bargaining, the Law and Unofficial Strikes: the Case of Sweden', *British Journal of Industrial Relations,* Vol. 16, No. 3 (1978) pp. 355–68.
47. W. Korpi and M. Shalev, 'Strikes, Industrial Relations and Class Conflicts in Capitalist Societies', *British Journal of Sociology,* Vol. 30, No. 2 (1979) p. 177.
48. A. Pizzorno, 'Political Exchange and Collective Identity in Industrial Conflict', in C. Crough and A. Pizzorno (eds.) *The Resurgence of Class Conflict in Western Europe Since 1968: Volume 2, Comparative Analyses,* Macmillan, London, 1978.
49. C. Huxley, 'The State, Collective Bargaining and the Shape of Strikes in Canada', *Canadian Journal of Sociology,* Vol. 4, No. 3 (1979) pp. 223–39.
50. *Loc. cit.*
51. *Ibid.,* p. 29.
52. *Ibid.,* p. 30.
53. *Ibid.*
54. *Ibid.*
55. E. Shorter and C. Tilly, *Strikes in France 1830–1968,* Cambridge University Press, Cambridge, 1974.
56. *Ibid.,* pp. 344–5.
57. *Ibid.,* pp. 106–7
58. *Ibid.,* p. 140.
59. *Ibid.,* p. 104.
60. *Ibid.,* p. 306.
61. *Ibid.,* pp. 330–1
62. *Ibid.,* p. 330.
63. *Ibid.*
64. *Op. cit.,* p. 181.
65. *Ibid.,* p. 181.
66. *Ibid.*
67. *Ibid.,* p. 182.

68. D.A. Hibbs, 'On the Political Economy of Long-Run Trends in Strike Activity', *British Journal of Political Science,* Vol. 8, No. 2 (1978) pp. 153–75.
69. *Ibid.,* p. 169.
70. *Ibid.,* p. 167.
71. D.A. Hibbs, 'Industrial Conflict in Advanced Industrial Societies', *American Political Science Review,* Vol. 70, No. 4 (1976) pp. 1033–58.
72. D. Snyder, 'Institutional Setting and Industrial Conflict', *American Sociological Review,* Vol. 40, No. 3 (1975) pp. 259–78.
73. *Ibid.,* p. 268.
74. *Ibid.,* p. 270.
75. *Ibid.,* p. 270.
76. *Ibid.,* p. 274.
77. *Ibid.,* p. 275.
78. B.E. Kaufman, 'The Determinants of Strikes in the United States 1900–1977, *Industrial and Labour Relations Review,* Vol. 35, No. 4 (July 1982) pp. 473–90.
79. *Ibid.,* p. 482.
80. *Ibid.*
81. Shalev, *op. cit.*
82. J.W. Skeels, 'The Economic and Organizational Basis of Early United States Strikes 1900–1948', *Industrial and Labour Relations Review,* Vol. 35, No. 4 (July 1982) pp. 491–503.
83. *Ibid.,* p. 502.
84. A. Gifford, 'The Impact of Socialism on Work Stoppages', *Industrial Relations,* Vol. 13, No. 2 (1974) pp. 208–11.
85. R. Bean, *Comparative Industrial Relations,* Croom Helm, Beckenham, Kent, 1985.
86. *Ibid.,* p. 143.
87. *Op. cit.* p. 40.
88. M. Paldam and P.J. Pederson, 'The Macro-Economic Strike Model: A Study of Seventeen Countries 1948–1975', *Industrial and Labour Relations Review,* Vol. 35, No. 4 (1982) pp. 504–21.
89. A.H. Hansen, 'Cycles of Strikes', *American Economic Review,* Vol. 11, No. 4 (1921) p. 618.
90. *Ibid.,* p. 620.
91. E.T. Hiller, *The Strike: A Study in Collective Action,* Arrow Press, New York (1969). Originally published in 1928.
92. A. Rees, 'Industrial Conflict and Business Fluctuations', *Journal of Political Economy,* Vol. 60, No. 5 (October 1952) p. 371–82.
93. J.I. Griffen, *Strikes: A Study in Quantitative Economics,* Columbia University Press, New York, 1939.
94. D. Yoder, 'Economic Changes and Industrial Unrest in the United States', *Journal of Political Economy,* Vol. 48 (1940) p. 222–37.
95. A.F. Burns and W.C. Mitchell, *Measuring Business Cycles,* National Bureau of Economic Research, New York, 1946.
96. E.H. Jurkat and D.B. Jurkat, 'Economic Function of Strikes', *Industrial and Labour Relations Review,* Vol. 2 (July 1949) pp. 527–45.

97. *Loc. cit.,* p. 381.
98. *Ibid.*
99. O.C. Ashenfelter and G.E. Johnson, 'Bargaining Theory, Trade Unions and Industrial Strike Activity', *American Economic Review,* Vol. 59, No. 1 (1969) pp. 35–49.
100. *Ibid.,* p. 48.
101. J.H. Pencavel, 'An Investigation into Industrial Strike Activity in Britain', *Economica,* Vol. 37, No. 147 (1970) pp. 239–56.
102. *Ibid.,* p. 243.
103. *Ibid.,* p. 255.
104. K. Mayhew, 'Economists and Strikes', *Oxford Bulletin of Economics and Statistics,* Vol. 41, No. 1 (1979) pp. 6–7.
105. K.G. Knight 'Strikes and Wage Inflation in British Manufacturing Industry 1950–1968', *Bulletin of the Oxford University Institute of Economics and Statistics,* Vol. 34, No. 3 (August 1972) pp. 281–94.
106. M.J. Mauro, 'Strikes a a Result of Imperfect Information', *Industrial and Labour Relations Review,* Vol. 34, No. 4 (July 1982) pp. 522–38.
107. *Ibid.,* p. 523.
108. *Ibid.,* p. 536.
109. *Loc. cit.*
110. *Ibid.,* p. 517.
111. *Ibid.,* p. 571.
112. M. Paldam, 'Industrial Conflicts and Economic Conditions', *European Economic Review,* Vol. 20, No. 2 (1983) pp. 231–56.
113. *Ibid.,* p. 252.
114. R.J. Davies, 'Economic Activity, Incomes Policy and Strikes—A Quantitative Analysis', *British Journal of Industrial Relations,* Vol. 17, No. 2 (July 1979) pp. 205–23.
115. *Ibid.,* p. 209.
116. P.I.C. Edwards, in G.S. Bain, *op. cit.,* p. 217.
117. *Ibid.*
118. E. Evans, 'On Some Recent Econometric Models of Strike Frequency: A Further Comment', *Industrial Relations Journal,* Vol. 8, No. 4 (Winter 1977–8) p. 73.
119. R.N. Stern, 'Methodological Issues in Quantitative Strike Analysis', *Industrial Relations,* Vol. 17, No. 1 (February 1978) pp. 32–42.
120. S.W. Creigh and D. Makeham, 'Strike Incidence in Industrial Countries: An Analysis', *Australian Bulletin of Labour,* Vol. 8, No. 3 (1982) pp. 139–49.
121. P.K. Edwards, in G.S. Bain, *op. cit.*
122. *Ibid.,* p. 215.
123. D.A. Hibbs (1976), *loc. cit.*
124. *Ibid.,* p. 1057.
125. *Op. cit.*
126. *Ibid.,* p. 107.
127. C.T.B. Smith *et al., Strikes in Britain,* Department of Employment, Manpower Paper No. 15, HMSO, London, 1978.
128 J. Shorey, 'Time Series Analysis of Strike Frequency', *British Journal of*

Industrial Relations, Vol. 15, No. 1, pp. 63–75.

129. *Loc. cit.*

130. R.A. McLean, 'Interindustry Differences in Strike Activity', *Industrial Relations,* Vol. 18, No. 1 (Winter 1979) pp. 104.

131. *Ibid.,* p. 109.

132. J. Shorey, 'An Inter-Industry Analysis of Strike Frequency', *Economica,* Vol. 43 (1976) pp. 349–65.

133. *Ibid.,* p. 364.

134. *Ibid.*

135. S. Creigh and P. Makeham, 'Variations in Strike Activity within UK Manufacturing Industry', *Industrial Relations Journal,* Vol. 11 (November–December 1980) pp. 32–7.

136. *Ibid.,* p. 34.

137. *Ibid.,* p. 36

138. B.E. Kaufman, 'Interindustry Trends in Strike Activity', *Industrial Relations,* Vol. 22, No. 1 (Winter 1983) pp. 45–57.

139. *Ibid.,* p. 56.

140. C.T.B. Smith *et al., op. cit.*

141. *Ibid.,* p. 73. Note that alternative explanations were also considered, some contradictory.

142. J. Shorey, 'The Size of the Work Unit and Strike Incidence', *Journal of Industrial Economics,* Vol. 23, No. 3 (March 1975) pp. 175–88.

143. See for example, R.W. Revens, 'Industrial Morale and Size of Unit', in W. Galenson and S.M. Lipset (eds.) *Labor and Trade Unionism,* Wiley, New York, 1960, pp. 259–300; Action Society Trust, *Size and Morale,* Action Society Trust, London, 1953; S. Talacchi, 'Organisational Size, Individual Attitudes and Behaviour: An Empirical Study', *Administrative Science Quarterly,* Vol. 5 (1960) pp. 398–420.

144. G.K. Ingham, *Size of Industrial Organisation and Worker Behaviour: An Empirical Study,* Cambridge University Press, London, 1970.

145. S.J. Prais, 'The Strike-Proneness of Large Plants in Britain', *Journal of Royal Statistical Society,* Series A (General), Vol. 141, Part 3 (1978) pp. 368–84.

146. P.K. Edwards, 'Size of Plant and Strike Proneness', *Oxford Bulletin of Economics and Statistics,* Vol. 42 (May 1980) pp. 145–56.

147. P.M. Marginson, 'The Distinctive Effects of Plant and Company Size on Workplace Industrial Relations', *British Journal of Industrial Relations,* Vol. 22 (March 1984) pp. 1–14.

148. *Loc. cit.*

149. P.K. Edwards, in G.S. Bain, *op. cit.*

150. L.C. Hunter, *The Economic Determination of Strike Activity: A Reconsideration,* Department of Social and Economic Research, Discussion Paper No. 1, University of Glasgow.

151. Creigh, Poland and Wooden, *op. cit.,* p. 58.

152. D. Sapsford, 'Strike Frequency: a Reply', *Industrial Relations Journal,* Vol. 8, No. 1 (Spring 1977) p. 71.

153. *Loc. cit.,* p. 215.

5 Explanations of Industrial Conflict

There is a range of literature which has examined industrial conflict, in its broadest sense, that has not been touched on so far. Although in specific instances this literature has sought to understand and explain strike activity, it has often looked beyond as well as at strikes, and its aim has been to develop a general understanding rather then to provide an explanation, say, for differences in the strike records between countries.

One of the strongest traditions in such literature springs from what is frequently referred to as the 'human relations school'.

HUMAN RELATIONS SCHOOL

The human relations school has its origins in the work of Mayo and the "Hawthorne Studies".[1] In this work Mayo highlighted the importance of social relationships in the workplace, and particularly the role of informal groups. Two different types of group were found. One that was found during the relay assembly test room experiments both provided personal satisfaction for its members and furthered management aims. In this latter connection the members of the group believed that they had a favoured position in the plant and that this could only be maintained by a high level of production. The group, therefore, chided members if they fell behind with their production quotas and helped to maintain discipline. The second kind of group was found in the bank wiring room experiment. In this case also the group provided personal satisfactions, but unlike the other group it acted against management aims. Production was restricted by informal agreement and output was regularly below what could have been achieved. The means used by the group to control those who produced too much included damaging complete work, hiding tools, and threats of physical violence.

The recognition of the importance of informal groups for the worker, then, was allied to a recognition that such groups could operate in line with or counter to management aims. They might operate in this latter fashion for a number of reasons. For example, because of 'the transference into the plant of habits or attitudes formed in the family or community', or because of 'the failure of the industrial organisation to provide a satisfactory social environment for the employee, with a resulting rise in "obsessive response", "individual futility" or "exasperation"', or they might operate in this way because of 'a failure of communication'.[2]

The role of management, from this standpoint, was not to try to deny the social needs of the worker, but to try to work within the boundaries they imposed and ensure that informal groups worked for, not against, them. Thus some members of the human relations school have held that managers should assist in the strengthening of informal groups and in protecting them from disruption. Management should encourage its lower supervisors to enter these groups, and, if possible, to become their leaders, in order to direct them 'consonant with the aims of the formal organisation'. Sometimes control of the informal structure will be impossible. In such circumstances the manager should aim to prevent the growth of the more harmful type of group, 'perhaps by encouraging a multiplicity of informal groups cutting across lines of potential conflict or disruption'.[3]

Perhaps the most authoritative review of the Hawthorne experiments is that of Roethlisberger and Dickson. They sought to identify the lessons that should be drawn for management and drew attention to what they saw as the essential link between the economic purpose of the enterprise and its social organisation. Thus, they said that the social and economic functions of the organisation are interrelated, and failure 'to obtain satisfaction from co-operation will prevent in time the effective achievement of the common economic purpose of the organisation'.[4]

A successful manager, then, needs to treat workers, not as 'economic men', as traditionally was the case, but as 'social men': any attempt to see workers, supervisors and executives apart from their social setting will be inadequate. Roethlisberger and Dickson identified three major problems to which management need to pay particular attention.

First, the problem of change in the social structure.

In summary . . . changes in the technical and in the formal organisation of the company are intimately related to the general problem of maintaining internal balance. These problems cannot be regarded as occurring in isolation from the total situation. They are intimately related to the social organisation of the company and have profound consequences not only in terms of the effectiveness with which the organisation as a whole functions but also in terms of employee relations.[5]

Second, the problem of control and communication. The formal structure of a plant specifies the way in which control should be exercised. Generally this function is performed by supervisory staff and specialist groups. The basic problem, in all of this, is one of communication.

In order to exercise intelligent control, the management of a concern must be continually provided with accurate information as to the manner in which the total organisation is functioning. This is one of the major functions of the supervisory hierarchy and depends for its successful functioning upon the accurate transmission of information down through the structure on the one hand, and of information pertaining to the work level and successive levels of supervision up through the structure, on the other. The problems involved in transmitting information from the top to the bottom are fairly well recognised, but some of the problems arising in the communication from the bottom to the top have not been so clearly indicated.[6]

One of the common sources of faulty communication, it was argued, is the inadequate orientation of the supervisor to his situation. He may view his role in rather narrow terms, concentrating on the usual criteria of efficiency and ignoring the social processes within his group. Another important source of faulty communications

relates to the nature of the informal organisation of the work group and the extent to which the informal organisation is at variance with the formal organisation. Any marked discrepancy between the actual situation and the formal organisation may place the supervisor in an awkward position. This problem was clearly seen in the Bank Wiring Observation Room. In order to maintain his own position the supervisor in such situations may tend to convey an inaccurate picture of the actual situation to his superiors.[7]

The third major problem relates to the difficulties of an individual's adjustment to the structure. In any organisation there is a continual movement of people.

A man is hired, he remains a member of the organisation for a time varying in length from a few hours to a lifetime, and then moves out of the structure to another organisation or to retirement . . .. During the time the person remains in the company he undergoes movement in terms of social space . . .. The structure of social organisation in terms of which his position is defined may *itself change,* thus altering the person's position in the structure.[8]

The problems caused by movement within the structure are particularly important for the personnel manager and success in dealing with them may be crucial for the social satisfaction of the worker and the efficiency of the organisation.

The stress that is placed, from the lessons of the Hawthorne experiments, both on the importance of social relationships for worker satisfaction and on the importance of harnessing them for the efficiency of the organisation, are worth emphasising. As far as industrial conflict is concerned the failure to meet social needs and the failure to harness them effectively can present real dangers.

One particular emphasis which was taken out of the early work of the human relations school (and which was highlighted by Roethlisberger and Dickson) was the emphasis on good communications as a way of avoiding conflict. This was an important element, for instance, in the study by Scott and Homans, mainly of car workers in post-war Detroit. They argued that, especially in large organisations, poor communications meant that workers felt they were being given the 'run around'. Workers 'use that phrase when they feel that what they consider is important is not being treated as such by people in authority'.[9] Some of the reasons suggested for poor communications were language problems, lack of time and the difficulties facing the 'link men', foremen.

A number of other studies have drawn attention to the importance of foremen. For example, Dalton argued that providing 'he learns to function flexibly and work out accommodations in response to imperatives playing on him' the foreman can be 'one of the major influences for reducing conflict within the organisation'.[10] However, it was recognised that foremen face major problems: they are expected, as members of the management team, to share in the responsibility for management decisions, but usually they have had no part in making them and may not even have been consulted about them. Later work has suggested that frequently foremen are bypassed by both management and unions: management, for instance, may talk directly to the union representative on the shop floor, going over the head of the foreman. The problems relating to the foremen are part of a more general concern about supervision. In this context they link with the argument put forward in Whyte's study of a steel container factory, where he suggested that conflict arose because of the autocratic attitude of the works manager.[11]

Many would accept the points made by the human relations school. Workers have social as well as economic needs: as a corrective to the assumptions of 'economic man' made by scientific management an important point was made and generally taken. Even Carey, who is strongly critical of the Hawthorne studies and argues that the evidence is 'surprisingly consistent with a rather old world view about the value of monetary incentives, driving leadership and discipline' rather than conclusions put forward by the Hawthorne researchers, is more concerned to attack the methodology than to argue for the view of 'economic man'.[12] Thus, he says: 'To make these points is not to claim that the Hawthorne studies can provide serious support for any such old-world view. The limitations of the Hawthorne studies clearly render them incapable of yielding serious support for any sort of generalization whatever'.[13] Similarly, few would argue with the desirability of 'good communications', though the words of caution of Kerr and Siegel[14] that improved communications will only 'solve' industrial conflict if that is where the real problems lie are important (if the problems lie elsewhere, improved communications may make the basic disagreement more visible and conflict worse). However, many have been concerned to point to the inadequacies of particular studies within the human relations school, to the proposition that not all workers want to gain social satisfaction from the workplace (or to be members of social groups) and, critically, to the other as well as to the social needs of workers. As far as industrial conflict is concerned the argument has been that meeting supposed social needs alone will not be a solution. In essence, the problem with the human relations school was that they never considered the other sources of conflict in the workplace.

The early human relations studies have been followed by others which are sometimes grouped under the heading of the 'neo-human relations school'. The argument is still that workers look for more than economic rewards from the workplace: however, now it is suggested that they may look for more than social rewards as well. One of the main propositions is that they will seek satisfaction from the work itself (writers who have put this forward are sometimes referred to as the 'self-actualisation school').

There are a variety of different interpretations of this point. For example, McGregor put forward his theory X and theory Y thesis.[15] This holds that managers frequently assume that workers seek financial reward from their work (theory X) and can only be motivated by the consideration of such factors. He contends that managers should pay more attention to the demands of workers and recognise that expenditure of effort is natural and will be readily accepted by workers providing certain conditions are met (theory Y). It is only, so the argument proceeds, by paying more attention to theory Y that managers will be able to motivate workers properly.

Similarly, Hertzberg[16] argues that a two-factor approach to worker motivation needs to be adopted: it needs to be recognised that satisfaction and dissatisfaction are not merely opposite sides of the same coin:

the factors involved in producing job satisfaction were *separate* and *distinct* from the factors that led to job dissatisfaction. Since separate factors needed to be considered, depending on whether job satisfaction or job dissatisfaction was involved, it followed that these two feelings were not the obverse of each other. Thus the opposite of job satisfaction would not be job dissatisfaction, but rather no job satisfaction; similarly the opposite of job dissatisfaction is no job dissatisfaction, not satisfaction with one's job.[17]

Hertzberg distinguishes between hygiene factors (such as good wages and working conditions) and satisfiers (responsibility, recognition, interesting work). Both hygiene factors and satisfiers are important, but they fulfil different roles. Hygiene factors prevent dissatisfaction but management cannot motivate workers simply by paying more attention to them: to motivate workers, attention also has to be paid to satisfiers.

Again, Maslow has discussed workers' 'needs' in terms of a hierarchy, ranging from needs that are essential for survival to those which enable workers to make full use of all their resources.[18] Self-actualisation is at the top of the hierarchy. Once lower-level needs have been met to a reasonable degree then managers will have to look further up the hierarchy if they are to motivate workers. The emphasis on met to a reasonable level rather than met completely, though, is important. Maslow recognised that 'most members of our society who are normal are partially satisfied in all their basic needs and partially unsatisfied in all their basic needs at the same time'. Similarly, the emergence of a new need after a lower-level one has been satisfied 'is not a sudden saltatory phenomenon but rather a gradual emergence by slow degrees from nothingness'.[19]

Recognition of the 'needs' of workers has an explicit management objective: it is not simply an academic matter. The aim, as with the early human relations school, is quite clearly to harness workers' energy to support management aims. McGregor explicitly argued that management should organise work so that employees would achieve their own aims 'by directing their own efforts towards organisational objectives'.[20] Another writer from the same 'school', Likert, probably most clearly linked worker satisfaction to increased efficiency.[21] The new system of management was one in which motivational forces were recognised and used to ensure that the objectives of the organisation were achieved.

The view that workers are concerned to obtain satisfaction from the work itself has led to the proposal that work should be restructured to allow it to resemble more closely the principles of 'craft work'. Such principles imply that workers should be able to identify with the product they are making and that they should have more control over it when they work. Ideally it should also mean that the worker sees little distinction between work and leisure. A number of moves have been suggested to try to achieve this goal and make modern industrial employment more like craft work: these include job enlargement, job enrichment and flexitime.

Few would oppose the move to make work more interesting. Nevertheless, major criticisms have been made of the assumptions of the self-actualisation school. Some have been made by other social psychologists who have questioned the idea of a set agenda for motives; rather, it has been argued, motives can vary according to the situation of the person concerned. One writer from the Massachusetts Institute of Technology, Bennis, has questioned the assumption in the work of the self-actualisation school about basic human needs.[22] Other objections have been raised by trade unions, who have been concerned that job satisfaction might be seen by management as an alternative rather than as a supplement to workers' other needs. Thus, one union leader has warned 'that any scheme for improving job satisfaction by changes in work organisation must not be regarded as a substitute for . . . improvements in the working environment and the terms and conditions of employment'.[23] Another criticism has developed from a major British study. The 'Affluent Worker' studies of Goldthorpe and Lockwood have questioned the extent to which all workers seek intrinsic satisfaction from their work.[24] In their study Goldthorpe and Lockwood claimed to find an instrumental orientation to work: the principal aim was to earn sufficient from work to gain satisfaction elsewhere. Although the 'Affluent Worker' studies have not themselves escaped criticism (some USA studies,[25] for example, have been able to point to aspirations for jobs that offer a high skill and interest content while others have questioned the whole notion of 'orientations to work'[26]) they served to draw attention to the fact that not all workers see obtaining an interesting job as their only or main aim: other needs have to be met if worker dissatisfaction is to be lessened, and some of these may be generated outside as well as within the workplace.

Other critics of the self-actualisation theories have questioned the assumption in much writing that the restructuring of work can be achieved to meet the needs of both the worker and the employer. Experiments, like those at Volvo's Kalmar plant in Sweden, it has been argued, do not prove the ability to meet both sets of needs in quite the fashion assumed by some of the more optimistic commentators. While it is accepted that Volvo has been able to modify the traditional system of work in the car industry without sacrificing efficiency or competitiveness in the market, it is suggested that the changes have not been as radical as is often assumed: the work is more varied in that an opportunity is given to perform a larger number of tasks, but the skill level of the work is not much greater.

TECHNOLOGY AND INDUSTRIAL CONFLICT

The concerns of the human relations school to recognise and harness the social needs of the worker, and of the self-actualisation school to modify the nature of modern industrial work, have links with the view that the kind of technology employed in an industry will help to determine worker satisfaction and the level of industrial conflict. The clearest link is through the concern about the impact of assembly-line production. A great deal of work was undertaken in America in the 1950s designed to show the impact of assembly-line technology. Studies of the motor vehicle industry by Walker and Guest[27] and Chinoy[28] pointed out that extreme specialisation led to fragmented and repetitive work tasks. They also showed how the technology used restricted the opportunities for social intercourse: for instance, noise and brevity of spare time between job cycles restricted any conversation between operators, while the range of people to whom an operator could talk was determined by his position on the line. Walker and Guest described the impact of assembly-line production in one of the factories they studied:

Most workers are located along the 'main line' according to the particular manpower requirements of each segment of the assembly process. Each operator works in a limited area completing his own operations independently of others as the car is carried by the conveyor down the line. A particular individual may talk with the men immediately around him, but these men cannot be said to comprise a bona fide work group in the usual sense of the term . . .

In our interviews these men exhibited little of what the sociologist would call 'in-group awareness'. Rarely, for example, did they talk about 'our team' or 'our group' or 'the men in our outfit'. Instead the following remark was typical: 'I've been here for over a year, and I hardly know the first names of the men in the section where I work'.[29]

Such views of assembly-line technology led the authors to propose changes which have been associated with the human relations and neo-human relations schools. Walker, for example, considered ways in which the foreman could become a group leader and harness the group's social needs for managerial ends: Chinoy suggested job rotation and job enlargement in an effort to overcome the monotony of assembly-line production. These views of assembly-line production, though, also have a link with the proposition that the kind of technology used helps to determine worker satisfaction. In this case one particular kind of technology was being examined but the way in which this technology was seen to determine social relationships, which in turn could affect satisfactions derived from work, is more generally important.

A variety of work fits into this school of thought. Again, many of the same issues recur, particularly the importance of social relationships and work groups. For example, Sayles tried to categorise work groups and explain differences between them in terms of the kind of technology used.[30] Sayles looked at 300 work groups, in a number of different industries in the USA. Four different types of group were distinguished. The first was what he termed the 'apathetic' group. Such groups had no clear leadership, little internal unity, played little part in union affairs and were not seen as co-operative with management or as high producers; they also had low levels of grievance activity. The second type of group were termed 'erratic'. Such groups were more united internally, leadership was often highly centralised, members often played an active part in unions and they were seen as unsatisfactory employees by management; they frequently engaged in grievance activity but it was not controlled well or necessarily linked directly to the goals of the group. The third type of group was called the 'strategic' group by Sayles. They tended to be composed of key workers and had a high degree of internal unity. Members of such groups participated regularly in union activities, frequently taking leadership roles, although they were also often viewed positively by management. This type of group had the highest level of grievance activity and such activity was clearly directed towards the group's own ends. The final kind of group was termed 'conservative'. These groups were highly united internally and highly valued by management. At the same time they paid little attention to union affairs and used 'restrained' pressure in support of their grievances.

Sayles sought to explain the differences between the groups not by reference to factors like the skills of the supervisor or management but by reference to the kind of technology employed. Technology, he argued, influences the extent to which the division of labour can be taken, and in turn the division of labour influences the formation and nature of work groups. Thus, Sayles argued, a division of labour 'which separates or eliminates workers doing identical tasks, reduces their tendency to engage in concerted activity'. The number of problems on which there can be consensus can be reduced 'by the simple expedient of reducing the number of similar jobs, or separating them in space so that communications barriers are created among the job-holders'.[31]

Work groups and technology both have an important role to play as well in the analysis of Kuhn.[32] He looked at workers in the rubber tyre and electrical equipment industries in the USA; his aim was to discover why workers in the rubber tyre industry participated more in fractional bargaining (the unauthorised pursuit of demands backed up by unofficial action) than workers in the electrical equipment industries. His argument centred on the idea that the type of technology used in the industries determined the willingness of workers to formulate, and their ability to press, demands; in the case of the rubber tyre industry it encouraged and aided workers to press demands whereas the opposite was the case in the elecrtical equipment industry.

In detail, and as a general hypothesis, Kuhn suggested that technology with the following four characteristics was more conducive to fractional bargaining. First, that which 'subjects a large proportion of workers to continued changes in work methods, standards or materials as they work at individually paced jobs'. Second, that which permits interaction between workers in the same task group. Third, that which 'groups most of the workforce into several nearly equal-sized departments'. Fourth, that which 'requires continuous rigidly sequential processing of materials into one type of product'. Kuhn argued that the first two characteristics stimulated the workforce to engage in fractional bargaining while the fourth increased their ability to press home demands by ensuring that the cost of work disruption would be much greater for management than workers. The third characteristic weakened the power of the union over the work group and as a result helped to ensure that action taken would be unofficial.

A simple view, though, that the kind of technology employed in an industry determines the level of industrial conflict faces problems, for there are variations in the level and nature of industrial conflict within industries. Goldthorpe's study of a 'deviant case' in the British motor vehicle industry (Vauxhall) drew attention to this problem.[33] Goldthorpe's solution was to place emphasis away from technology on to the orientations of workers. Technology was not discarded altogether as an explanation, but it was not seen as *the* explanation. The type of technology placed constraints on behaviour but did not determine it. Different meanings can be attached to the same 'objective factors' by different workers and if one is to understand these different meanings then one has to look beyond the workplace itself, to the social lives of the workers involved.

Sayles and Kuhn both recognised the problem that had to be faced if their explanation were to be tenable. Sayles, in particular, seemed to move away from technological determinism at one stage. He noted the importance of leadership within work groups and, as Eldridge has argued, this 'would seem to lead us away from the doctrines of technological determinism when discussing the question of strike-proneness as between firms'.[34] However, Sayles' conclusion is fairly rigid: thus, he argues that 'the conclusions of the study' show that the technology of the plant 'moulds the type of work groups that evolve', and 'the human element, so-called, is a resultant of the technological decisions and, in part at least, predictable from them'.[35]

Other writers have been much clearer in their attempt to move away from technological determinism. For example, Woodward, in an early study, looked at the organisational structure of a hundred British firms.[36] This suggested that organisational characteristics were not directly related to factors like size, broad industrial classification or the degree of business success enjoyed, but were directly related to the technology used. Three main groups of technology were identified: those producing units or small batches for customer orders, those working on the basis of large batch or mass production and those operating on the basis of continuous process production. 'When the organisational characteristics of firms were related to these technical categories, it was found that specific organisational patterns were associated with each category'.[37] The unit/small batch method of production and the continuous process method of production appeared to produce structure and behaviour 'more consistent and predictable' than large batch or mass production. Woodward went on to argue that the attitude and behaviour of management and supervisory staff and the 'tone' of industrial relations was determined by the type of technology. For example, pressures seemed to build up in an assembly-line technology and these adversely affected industrial relations.

However, Woodward took these issues further in a later study and recognised that the relationship between technology and behaviour might be more complex than initially thought. First, although the behaviour of an employee may be limited or constrained by technology 'these limitations will not be the only ones, for he will also be limited by the requirements of the administration, by the demands of his colleagues and by other factors'. Second, the interplay between the individual operator and his technological surroundings will not necessarily be one-way; 'often he may be able to bring about changes in his immediate technical situation, over and above those changes which he is expected to carry out as part of his job'.[38]

Woodward went on to argue that industrial organisations can best be studied through a socio-technical system approach. This approach implies that theories about industrial organisations will be incomplete and relatively unhelpful 'if they are limited solely to the technical aspects, or solely to the social aspects of organisations'[39]: the study of industrial organisations rather should give due regard to the interaction between the social and the technical. The socio-technical systems approach, however, also implies that study can be constrained within the boundaries of a social system. Woodward argued, explicitly, that technological systems can be isolated and their boundaries fairly easily determined.

A range of work has been produced utilising the concept of the socio-technical system; much has arisen from researchers at the Tavistock Institute of Human Relations. For example, Trist has looked at labour relations in the coal-mining industry.[40] This research centred on three main mining systems. The first was the traditional system of single-place working. In this

. . . the miner possesses the necessary range of skills to undertake all facework tasks in a self-contained work place. His role is that of a multi-skilled, self-supervising workman towards whom the deputy stands in a service rather than a supervisory relation. Groups of up to six men share a place, the men selecting their own mates. Since all members do all jobs, either on the same or different shifts, they share equally in the same paynote.[41]

The second was the conventional longwall system. This marked a sharp break with the single-place working for there was 'a formal division of labour with specialised tasks carried out by a number of groups of varying size'. Further, although there were task groups each had 'its own customs and agreements, including separate paynotes, so that each' was segregated 'from the other and bound within its own field of interest'. Since the groups did not spontaneously work together, co-ordination and control had to be provided 'entirely from outside—by management'.[42] The third mining system was the composite longwall system. This had some similarities with conventional longwall mining, in that the same basic technological devices were utilised; however, it differed in the way the men were organised to carry out these similar tasks. Thus, although the task groups were the same as on conventional longwalls with regard to the activities they carry out, they were not segregated from each other, but interchangeable in memberships.

As soon as the scheduled work of a shift is completed, men spontaneously carry on with whatever activity is next in sequence so that subsequent groups gain time in hand against unpredictable interferences with the progress of the cycle, always to some extent likely in the underground environment.[43]

Such a method of work organisation, Trist argued, results in the development of self-regulation and continuity characteristics which parallel those of single-place working.

Under these conditions the deputy is liberated from detailed 'progress chasing' and seam management is able to concentrate on planning and maintaining the conditions and services which permit the cycle to proceeed without disruption and work groups to aim for higher production targets.[44]

Trist drew two important conclusions from this analysis. The first was that the kind of organisation associated with the single-place system and the composite longwall system has both technical and social benefits; it was found to possess characteristics conducive 'to productive effectiveness, low cost, work satisfaction, good relations and social health'.[45] They appeared to be able to overcome the disadvantages associated with conventional longwall mining, such as work isolation, conflict, supervisory problems, and low productivity. The second, and probably even more important conclusion, was that the technical system need not determine precisely the form of work organisation. The same basic technical system, longwall mining, could be used in a number of different ways, two of which have been highlighted. The aim, therefore, should be to recognise the consequences of different methods of work organisation and to select the one which provides the best fit between the social and technical objectives.

The emphasis in this writing on the way in which technical systems can be affected by other variables, and the move away from a deterministic stance, is welcome. Nevertheless, it is open to question whether too much emphasis is still given to the importance of social satisfaction within the workplace. The criticism here has to return to the kinds of issue discussed in the analysis of the human relations school: other sources of conflict need to be considered.

MARXIST EXPLANATIONS OF INDUSTRIAL CONFLICT

A clear challenge to the assumptions of both the human relations school and the technological school is provided by the Marxist approach to industrial conflict. The central problem from this point of view lies in the economic rather than the social sphere. In essence the problem lies in the division of economic resources and the existence of a capitalist class.

One of the leading exponents of the Marxist view of industrial conflict argues that industrial relations occur 'within a dynamic conflict situation which is permanent and unalterable so long as the structure of society remains unaltered'.[46] The conflict situation is viewed as a product of the labour market, in which on the one hand there are workers who have to sell labour power in order to subsist, while on the other hand there are buyers of labour power who own the means of production and purchase labour power (for them the cost of labour power is an important factor in the cost of production).

These two interests are irreconcilable. They are engaged in a perpetual conflict over the distribution of revenue. It might be stated that the interests have a common purpose increasing total revenue and so they have. But the conflict over distribution is in no sense lessened by this for the actual distribution of additional increments of revenue is determined by the power situation. Employees with no power may get nothing. There is no automatic distribution based on a sense of fairness or equity. Shares have to be fought for sometimes bitterly.[47]

Of course, this picture may well not be recognised by all of the participants, crucially by all of the workers: they may view conflict on a much narrower front and on a more parochial basis. However, this does not invalidate the picture that has been drawn, it merely draws attention to the problem of 'consciousness' which is highlighted in a great deal of Marxist writing. Absence of consciousness on the part of the workers, and false class consciousness, may affect the outcome, but it does not affect the assessment of the basic cause of conflict.

When one turns to look at the strike and the role it plays, though, the Marxist view becomes more difficult to state in a straightforward fashion. Marx and Engels clearly saw a role for strikes in raising consciousness: Engels described strikes as 'the military school of the working man in which they prepare themselves for the great struggle which cannot be avoided'.[48] Yet Marx and Engels both saw dangers as well in the 'injudicious use of power'. There was a danger, they argued, that workers would be limited to 'petty warfare against the existing system' rather than attempting to change it. There was also a danger, so it was argued, in adopting elements of the syndicalist tradition which elevated strike action, particularly the general strike, to a critical role in bringing about revolutionary social change. Support for the general strike frequently paid insufficient attention to the organisational demands for successful action. Engels portrayed this position as too simple and unrealistic. It assumed that

one fine day all the workers in a country or even maybe throughout the world will stop work and force the wealthy classes in at most four weeks either to give in or attack the workers, who in turn will have the right to defend themselves and so can overturn the whole of the old society.[49]

In practice Marx and Engels took a view in between the two extremes put forward: they saw strikes neither as meaningless nor as the single important weapon. Yet their middle way has not always been accepted, and in the years since their writing was first published there have been many debates within the Marxist tradition about the value of strike action.

In a similar fashion Marxist writers have debated the role that trade unions can and do play. Early Marxist writers clearly saw a role for trade unions: trade unions were seen as an expression of the common interest of the working class (recognition that workers had a common interest in fighting the ruling class, rather than fighting amongst themselves was an important stage in the movement towards revolutionary social change). However, Marx and Engels recognised some dangers in trade union activity and this caution was taken up by later writers.

Lenin, for example, argued that trade unions tended to concentrate on economic matters which were of only sectional interest (such as the improvement of conditions in their own factory or industry).[50] This was a mistake because it meant that workers often ignored non-economic issues and it hindered the development of class consciousness. Others, writing at the same time, expressed similar reservations. Trotsky, for example, argued that trade unions might be ineffective because they would be 'incorporated' into the state: trade unions in all societies competed with capitalists to obtain the favour of the state.[51] However, both Lenin and Trotsky stopped short of adopting the position put forward by some others, that trade unions were at best irrelevant, and at worst their action was counterproductive in the drive to achieve radical social change. Writing in 1938 Trotsky said that the 'powerful growth of trade unionism in France and the United States is the best refutation of the preachments of those ultra-left doctrinaires who have been teaching that trade unions have "outlived their usefulness"'.[52]

The debate within the Marxist tradition, while important and worth stressing, has still been less critical than the debate between the Marxist tradition and other schools of thought. This is well exemplified in the discussion of alienation, in which divergent approaches and even definitions of the term can be seen in the positions taken by Marxists and non-Marxists.

Alienation was one of the important themes in the early writings of Marx. It was central to his argument that alienation arises from the fact that in the capitalist system labour is sold; it is bought by the capitalist and used to satisfy his needs rather than those of the worker. Thus the worker is estranged from the things he creates and this, in turn, violates the essential nature of man. Marx wrote: 'the alien character of work under capitalism emerges clearly in the fact that as soon as no physical or other compulsion exists labour is shunned like the plague. External labour, labour in which man alienates his self, is a labour of self-sacrifice, of mortification'.[53]

Alienation is most vividly seen in modern industrial labour. Two aspects are particularly crucial. The first is the division of labour, which is seen by Marx as a means of promoting wealth for the capitalist but restricting even more closely the freedom of the worker. The second is the factory system of production, which is viewed as the most complete method of domination of the worker by the capitalist for he can control in detail every activity of labour. However, it is crucial to appreciate that neither the division of labour nor the factory system were seen by Marx as important in their own right; they were only important because they represented the most developed form of treating workers as a commodity.

Alienation will not be overcome simply by increasing wages; while from some points of view this might be desirable, it will not result in freedom, but merely make the worker 'a better paid slave'. Similarly, social reforms, and even workers' co-operatives, unless they are entirely the creation of workers and receive no state aid, will not help to overcome alienation. Alienation will only be overcome, according to Marx, with the overthrow of the capitalist system, when labour stops being treated as a commodity.

Discussion of alienation frequently becomes confused, because when the term has been used by other writers it has been interpreted in a different fashion. For example, although Weber rarely used the term he clearly had an interest in the area and commented on related issues at length. Yet Weber differed from Marx fundamentally in his analysis of the subject. As has already been noted, for Marx alienation was a consequence of capitalism; for Weber it was much more a product of industrialisation and bureaucracy. As a result, although the abolition of private property is crucial in order to overcome alienation from the Marxist viewpoint, it is of little moment from the Weberian perspective.

Blauner[54] has also given a different emphasis in his discussion of alienation; he has linked it to particular types of technology. His starting point is to suggest that there are four dimensions of alienation, each of which can be contrasted with non-alienative states. One is powerlessness, which is contrasted with control; a second is meaninglessness which is contrasted with purpose; a third is isolation which is contrasted with social integration; and the fourth is self-estrangement which is contrasted with self-improvement. Each of these dimensions is, in Blauner's view, linked, for each inhibits an essential and basic activity of man. Alienation was studied by Blauner in four industries (printing, textile, motor vehicles and chemicals) which were viewed as examples of four different technologies (craft, machine tending, assembly line and process respectively). His conclusion was that alienation in these different technologies could be looked at on the basis of an inverted 'U' curve; craft technology represents maximum freedom for the worker, a freedom which is sharply diminished in machine tending and assembly-line production, but which is largely regained through process technology. In this latter system, the progress of the division of labour is halted and may even be reversed, while automation enables the employee to increase his control over the work process.

Blauner's thesis is in many ways essentially optimistic. Although he adds caveats, such as that further automation may not necessarily reduce alienation because it may take forms other than process technology, he nevertheless holds out hope for improvements in the future. However, Blauner is only able to do so because of the particular view he adopts on the nature of alienation. For him it centres on a conception of 'basic human needs' which views the craft ethic as the ultimate aim; he is, in other words, taking the view put forward by the 'self-actualising' and 'neo-human relations' schools. This means that Blauner is able to postulate a reduction in alienation without fundamental changes to the ownership of industry or the nature of work organisation.

It is worthwhile referring here to the distinction made by Wright Mills,[55] and supported by Eldridge,[56] between objective (structural) and subjective (feeling states) factors. Blauner's discussion concentrates on subjective factors, assessing feelings of powerlessness, meaningless, normlessness and isolation; if a worker expresses satisfaction on these issues then he is assumed to be non-alienated. However, other sociologists would want to argue that the social structure may affect the individual in ways he would not perceive. Thus, 'if the sociologist wants to argue that social structures affect people's lives in ways which the people themselves only partially comprehend, then the actor's definition of the situation, whilst of great importance in sociological analysis, does not exhaust the sociologist's task'.[57]

Mills clearly adopts this latter position. Workers may express satisfaction with their present job, he says, but this does not mean that they have power, economic or political. Neither does it mean that the basis of alienation or industrial conflict has been removed. It merely means that employers have been able to manipulate workers into believing that they are satisfied: in fact, he says, 'the satisfaction thus expressed may be nothing other than "the morals of the cheerful robot"'. Similarly he goes on to argue that 'current managerial attempts to create job enthusiasm . . . are attempts to conquer work alienation within the bounds of work alienation. In the meantime, whatever satisfaction alienated men gain from work occurs within the framework of alienation'.[58]

Blauner's use of the term alienation is a link back to the discussion of technology. Another, and one which links more clearly to the Marxist perspective, is provided by Braverman.[59] His book, published in 1974, has had a major impact. Braverman quite explicitly acknowledges his reliance on a Marxist perspective: as he says the 'intellectual influence under which [the] work was composed [was] that of Marx'.[60] However, it is also worthwhile noting that although Braverman explicitly acknowledged his Marxist perspective he said he owed little debt to anything that has been written by Marxists since Marx. He argued that in his writing Marx

shows how the processes of production are, in capitalist society, incessantly transformed under the impetus of the principal driving force of that society, the accumulation of capital. For the working population, this transformation manifests itself, first, as a continuous change in the labor process of each branch of industry and second, as a redistribution of labor among occupations and industries.[61]

However, since Marx completed his work in the 1860s, it is suggested, Marxists have added little to his body of work in this respect. 'Neither the changes in productive processes throughout this century of capitalism and monopoly capitalism, nor the changes in the occupational and industrial studies of the working population have been subjected to any comprehensive Marxist analysis since Marx's death'.[62]

Braverman's Marxist perspective was used for a survey of development of capitalism in the USA. Considerable emphasis was placed on the impact of Taylor's scientific management and the way that its principles have been used to guide the introduction of new production techniques. One particularly important and distinctive feature of scientific management was the concept of control. Braverman recognised that the issue of control was not new but had been an essential feature of management throughout its history: the argument was that with Taylor the issue of control assumed unprecedented dimensions. Taylor, it was argued, 'raised the concept of control to an entirely new plane when he asserted as an *absolute necessity for adequate management the dictation to the worker of the precise manner in which work is to be performed.* That management had the right to 'control' labour was generally assumed before Taylor, but in practice this right usually meant only the general setting of tasks, with little direct interference in the worker's mode of performing them. Taylor's contribution was to overturn this practice and replace it by its opposite. Management, he insisted, could only be a limited and frustrated undertaking so long as it left to the worker any decision about the work. His 'system' was 'simply a means for management to achieve control of the actual mode of performance of every labour activity, from the simplest to the most complicated'.[63] The application of Taylor's principles meant that the labour process was divorced from the skill and autonomy of the individual worker; it also meant a clear break between manual and mental labour and the monopoly of knowledge by management of every step of the labour process. The result, according to Braverman, has been the progressive degradation and deskilling of labour.

Braverman also recognised the impact of new technology. Methods of production have been revolutionised: 'modern production constantly overhauls all aspects of its peformance, and in some industries has completely reconstituted itself more than once in the space of a hundred years'.[64] The drive for greater productivity has led to faster and more efficient methods and machinery. However, it is the way that new technology is used by management within capitalism, and the implications for control, that are important. In the capitalist mode of production

new methods and new machinery are incorporated within a management effort to dissolve the labor process as a process conducted by the worker and reconstitute it as a process conducted by management. In the first form of the division of labor, the capitalist dissassembles the craft and returns it to the workers piecemeal, so that the process as a whole is no longer the province of any individual worker . . . [But it] is in the age of the scientific-technical revolution that management sets itself the problem of grasping the process as a whole and controlling every element of it without question.[65]

The changes that Braverman noted are not restricted to manual labour in factory production. Increasingly, Braverman argued, the nature of both clerical and service work is being changed. The use of new technology in offices has transformed the work of clerks, and the use of new technology in shops is now being developed so that 'a revolution is now being prepared which will make of retail workers, by and large, something closer to factory operatives than anyone had ever imagined possible'.[66] These changes have implications for control, but also for the class structure. For example, when looking at clerical workers, Braverman argued that the problem of white-collar workers 'which so bothered early generations of Marxists, and which was hailed by anti-Marxists as a proof of the falsity of the "proletarianization" thesis'[67] has been unambiguously clarified. The conditions of work of the clerk have lost all their former superiorities and the clerk has become part of a large proletariat in a new form.

The Braverman thesis has excited considerable debate. Hill has reviewed the Braverman thesis and noted a number of the criticisms made of it.[68] Initially three are highlighted. The first is that it is too single-minded in its emphasis on the conflict of interests between labour and capital as the source of managerial control needs, and of these needs as determining productive technique. 'Capitalism is concerned with the making of profit, and to this end it has increasingly transformed the forces of production. One way of improving profitability is to create a production process which prevents the conflicts of interest in industry from hindering accumulation. But this is by no means the only impetus towards new techniques'.[69] Second, Braverman exaggerates the extent to which managers actually succeed in imposing control through the design of new work methods, at least in the short and medium term. Third, Braverman is too concerned with the consciously intended consequences of management activity. The origins and the outcome of the use of new technology are more complex than he imagines.

Hill goes on to suggest that there are 'alternative explanations of why managers have transformed the work process which are more appropriate in most instances than Braverman's'.[70] Senior managers obviously aim to use the resources at their disposal in the most efficient manner, so as to increase profit and the rate of capital accumulation. However, increasing their control over the workforce is only one means of doing that. New production techniques may be put forward not because they increase control but because they allow production to be carried out more efficiently than if human capability had to be relied on.

Hill also argues that Braverman exaggerated the inevitability of the transformation of the work process and 'underestimates the potential resistance of workers to work degradation'.[71] He points to evidence, particularly from Western Europe, of worker resistance to new production methods in the 1960s and 1970s. The resistance of workers in the car industry, for example, was manifest through recruitment difficulties, high rates of labour turnover and absenteeism. In the Swedish car industry such resistance forced management to move back from the strict application of assembly-line techniques.

Similarly, Hill argues that Braverman made an error in interpreting the tendency of production technology to give management responsibility for the organisation of the work process to mean that technology allows for management control of the whole of work in its broadest sense. 'In Britain, for example, where organised labour has rarely disputed the *principle* of management's right to extend its direction of work processes and rationalise production, there have been challenges to managerial control over other aspects of work'.[72]

One of the most wide-ranging reviews of the Braverman thesis has been undertaken by Littler.[73] He recognised that Braverman had made a major contribution by updating Marx and attempting to link the phase of monopoly capitalism and the transformation of the labour process. Nevertheless, Braverman, according to Littler, has created a number of impediments to further analysis. First, while

Braverman appears to offer an historical argument starting with the development of management in the late nineteenth century, in fact the work is largely devoid of historical or empirical content. This has a number of consequences, of which the most important is that the work is permeated by an idealized conception of the traditional craft worker.

Second Braverman assumes that the separation of the conception and execution of work tasks is inimical to the essential character of human work, with the result that labour will continuously try to subvert such arrangements. Workers therefore come to their job opposed to capitalist authority. This means that Braverman 'ignores the fact that areas of influence and control may be the school, the family and other non-work social institutions' so that workers come to the factory prepared to work within the established arrangements. It also means that by assuming a universal recalcitrance on the part of labour he is able to avoid consideration of specific trade union or shop-floor existence and minimise the role of class struggle in shaping the labour process. Third, Braverman presents a view which has within it a strong strain of Marxist functionalism.

Reorganisations of the labour process are presented 'as the outcome of a conscious design rather than of the product of the struggle of contending groups'. This perspective leads to an almost conspiratorial concept of capitalism in which every event is planned by the capitalist class and is in the interests of each and every unit of capital.[74]

Finally, Braverman equates the logic of Taylorism with the logic of capitalism. He seems to assume that what Taylor argued in theory actually happened on the shop floor.

These impediments lead Littler to suggest the need for a less rhetorical and better grounded theory of labour process. The elements of this theory involve a concern for employer strategies, a recognition of the diversity within capitalism and the need for any system of control to take account of the consciousness of workers.

Within capitalism there is a perpetual tension between treating workers as a commodity to be hired and fired and harnessing their ingenuity and cooperativeness. Thus there is a twofold nature to the capital/labour relationship. If the contradictory nature of the capital/labour relationship is accepted, then this changes the nature of the control relation. Control should be seen in relation to conflict and sources of conflict and in relation to the potential terrain of compromise, bargaining and consensus'.[75]

Littler's comparative study of USA, Britain and Japan serves to emphasise and illustrate this approach. It shows, for example, variations in the impact of Taylorism and in the strategies developed by employers.

Littler's criticisms follow those of a number of other writers who took part in the debate over Braverman in the 1970s. For example, both Friedman[76] and Edwards[77] drew attention to the way in which worker resistance can mean that managements have to develop fresh strategies to maintain control. Friedman talked about the way in which managements can develop 'responsible autonomy strategies' which have meant that the direct control approach of Taylorism has not been necessary. Edwards has pointed to different types of management strategies, such as the use of industrial relations procedures, attempts to channel and contain conflict, and the use of labour market strategies which divide and segment the working class.

Wood has edited a volume designed to evaluate the deskilling thesis.[78] In his introduction Wood argues that the Braverman thesis was accepted excessively enthusiastically in Britain. He also argues that the Friedman and Edwards criticisms do not go far enough: 'the kinds of omission which critiques of Braverman have highlighted in his analysis involve fundamental questions: to incorporate worker resistance, labour and product markets and extra-economic factors involves more than simply extending one's analysis; it amounts to a theoretical reconsideration'. The deskilling which has occurred 'must be located in a context which is far broader than Taylorism and certainly more complex than a straightforward managerial conspiracy'.[79]

Wood's argument, then, is that the flaws in the Braverman thesis are more fundamental than has frequently been recognised. He also suggests that the Braverman thesis was not so novel as the author suggests and that in fact other Marxists have paid attention to the issues Braverman discusses. Wood's overall judgement is perhaps a little harsh. Braverman raised an area of debate and pertinent questions. A conclusion which suggested that he drew attention to some important processes rather than *the* important process might be a better summary of the debate which has surrounded his work.

Conclusions

The human relations school provided an essential corrective to the assumptions made by scientific management. The recognition that some workers look for social as well as economic rewards from their work and the recognition of the importance of informal work groups was a major step forward. In the same way, the recognition by the neo-human relations and self-actualisation schools that some workers could look for an interest in the job itself was also important. Few would deny the relevance of such comments: the criticisms have arisen from the failure to see that not all workers look for such rewards, not all workers look for the same rewards, and if one is to understand industrial conflict then one needs to look at other factors, and beyond the workplace.

There are clear links between the human relations and neo-human relations schools on the one hand and those who have sought to explain the level of industrial conflict by reference to the kind of technology employed on the other. The most obvious links are through the emphasis on the dehumanising aspects of assembly-line technology and on the importance of social relationships at work. The relevance of such matters to an understanding of industrial conflict is beyond dispute. However, the amount of emphasis that should be put on them is contentious. It is arguable that technology should be taken as an influence on relationships at work in general and industrial conflict in particular rather than a determinant of either.

The Marxist approach to industrial conflict supplies an ingredient missing in other analyses; a consideration of the broader social/political context in which relationships at work have to be seen. The recent interest in the work of Braverman provides a useful link between a concern with technology and a concern with broader power relationships in society.

The discussion of industrial conflict reviewed in this chapter has relevance to an understanding of strikes. It is not a substitute but a supplement for the consideration of the kind of factors looked at in the last chapter. It is part of the patchwork that needs to be built up to gain a greater understanding of the causes of strikes. This is far from suggesting, though, that even with the addition of this material, one can produce one explanation or a grand theory of strikes.

NOTES

1. E. Mayo, *The Human Problems of an Industrial Civilization,* Harvard University Press, Cambridge, Mass., 1946.
2. E.V. Schneider, *Industrial Sociology,* McGraw-Hill, London, 1971, p. 92.
3. *Ibid.,* p. 93.
4. F.J. Roethlisberger and W.J. Dickson, *Management and the Worker,* Harvard University Press, Cambridge, Mass., 1939, p. 569.
5. *Ibid.,* p. 580.
6. *Ibid.,* p. 581.
7. *Ibid.,* p. 583.
8. *Ibid.,* p. 585.
9. J.F. Scott and G.C. Homans, 'Reflections on the Wildcat Strikes', *American Sociological Review,* Vol. 12 (1947) p. 281.
10. M. Dalton, 'The Role of Supervision', in A. Kornhauser, R. Dubin and A.M. Ross (eds.) *Industrial Conflict,* McGraw-Hill, New York, 1954, p. 185.
11. W.F. Whyte, *Pattern for Industrial Peace,* Harper and Row, New York, 1951.
12. A. Carey, 'The Hawthorne Studies: A Radical Criticism', in J.M. Shepherd (ed.) *Organizational Issues in Industrial Society,* Prentice Hall, Englewood Cliffs, N.J., 1972, pp. 297–315.
13. *Ibid.,* p. 315.
14. C. Kerr and A. Siegel, 'The Inter-Industry Propensity to Strike', in A. Kornhauser, R. Dubin and A. Ross (eds.) *op. cit.*
15. D. McGregor, *Leadership and Motivation,* MIT Press, Cambridge, Mass., 1966.
16. F. Hertzberg, *Work and the Nature of Man,* Stapes Press, London, 1968.
17. *Ibid.,* p. 79.
18. A.H. Maslow, *Motivation and Personality,* Harper and Row, New York, 1954.
19. *Ibid.,* p. 54.
20. *Ibid.,* p. 15.
21. R. Likert, *New Patterns of Management,* McGraw-Hill, New York, 1961.
22. W.G. Bennis, *Changing Organisations: Essays on the Development and Evolution of Human Organisations,* McGraw-Hill, New York, 1966.
23. K. Graham, 'Union Attitudes to Job Satisfaction', in M. Weir (ed.), *Job Satisfaction,* Fontana, Glasgow, 1976, pp. 267–8.
24. J.H. Goldthorpe, D. Lockwood, F. Beckhofer and J. Platt, *The Affluent Workers,* Cambridge University Press, London, 1968.
25. H.L. Sheppard and N.Q. Herrick, *Where Have All the Robots Gone?,* Free Press, New York, 1972.
26. R.M. Blackburn and M. Mann, *The Working Class in the Labour Market,* Macmillan, London, 1979.
27. C.R. Walker and R.H. Guest, *The Man on the Assembly Line,* Yale University Press, New Haven, 1957.

28. E. Chinoy, *Automobile Workers and the American Dream,* Doubleday, New York, 1955.
29. W.A. Faunce (ed.), *Reading in Industrial Sociology,* Meredith, New York, 1967, pp. 258–9.
30. L.R. Sayles, *Behaviour of Work Groups,* Wiley, New York, 1958.
31. *Ibid.,* p. 127.
32. J.W. Kuhn, *Bargaining in Grievance Settlement: The Power of Industrial Work Groups,* Columbia University Press, 1961.
33. J.H. Goldthorpe, 'Attitudes and Behaviour of Car Assembly Workers: A Deviant Case and a Theoretical Critique', *British Journal of Sociology,* Vol. 17, No. 3 (September 1966).
34. J.E.T. Eldridge, *Industrial Disputes,* Routledge and Kegan Paul, London, 1968, p. 50.
35. *Op. cit.,* pp. 4–5.
36. J. Woodward, *Industrial Organisation: Theory and Practice,* Oxford University Press, London, 1965.
37. J. Woodward (ed.), *Industrial Organisation: Behaviour and Control,* Oxford University Press, London, 1970, p. ix.
38. *Ibid.,* p. 5.
39. *Ibid.,* p. 4.
40. E.L. Trist, G.W. Higgin, H. Murray and A.B. Pollock, *Organisational Choice,* Tavistock, London, 1963.
41. *Ibid.,* p. 289–90.
42. *Ibid.,* p. 290.
43. *Ibid.,* p. 291.
44. *Ibid.*
45. *Ibid.*
46. V.L. Allen, *The Sociology of Industrial Relations,* Longman, London, 1971, p. 39.
47. *Ibid.*
48. F. Engels, 'Labour Movements', in T. Clarke and L. Clements (eds.) *Trade Unionism Under Capitalism,* Fontana, Glasgow, 1977, p. 40.
49. *Collected Works of Marx and Engels,* Institut für Marxismus-Leninismus, East Berlin, Vol. 18, p. 474.
50. V.I. Lenin, 'Capital and Labour', in T. Clarke and L. Clements (eds.), *op. cit.,* pp. 64–76.
51. L. Trotsky, 'Marxism and Trade Unionsim', in T. Clarke and L. Clements (eds.), *op. cit.*
52. *Ibid.,* p. 81.
53. Quoted by J.E.T. Eldridge, *The Sociology of Industrial Life,* Nelson, London, 1973, pp. 140–1.
54. R. Blauner, *Alienation and Freedom,* University of Chicago Press, Chicago, 1964.
55. C. Wright Mills, *White Collar,* Oxford University Press, London, 1959.
56. *Op. cit.*
57. *Ibid.,* p. 193.
58. Quoted *Ibid.,* p. 195.

59. H. Braverman, *Labor and Monopoly Capitalism,* Monthly Review Press, New York, 1974.
60. *Ibid.,* p. 8.
61. *Ibid.,* p. 8–9.
62. *Ibid.,* p. 9
63. *Ibid.,* p. 90.
64. *Ibid.,* p. 170.
65. *Ibid.,* p. 170–1.
66. *Ibid.,* p. 371.
67. *Ibid.,* p. 355.
68. S. Hill, *Competition and Control at Work,* Heinemann, London, 1981.
69. *Ibid.,* p. 112.
70. *Ibid.*
71. *Ibid.,* p. 113.
72. *Ibid.,* p. 115.
73. C.R. Littler, *The Development of the Labour Process in Capitalist Societies,* Heinemann, London, 1982.
74. *Ibid.,* p. 27–8.
75. *Ibid.,* p. 34–5.
76. A. Friedman, 'Responsible Autonomy Versus Direct Control over the Labour Process', *Capital and Class,* No. 1 (Spring 1977) pp. 43–57.
77. R. Edwards, *Contested Terrain,* Heinemann, London, 1979.
78 S. Wood (ed.), *The Degradation of Work?,* Hutchinson, London, 1982.
79. *Ibid.,* p. 21–1.

6 The Impact of Strikes

Strikes can have an impact on a wide variety of individuals and organisations; the impact may be direct or indirect; it may be a major cause of concern or hardly noticed. Chermesh has produced a model of what he terms 'strike damage' which uses eight different reference categories: union, management, owners, involved workers, suppliers, clients, uninvolved workers and the public.[1] The model, which he sees as the inverse of the Blau and Scott[2] analysis of formal organisations based on 'cui bono', allows him to discuss who is the victim of a strike and to what degree.

Chermesh's model is useful in this context in that it serves to emphasis the breadth of coverage necessary if one is to examine the impact of strikes. There is not the space in this chapter to examine each of Chermesh's categories independently though all of them will be touched on at some stage. The broad division that will be adopted is to look first at the directly involved participants, second at what might be termed the directly related non-participants and finally at society in general.

IMPACT OF PARTICIPANTS

Strikes, in the nature of things, will almost always have some effect on both employees and employers in the firm concerned. When they go on strike workers have to make a financial sacrifice in the sense that they are forgoing their wages. In Australia though not in the UK or USA, statistics are regularly published with an estimate of 'wages lost' as a result of strikes. In the 1970s the estimate of wages lost ranged from A$30.9 million (in 1970) to 148 million (1979). However, calculations like this are only a first move in determining the financial cost of strikes to workers. A more complete assessment will also need to take into account, for example, the extent to which lost wages can be made up after the strike, either through overtime working or higher rates of pay gained as a result of the strike, and of the extent to which the financial sacrifice of the strike can be cushioned by assistance from family or friends, by strike pay or by state social security benefits.

Attempts to assess these matters face major problems not simply because of the variety of different possible circumstances that might be brought into play but also because of the complex methodological issues raised. It should not be surprising then that the available studies fail to point to a clear and unanimous conclusion.

One of the most comprehensive studies has been undertaken by Gennard and has been reported to in a number of different publications. In one of them Gennard sought to identify the sources of assistance for strikers and the costs of strike action for them.[3] His assessment of the net return from strike action in four different instances is given in Table 6.1. In all cases except one, the stoppage cost the strikers more than they received from that action and the assessed 'pay back period', the time taken to recoup losses, was up to five years (in the case where there was a five-year-pay-back period a proportion of the strikers were due to retire within that period).

In another publication Gennard looked at the sources of support for the same workers during the four strikes.[4] His results are summarised in Table 6.2. From this table it can be seen that the strikers' own resources were almost always the most important source of income during a strike. The comparison with state subsidies (in this case supplementary benefit) is particularly interesting for in no case did the state subsidy exceed one fifth of the income during strikes, nor did it outweigh the strikers' own resources. Payments by unions differed widely as a source of income. In one case these accounted for about a fifth of income received but in all other cases such payments were negligible or non-existent.

Table 6.1: Net Return on Strikes

| | Post Office Dispute | | Chrysler Dispute | Dunlop Dispute | | Chamberlain Dispute |
	All Male Groups	All Female Groups		All Male Strikers	All Female Strikers	
	£	£	£	£	£	£
Gross cost	193.63	135.13	748.36	183.04	151.10	220.71
Total offsets	89.95	36.49	340.93	46.53	32.54	73.48
Net cost	107.68	98.64	407.43	136.51	118.56	147.23
Gross return	24.51	44.81	115.25	84.95	136.05	35.81
Net return	−83.11	−53.83	−292.18	−51.56	+17.49	−111.42
Net return as % of Gross cost	−77.2	−54.6	−71.7	−37.8	+14.8	−75.8

Notes

Gross cost — Earnings foregone for the period of the stoppage.

Net cost — Gross Cost —OFFSETS (such as strike pay, tax rebates, supplementary benefit, jobs taken by additional members of the family because of the strikes).

Gross return — the sum of higher earnings, extra overtime earnings and extra back pay as a result of striking − / + adverse/positive employment effects, for the 'First Period'

Net return — Gross Return − Net Cost

Source: J. Gennard, 'The Financial Costs and Returns of Strikes, British Journal of Industrial Relations, Vol. 20, No. 2 (July 1982) p. 252.

A North America study by Curtis Eaton seems at first sight to call one aspect of Gennard's work into question.[5] The aspect looked at in the North American study was the cost of strikes to workers taking part in them. In this study Curtis Eaton looked at a sample of 26 strikes drawn from stoppages in the Vancouver area which were settled between 1 June 1967 and 1 June 1970, and which involved at least 100 employees (in fact the data collected only allowed discussion of 20 out of the 26 strikes). The conclusion reached, that 'for this group of strikes, net benefits, are greater than zero; that is, in most cases the strike appears to be profitable to the employee' clearly contradicts that of Gennard. This conclusion was reached even though 'the strike-induced benefits were discounted at a relatively high rate (20 per cent); it was assumed that strike-induced benefits were rapidly dissipated; the uncertainty of continued employment was taken into account, and supplemented earnings during the strike period were ignored'.[6]

There are a number of possible explanations for the different conclusions of Gennard and Curtis Eaton. It might be that they are a reflection of the different contexts in which the studies took place; it might be that they are a reflection of the fact that both are based on small samples. It might also be that the differences are in some sense a reflection of the methodological difficulties in this area. In his conclusion Curtis Eaton reflects on some of these methodological difficulties. He opens up the possibility that the supposed 'net gain' of the striker may be nothing more than an illusion.

Finally, the empirical results might reflect a scenario in which the employer, in anticipation of a strike, makes a final offer which is substantially less than the wage rate at which he anticipates settlement. He does this in order to maintain flexibility to offer wage concessions and hopefully shorten the duration of a strike that he thinks is inevitable. The employer's last offer is, in a sense, not an offer at all but a bargaining ploy. This interpretation would indicate that the profitability of the strike is merely an illusion.[7]

Despite the methodological problems involved in assessing the costs and benefits of strike action, the workers' perception of them may be critical in determining the decision whether or not to go on strike. One topic which has received particular attention in the literature has been the extent to which state

Table 6.2: Source of Income Received by Households Affected by a Strike

| Source of Income | Post Office | | Chrysler | Dunlop Dispute | | Chamberlain |
| | All Male Groups | All Female Groups | | All Male Strikers | All Female Strikers | |
	%	%	%	%	%	%
State subsidies	16.2	0.0	15.1	0.0	0.0	14.0
Union payments	1.4	2.8	21.9	0.1	0.3	0.0
Payments from employers	14.7	54.7	9.8	0.0	0.0	25.3
Debts to financial institutions	10.2	0.0	8.2	9.6	7.2	17.3
Own Resources	58.0	42.5	45.0	90.3	92.5	43.5

Source: J. Gennard, 'The Effects of Strike Activity on Households', British Journal of Industrial Relations, Vol. 19, No. 3 (November 1981) p. 330.

support to strikers during stoppages may reduce the costs of such action and thereby encourage workers to take part in it. There have been a number of British studies of this matter. One by Durcan and McCarthy looked at the macro level at the relationship between strike trends, income tax rebates, family allowances and supplementary benefits for the period 1956–70.[8] Their conclusion was that 'as a general explanation for variations in the strike pattern, benefit payment variations appear to be as unsatisfactory as tax remissions'.[9] In particular they said that such matters failed to provide any explanation for the significant rise in the number of strikes between 1967 and 1970 or for the increase in working days lost over the same period. They also argued there is little evidence 'that even the total abolition of these forms of state benefit to strikers would make much impact on the overall strike pattern'.[10]

The methodological problems associated with such work were highlighted by Hunter in a debate over the Durcan and McCarthy findings.[11] Hunter's criticism led him to question Durcan and McCarthy's conclusions but he did not take the issue so far as to claim that there was a relationship between strikes and state benefits: rather he was content to suggest that the Durcan and McCarthy study had not satisfactorily shown that there was no relationship.

In the present case there is some risk that certain conclusions drawn by Durcan and McCarthy may be misleading. This is particularly so in the case of their findings that the strike pattern would not be much affected by the total withdrawal of state payments . . . To be quite clear, this is not to say that there is any reason to believe that there *is* a positive and systematic relation between strikes and state payments nor is it a reason to give any support to the implied policy change that would reduce or eliminate such payments . . . So far, however, we do not have enough information to have complete confidence in the negative conclusion to which Durcan and McCarthy tend.[12]

Another British study took a different approach to the issue, centring not on macro data but on case studies. This narrower focus allowed attention to be paid to what actually happens when a worker is on strike. The interviews conducted suggested that unions, and individual strikers, had limited knowledge of what state benefits would be available during a strike. The authors said that 'some of the strikers to whom they spoke had no idea how much benefit they would receive when they made a claim' during a strike. This finding, they went on to suggest, means 'that it is highly improbable that workers are able to calculate meaningfully the amount of earnings foregone through strike action offset by supplementary benefit'.[13]

The impact of a strike on the workers who take part in it is not simply restricted to the economic arena. Participation in a strike can have broader social-political consequences for the employees involved. This is particularly true in the case of a lengthy strike when the strains are greatest and when collective support may be most important. Strikes can lead individuals to become involved in labour relations activities beyond anything they have previously experienced. This very involvement may be critical in developing and changing attitudes. The effect may be particularly noticeable in areas of industry that have no history of militancy and where trade unionism has been weakest. In such instances individuals may be entering a totally new arena and their experience may colour their attitude to future relations in their own industry and to workers in other industries. For example, white-collar workers who have previously been sceptical of the need for industrial action and the relevance of a 'two-sides view' of industry both within their own workplace and in society more generally, might change their attitudes if during a strike they experience behaviour from management that seems to them to be intransigent and combative. One study which looked at workers who had no previous experience of strike action referred to the strike as a critical incident 'giving a powerful twist to men's experience and hence future attitudes and behaviour'.[14] Fantasia has taken this further by arguing that the experience of a successful strike may encourage workers to take similar action again. Thus, he said: 'a successful wildcat strike can represent an impetus to further collective action to the extent that the workers perceive their victory to be the result of their own unity and perseverance'.[15] It is, of course, difficult to measure this kind of impact in a statistical fashion, yet it is potentially as important as the economic impact and may have longer-term implications.

The most obvious impact of a strike on an employer is in economic terms. A strike may lead to the loss of production and as a result a loss in profit. Certainly when workers undertake strike action they calculate that employers as well as themselves will suffer economically. If they believe that employers will suffer more, then they will see this as a strong bargaining counter. However, the calculation of the likely economic cost of strike action for an employer is just as difficult as the calculation of the economic costs of strike action for an employee. The starting point will be to refer to production lost as the result of a strike, and the number of working days lost may be taken as a guide. In particular cases, though, such calculations may either grossly underestimate or grossly overestimate the costs of a strike to an employer.

In highly interdependent industries the impact of a strike may extend well beyond the group initially involved, and the costs to an employer may be far greater than indicated by the number of working days lost. In industries like motor vehicles, for instance, a strike by a small group of workers may bring a whole workplace to a halt. The power of 'key' workers in such circumstances is well recognised and employers may be particularly careful to avoid open conflict with them. Nevertheless such workers clearly take strike action on occasions, and when they do an assessment of the economic costs based on days lost will almost certainly be an underestimate. An estimate of economic cost which is based on production lost during a strike may be an underestimate in another important way. A prolonged strike may mean that an enterprise loses markets. As one study noted, the failure to 'meet sales commitments and production target dates incurs goodwill costs for suppliers'.[16] Customers may find new suppliers whom they perceive either to be more reliable or to produce a better/more cost-effective product. Unless new markets can be captured, the economic effect of a strike on the firm where it occurred may be far greater than simply the immediate loss of production.

In other instances, though, the use of days lost as a guide to lost production and economic cost will almost certainly be an overestimate. This will be the case, for example, where a strike takes place when an employer has a stock of goods that cannot be sold. In some instances it may be that an employer will not be hurt financially at all by strike action; in an extreme case an employer may be better off financially. One study of the motor vehicle industry has suggested that firms sometimes welcome a strike as a way of dealing with problems of over-production.

One can readily imagine that a management which has reached the limits of its ability to stock finished cars or persuade its dealers to take more, and is afraid that sufficient short time will be difficult to organise but that layoffs will result—if not in official strikes or public criticism—in a labour shortage when trade recovers, may accept an unofficial dispute as a heaven sent occasion to suspend production temporarily[17]

Accusations have been made that in other circumstances employers have provoked strike action so as to provide a justification for dismissal and as a way of avoiding liabilities for severance or redundancy pay.

Other less dramatic instances may enable an employer to cushion if not eliminate the economic costs of strike action. Neumann and Reder point out that lost production may not be lost for ever.[18] For example, in some cases it may be possible to make up lost production at the end of a strike: this can reduce the costs of the strike to both the employer and the employee. In other instances, an employer may be able to reduce costs. As well as saving wage costs an employer may also be able to save costs in purchasing raw materials and, depending on the kind of operation undertaken, may be able to save some overhead costs. The least damaging strike economically, as far as the employer is concerned, will be where labour costs are a high proportion of total costs. In the public sector the employer may very clearly 'gain' economically as the result of a strike. A strike by school teachers will have very little economic impact on a public-sector employer other than that the wage bill will be reduced, because in this case the employer is not directly selling anything and therefore does not stand to lose income. This is not to argue that such strikes have no costs, even economic costs: they may have economic costs for parents who have to take time off work to look after children, but the direct economic effect will not fall on the employer.

One way of measuring the economic costs of a strike to an employer is to look at the reaction of the stock market. If the values of a shareholder's investment in a company declines as the result of the stock market's re-evaluation of the economic fortunes of that company then this may be both a cost to the shareholders directly and an indication of the stock market's assessment of the economic costs to the enterprise. The methodology involved raises problems: the assumption cannot always be made that the stock market can accurately assess the costs of a strike, for the market does not have perfect information and reacts to sentiment as well as logic. Further, how does one use the information about changes in share values: should the value of one firm's shares be compared with general movements in the market and the assumption be made that the difference is the result of the strike (when it clearly could be the result of other factors), and should the bench marks against which changes in the value of the firm's shares are tested be the value immediately before the strike or at the beginning of the period from which a strike was first seriously discussed (from when the market might have started to react and allow for some of the costs of the strike)? Clearly answers to these questions have to be based on judgement and will always be open to challenge. Nevertheless, while recognising the difficulties involved, an exercise undertaken by Becker and Olsen using stock market values is still interesting.[19] They looked at strikes in the USA between 1962 and 1982 that each involved 1,000 workers or more. Eventually a sample of 699 strikes was obtained and an analysis was made of the effect of strikes on share-holder equity as measured by the change in stock prices. Becker and Olsen concluded that the average strike resulted in a 4.1 per cent drop in share-holder equity, or about $72-87 million at 1980 values. They also argued that smaller firms tended to have higher than average strike costs.

It is important, though, in this context to remember that strikes are only one possible manifestation of industrial conflict. A strike in some circumstances may be an alternative to other kinds of action. The other kind of action will also have costs. If a group of workers slow down production or if absenteeism rises then this may have just as great an impact on production, and on the profitability of a firm, as a strike. Of course, strikes are a very visible expression of discontent and the stock market may take more notice of strikes than of some other factors. Nevertheless, failure to recognise that strikes are not the only way in which discontent can be manifest can lead to erroneous calculations about the real economic impact of strikes on firms.

Strikes may have an effect on employers in another way which initially may not have economic consequences though arguably eventually it might do so. In industries, or in firms, which have experienced a relatively large number of strikes management may begin to doubt its ability to plan its business and to control production. The unpredictability of strikes, particularly unofficial or wildcat strikes, is a special problem. Thus, it has been argued that 'in the small number of establishments where there is what might be termed an "endemic" strike situation . . . managers and supervisors are in a constant state of anxiety lest they do something which might inadvertently lead to a strike'. The economic implications of this, it is argued, 'are obvious and serious': they can have a 'crippling effect on managerial attitudes in relation to the pace of innovation and technological advance in industry'.[20] The view that is being put forward here about the effect on managerial confidence can also mean that management reacts, or from this point of view, over-reacts, to the subsequent threat of strike action.

If an employer forestalls a strike by making concessions in the face of threats which it might have been better to resist, or by refraining from introducing changes which he believes to be necessary in the interests of efficiency, then the economic consequences of his doing so may be more serious than those to which a strike would have given rise.

The difficulty which has recurred throughout this chapter is recognised in this case when it is added: 'Naturally, however, it is impossible to measure such consequences statistically'.[21]

In another study, this time by Sayles, similar problems were identified as the result of wildcat strikes. He referred to the problems ('perhaps more serious than the financial loss') of plant discipline. 'A clear-cut victory for a group of wildcat strikers may well be demoralizing for the rest of the employees in the plant'.[22] Similarly, Maki has discussed the possible effects of strikes on productivity, using empirical evidence from Canada. He suggested a number of possible effects on the struck firm. 'Recurrent strikes or threats of strikes can have a productivity effect . . . due to practices such as having large numbers of "supervisory" workers on the payroll to take over services in case of strike, or carrying larger finished goods inventories than would otherwise be optimal'.[23]

IMPACT ON DIRECTLY-RELATED NON-PARTICIPANTS

In most circumstances the impact of a strike is likely to be the greatest on those directly involved in it. However, normally others who have a close relationship with either the employee or the employer will also be affected, and in some cases they may be more severely affected than the participants themselves.

Frequently workers in the same firm or industry as those directly participating in the strike will be involved. In some industries and in some communities there is a history of solidarity which means that workers need little encouragement to take sympathetic action. There will be a presumption that the workers on strike deserve support and it will be offered. This is seen in many countries in the coal-mining and port-transport industries. The reasons for such solidarity have been extensively discussed and go beyond the mere industrial setting. Whether such solidarity should be applauded or derided depends on the perspective in which industrial relations is viewed. In these circumstances, though, the solidarity of other workers can ease the burden of a strike and be an important weapon in bringing it to a successful conclusion.

On other occasions workers will not react spontaneously to calls for support. Some may eventually join a strike but they may need persuading that it is justified and that their support will lead to a successful conclusion. In many other instances workers will not join a strike but will be affected nevertheless. This is particularly likely to be the case in highly interdependent industries where a stoppage in one section is likely to spread quickly to others. Large numbers of workers may be asked to work short-time or be laid off for the period of the strike. If this happens then the economic consequences of a strike for labour will increase; it may be that the other side of the coin is that the economic costs to the employer will decrease. The burden which a strike in one section of a firm or industry places on other workers may well be one of the weapons used by employers. The threat to 'lay off' other workers may lead to increased pressure on strikers to settle the dispute.

The impact of strikes on other firms may also be important. In many instances the impact will be a negative one. A strike, for example, is likely to adversely affect customers and suppliers. As Chamberlain and Schilling noted, there may be a series of chain reactions:

[producers] who rely on the struck product, and other producers who depend on goods made with the struck product, as well as suppliers of the struck unit, and other firms who supply not only the suppliers of the struck unit but also the directly and indirectly affected producers are all caught in the backwash of a stoppage.[24]

The extent of the impact on other firms in contact with the organisation will of course vary enormously from strike to strike. One factor will be the duration of the stoppage. In his discussion of the economic consequences of strikes, Turner drew attention to the threshold effect.[25] Short strikes, he argued, have little effect on, say, suppliers or customers because arrangements can be made to stockpile or rely on reserves of the goods concerned. Once strikes pass a particular threshold, though, in terms of length, their effect increases markedly. Suppliers can only stockpile for so long, customers eventually exhaust reserves, and a strike in one establishment can thus begin to have consequences over a wide area, in this way possibly exceeding the direct impact.

On the other hand the impact on other firms will not always be negative. In some instances other firms will benefit, say because they are able to capture the markets of the struck firm. Neumann and Reder examined the impact of strikes in manufacturing industries in the USA.[26] Their emphasis was on the effect on output of the industry as a whole rather than on the output at the struck firm. They argued that in most industries the impact of a strike on output was negligible: in 38 of the 63 industries analysed the estimate of the industry cost of strike activity was zero. Even in the industries where strikes were seen to have some impact on output, that impact was small. The major reason for this finding was the ability of other firms to make good the output lost at the struck firm.

IMPACT ON SOCIETY IN GENERAL

Some strikes, particularly though not exclusively large and lengthy ones, can have an effect well beyond the participants and the directly related non-participants. Two kinds of strike might be highlighted in this context. The first is a strike in a public-service area, like transport, which will arguably have a greater impact on the consumer than the employer. Such strikes are very visible, are likely to cause considerable inconvenience and are likely to be the subject of extensive discussion in the media. In some cases they may be more than simply inconvenient. Strikes in transport may mean that many people cannot reach their place of employment. However, the emphasis in this first example is on inconvenience and the effect of the strike on the public at large. The second kind of strike is one where the emphasis is much more on the general economic consequences. In this instance the strike may be in a key industry, say fuel and power, so that the dispute in that one industry may affect all others. Stoppages which centre on imports or industries whose work is connected with imports 'will occasion greater concern, particularly in periods of balance of payment difficulties'.[27] Again such stoppages may overlap with the first kind identified, in that they may cause some inconvenience as well as economic disruption: a strike in the electricity supply will affect private householders as well as industrial consumers while a strike affecting imports may result in the shortage of certain goods for the general public. There are stoppages, though, where the emphasis is on the general economic impact rather than the inconvenience caused.

Although one can identify general problems of these kinds that may result from strike action it is more difficult to quantify them. Inconvenience to the general public or the consumer is visible enough but the impact on the economy in general of a strike is very difficult to identify. For example, even if one can say that a strike in the fuel and power sector leads to firms closing down for a period, as occurred in Britain with the miners' strike in the early 1970s, one cannot simply translate the number of days' production lost into economic cost. It may be that workers and employers ensure that more work is produced during the shorter period allowed; it may be that production is made up at the end of the strike; and it may be that there was not a market for some of the goods and services that would have been produced anyway. The problems that face calculation of the economic cost to the participant employer of strike actions are mirrored in this case. It is similarly difficult to estimate the costs arising from an interruption to exports. Hudson attempted to quantify the effect of three British dock strikes (in 1967, 1970 and 1972).[28] Although he concluded that dock strikes cause a reduction in trade flows (particularly a reduction in exports) which is not made up by increased subsequent trade or by anticipatory trading in advance of a strike, he also recognised the difficulties involved in making such estimates: he referred to 'a substantial but unknown, margin of error'.[29]

Some attempts have been made to estimate the loss of production to the economy as a whole as a result of strikes. In some instances this attempt has been made on the basis of one particular strike: for example, it is estimated that a fifty-eight-day strike at General Motors cost the USA economy $7 billion in the fourth quarter of 1969.[30] Other attempts to estimate costs have covered more than just one particular strike. For instance, Hammeed and Lomas looked at production loss due to strikes in a range of industries, in Canada in 1967. They concluded that 'even if all economic effects of a strike, both within the industry itself and in related industries, are taken into account, the result would still be extremely small, probably not exceeding 1 per cent of GNP'.[31]

Any costs that might be calculated also need to be put into context. The loss of production through strikes is spectacular but relatively small (Whittingham and Towers[32] estimated that in 1970, one of the peak years for strike activity in the UK, the loss of output as a direct result of strikes only amounted to 0.2 per cent of GNP), and anyway other causes of lost production may be just as important. Reference is frequently made, for example, to the loss of production through sickness, other forms of absenteeism, occupational injury, and unemployment. Dabscheck and Niland argue that industrial accidents are a more significant cause of lost work and output than strikes, in Australia. They also claim that 'production losses through strikes pale in comparison with losses to production resulting from unemployment',[33] Similar comments can be, and have been, made about most other industrial nations.

Enderwick has also pointed to the positive role that strikes can play in the bargaining process, and argues that as a result strikes cannot merely be seen as a burden on society: 'The elimination of strike losses', say by outlawing strikes, 'might not represent a net gain for society. Such gain would have to be offset against the costs of an alternative procedure for reconciling bargaining interests'.[34]

In policy terms, though, whether or not strikes have a negative effect in this way of whether or not any such effect can be measured may not matter: the perception may be more important. If policy-makers and/or the general public perceive that strikes have a major negative impact then this alone may be sufficient to produce a push for a policy change. In many instances one can see that the perception of a 'strike problem' has brought about changes in national policy on industrial relations. Three examples might be given each from a different national context.

The first example is taken from the USA in the immediate post-Second World War years, Chamberlain and Schilling's classic study *The Impact of Strikes* highlighted the effect of strike action on the public in the immediate post-Second World War years, and linked this explicitly to attempts to regulate such action.[35] They saw the strike wave of 1945 and 1946 in the USA as being directly related to public support for strike-control legislation. In 1947 the Taft-Hartley Act was introduced giving the President authority to restrain strikes or lock-outs which would 'imperil the national health and safety'. Ten states also introduced legislation in the same year limiting the right to strike in certain industries and in most instances providing for seizure or compulsory arbitration. Chamberlain and Schilling argued that the 'connection between these federal and state acts and public disquiet over the turn of events in the preceding years seems clear and direct'.[36] In another study it was pointed out that public concern about industrial relations in the USA 'was heightened by the large number of strikes that occurred in the year immediately following the war's end, when a record, which still stands, was set for the amount of working time lost in one year as a result of labour-management disputes'. The same study went on to argue that the 'response of political leaders to this popular concern was to erect, in 1947, the Taft-Hartley Act', which sought to 'swing the pendulum of power in labour-management affairs back (but not too far back) in the direction of employers'. A number of the tactics used by unions (the closed shop, secondary boycotts, and picketing) to obtain the recognition of employers were prohibited, a list of unfair practices by unions was added to the law and supervisors were 'removed from the legal protection of union and bargaining'.[37] As Burtt argues, the Taft-Hartley Act 'provided a highly complex and detailed system for regulating union and collective bargaining in the United States'.[38]

The assumption about the impact of strikes on society in general that was implicit in the move towards the Taft-Hartley Act has not gone unchallenged. Warren's study of major stoppages in the USA between 1914 and 1949 led him to conclude that few had threatened public health or safety.[39] He argued that it was only in the field of public utilities and transportation that national emergencies could be found and even in those industries there were few 'real crises'. Chamberlain and Schilling challenge some of Warren's conclusions. However, in this context it is worthwhile reinforcing the point made earlier that the important issue for policy-making is not whether the strikes had a major impact but whether that was perceived to be the position. There is less distance between the contributors on that question.

The second example is taken from Australia at the end of the nineteenth century. The 'strikes of the 1890s', as they have been referred to, played an important role in the formation of the institutions of industrial relations in Australia. This period of industrial conflict in Australia was initiated by the maritime strike of 1890. The initial cause of that strike, which started in Melbourne in August 1890, was the decision of Mercantile Marine Officers' Association to ignore the warning of the ship-owners and affiliate to the Trades Hall Council in Melbourne. The ship-owners had taken the view that in order to preserve discipline the officers should not be associated with a body that was representative of the employees, who were under their authority at sea, and when the officers ignored their advice they refused to negotiate with them. Action also started in Sydney in

August 1890 but on a rather different basis: in this case it was the result of a decision of the wharf labourers' union not to handle work by non-union labour. Sutcliffe records that from 'the date of the commencement of the strike to the day it was declared off a little over two months elapsed', and during this time 'tension was extreme': every day 'brought forth some new phase of the fight and industry was paralyzed'.[40] The eventual collapse of the maritime strike 'led many employers to consider the time opportune for further attempts to secure acceptance by the unions of the principle of freedom of contract',[41] and in the next few years this was the main cause of the range of industrial disputes across a wide variety of industries.

The public perception of these disputes, it has been argued, was frequently to blame the union. Sutcliffe says that

it was difficult for many members of the public to realise all that lay behind the outward and visible signs of the maritime strike; in particular it was difficult to understand why the mere fact that a few marine officers were refused permission to join the Trades Hall Council should be made the cause of such an industrial upheaval.

Many took the view 'that this was but another instance of the tyranny of Trade Unionism. This view was not only advanced by the employers, but also largely by the press, and therefore it is not difficult to understand that it would also be endorsed by many of the public'.[42]

Isaac directly linked the strikes of the 1890s, and the public attitude towards them, to the development of the system of compulsory arbitration in Australia. The central aim of this system, Isaac contends, is the speedy settlement of industrial disputes. The desire for a speedy settlement rather than the encouragement of collective bargaining, he goes on to argue, 'derives from the troubled years of the 1890s, when public opinion, greatly disturbed by lengthy stoppages in strategic industries, demanded government intervention to end such stoppages, if necessary by the imposition of the terms of settlement'.[43]

Isaac accepts that the unions stood to gain something from this development; compulsory arbitration served, to some extent, to rehabilitate and stimulate unionism. Trade unions that had previously opposed such legislation now accepted it. As Gollan argues,[44] before the maritime strike 'both workers and employers (despite some instances of successful voluntary arbitration) were generally against arbitrators', but 'in the hard times after the strike unionists increasingly favoured arbitration as a means of forcing employers to acknowledge the rights of unions to be a party to the determination of conditions'.[45]

Nevertheless, government action cannot be understood simply by referring to trade union preferences. Isaac makes it clear that in his view public reaction to the strike of the 1890s was also important.

the early Australian preference for speed in the settlement of disputes by imposing government awards can be understood and justified in terms of the long drawn out emergency stoppages with widespread economic loss and personal inconvenience, and with the very existence of trade unions threatened by the refusal of employers to take part in collective bargaining.[46]

The emphasis on the importance of public concern about the impact of strikes on the development of compulsory arbitration in Australia is if anything stronger in Niland's account.[47] He argues explicitly that the current system 'arose primarily out of two coinciding events around the turn of the century'. The first of these was the 'traumatic experience with major industrial disputes during the 1890s which remain some of the most bitter and severe disputes in the whole Australian background'. At the same time a series of constitutional conventions were considering the constitutional basis for Australia's independence. 'Because concern for industrial disputes occupied such a prominent place in public anxiety of the time, it is natural that the framers of the constitution should have considered and eventually incorporated an industrial relations power for the Federal Parliament'.[48]

The final example is taken from the UK in the 1960s. This period saw extensive discussion of Britain's 'strike problem'. There was widespread use of the idea that Britain was particularly strike-prone. Strikes were sometimes referred to as 'the British disease'. The concern about strikes was one of the reasons for the setting up of the Donovan Commission in 1965. In its report, issued three years later,[49] the Commission was able to temper some of the debate: it showed that Britain was not so severely affected when compared to some other countries as had been popularly imagined. Judged by the number of working days lost, it said, the UK's recent record was 'about average' compared to other countries; judged on the basis of the number of strikes, the UK did less well 'though five other countries listed had more—Australia very many more'.[50] The report, however, did not dismiss the problem, particularly of unofficial strikes, but its proposals for a reform of the system of collective bargaining fell short of what some hoped for. In this context it is worthwhile noting the reservation published by a member of the Commission, Andrew Shonfield. He argued that while he could support many of the proposals of the majority report, they did not go far enough. Trade unions should be required to maintain certain minimum standards if they were to receive the protection enjoyed as registered trade unions and there should be an express duty on trade unions to conduct industrial relations 'in such a way as not to hold back improvements in the standard of living of the community as a whole',[51] Shonfield made these proposals because he believed the main report failed to address itself to the long-term problem of 'accommodating bodies with the kind of concentrated power which is possessed by trade unions'.[52] In this context he noted 'the growing dependence of people on the reliable performance of services required for tolerable living in crowded urban communities', and the ability of 'groups of producers to disrupt the lives of people who have no means of helping themselves'. He also pointed to the way in which increasingly 'a large complex of inter-related industrial operations located in different concerns may suddenly be placed at the mercy of the impulse of some small groups somewhere along the line'.[53]

Shonfield's view that the majority report, by arguing against legal remedies, in favour of public scrutiny and persuasion, did not go far enough, found widespread political support. As a result the Donovan Commission's report was never accepted by the government of the day as a satisfactory solution to the perceived problem. Instead the government brought out its own proposals in a White Paper called *In Place of Strife*.[54] These proposals differed significantly from those of the Donovan Commission: in particular, it was suggested that legal penalties might be used to force compliance with demands that the government might make. For example, the Secretary of State would be given the power to enforce recommendations made by a new body, the Commission on Industrial Relations. Following investigation of 'inter-union conflict' a 'conciliation pause' could be ordered (strike action had to be suspended and the status quo accepted) for twenty-eight days and a strike ballot could be required. Further, trade unions could be forced to register with a new Registrar of Trade Unions and Employers Association (the Registrar would have the power to require the revision of certain rules, notably those governing elections and discipline).

In the event the proposals made in the White Paper were never translated into action. Nevertheless the fact that they should have been made at all by a Labour government closely tied to the trade union movement is an indication of the extent of the belief that the position was so serious that radical and previously unthinkable action should be contemplated. The defeat of the Labour government's proposals 'to introduce the law' into industrial relations did not spell the end for such moves. The Conservative government which was elected in 1970 was pledged to introduce a similar package of measures. These formed the basis of the 1971 Industrial Relations Act. Whittingham and Towers have observed that one of the main aims of that Act was 'the curbing of the incidence of strikes'.[55]

England and Weekes, in a comment on the motives for state intervention over this period, highlighted a number of concerns including the slow growth of the economy and the high rate of inflation. The policy reaction they argued was a 'recognition that a political response was required to the increasingly popular view that unions were the major factor in the country's misfortunes'.[56] As a footnote it might be recorded that England and Weekes also argued that the moves towards greater state intervention in industrial relations in the late 1970s were influenced by the strikes of 1978–9 in the public sector: the 'winter of discontent' in 1979 gave further strength to the view that legal compulsion and authoritarian state regulation were necessary to restore order'.[57]

The three examples discussed above were deliberately taken from different national contexts. The details, of course, differed, yet a similar lesson can be drawn from all of them. Strikes are highly visible and a focus for media attention. In some cases it can be argued that the attention given is out of proportion to, or exaggerates, their importance. Nevertheless, the perception that can be created of the impact of strikes is critical. In each of the cases examined, major initiatives in public policy were introduced because of the perception that strike activity was creating major problems for the societies in which it occurred.

It would be a mistake, though, if it were to be imagined as a result of these comments that strikes, or say major strikes, necessarily gain such attention or necessarily lead to policy initiatives to curb such action. There are other examples that could be quoted which show that this is not necessarily the case. While some major strikes do not go entirely unnoticed, they do not lead to policy initiatives and other strikes which may lead to political action do not lead to initiatives which result in legislation designed to curb strikes. For instance, the miners' strike in Britain in 1974 did not lead to a policy initiative to curb strike action: on the contrary, it led to the defeat of the government, and the incoming administration introduced legislation which, amongst other things, enhanced the rights of trade unions and trade unionists.

The point that is being made, then, is not that strikes necessarily result in policy initiatives, and certainly not that they result in policy initiatives of a particular kind. The point is that strikes are highly visible and the perception of them *can* influence policy-makers and result in new initiatives. Such initiatives are one possible implication of strike activity and this possible implication needs to be noted, but one cannot go further than that.

CONCLUSIONS

A recurring theme throughout this chapter has been the difficulties involved in assessing the impact of strikes, at any level, whether one is referring to economic or broader social/political consequences; and whether one is referring to the direct participants, or others less directly involved, measurement is beset with problems. This issue, though, despite its difficulties cannot be ignored if only because the impact of strikes is of such general concern. Attitudes and policies towards industrial relations are critically affected by the perceptions of the impact of strikes. This can be taken one stage further. The argument being put forward here about the impact of strikes would suggest that strikes should not simply be seen against a particular social, economic or political background (for example, the way in which some authors have seen such backgrounds as the cause of strikes); strikes themselves can help to influence the nature and even in certain circumstances can help to change the social, economic or political environment. In other words, it is important to recognise that the relationship between strikes and the social/economic/political environment can be two way: each can influence the other.

NOTES

1. R. Chermesh, 'Strikes as Social Problems: A Social Matrix Approach', *British Journal of Industrial Relations,* Vol. 23, No. 2 (July 1985) pp. 281–308.
2. P.M. Blau and W.R. Scott, *Formal Organisations,* Routledge and Kegan Paul, London, 1963.
3. J. Gennard, 'The Financial Costs and Returns of Strikes', *British Journal of Industrial Relations',* Vol. 20, No. 2 (July 1982) pp. 247–56.
4. J. Gennard, 'The Effects of Strike Activity on Households', *British Journal of Industrial Relations,* Vol. 19, No. 3 (November 1981) pp. 327–44.
5. B. Curtis Eaton, 'The Worker and the Profitability of the Strike', *Industrial and Labour Relations Review,* Vol. 26, No. 1 (October 1971) pp. 670–9.
6. *Ibid.,* p. 679.
7. *Ibid.*
8. J.W. Durcan and W.E.J. McCarthy, 'The State Subsidy Theory of Strikes: an Examination of Statistical Data for the Period 1956–70', *British Journal of Industrial Relations,* Vol. 12, No. 1 (March 1974) pp. 26–47.
9. *Ibid.,* p. 41.
10. *Ibid.,* p. 45.
11. L.C. Hunter, 'The State Subsidy Theory of Strikes: a Reconsideration', *British Journal of Industrial Relations,* Vol. 12, No. 3 (November 1974) pp. 438–44.

12. *Ibid.,* pp. 443–4.
13. J. Gennard, *Financing Strikers,* Macmillan, London, 1977, p. 129.
14. S. Wood and M. Pedar, 'On Losing their Virginity: the Story of a Strike at the Grosvenor Hotel, Sheffield', *Industrial Relations Journal,* Vol. 9, No. 2 (Summer 1978) pp. 15–37.
15. R. Fantasia, 'The Wildcat Strike and Industrial Relations', *Industrial Relations Journal,* Vol. 14, No 2 (Summer 1983) p. 76.
16. P. Enderwick, 'Strike Costs and Public Policy', *Journal of Public Policy,* Vol. 2, Part 4 (October 1982) p. 351.
17. H.A. Turner, G. Clack and G. Roberts, *Labour Relations in the Motor Industry,* Allen and Unwin, London, 1963, p. 118.
18. G.R. Neumann and M.W. Reder, 'Output and Strike Activity in US Manufacturing: How Large are the Losses?'', *Industrial and Labour Relations Review,* Vol. 37, No. 2 (January 1984) pp. 197–211.
19. B.E. Becker and C.A. Olsen, 'The Impact of Strikes on Shareholder Equity', *Industrial and Labour Relations Review,* Vol. 39, No. 3 (April 1986) pp. 425–38.
20. Royal Commission on Trade Union and Employers' Associations, 1965–68, *Report,* Cmnd 3623, HMSO, London, 1968, p. 122.
21. *Ibid.,* p. 111.
22. L.R. Sayles, 'Wildcat Strikes', *Harvard Business Review,* No. 32 (November-December 1954) p. 48.
23. D.R. Maki, 'The Effects of Unions and Strikes on the Rate of Growth of Total Factor Productivity in Canada', *Applied Economics,* Vol. 15, No. 1 (1983) p. 32.
24. N.W. Chamberlain and J.M. Schilling, *The Impact of Strikes,* Greenwood Press, Westport, Connecticut, 1954, p. 251.
25. H.A. Turner, *Is Britain Really Strike Prone?.* Cambridge University Press, 1969.
26. *Loc. cit.*
27. P. Enderwick, *loc. cit.,* p. 351.
28. R. Hudson, 'The Effects of Dock Strikes on UK International Trade', *Applied Economics,* Vol. 13, No. 1 (March 1981) pp. 67–77.
29. *Ibid.,* p. 77.
30. Estimate in *Time,* 23 November 1970, quoted by S.M.A. Hammeed and T. Lomas, 'Measurement of Production Losses Due to Strikes in Canada: An Input-Output Analysis', *British Journal of Industrial Relations,* Vol. 15, No. 1 (March 1975) pp. 86–93.
31. *Ibid.,* p. 93.
32. T.G. Whittingham and B. Towers, 'Strikes and the Economy', *National Westminster Bank Quarterly Review,* November 1971, pp. 33–42.
33. B. Dabscheck and J. Niland, *Industrial Relations in Australia,* Allen and Unwin, London, 1981, p. 45.
34. P. Enderwick, *loc. cit.,* p. 360.
35. *Op. cit.*
36. *Ibid.,* p. 4.
37. N.W. Chamberlain, D.E. Cullen and D. Lewis, *The Labour Sector,* McGraw Hill, New York, 1980, p. 115.

38. E.J. Burtt, *Labour in the American Economy,* Macmillan, London, 1979, p. 279.
39. E.L. Warren, 'Thirty-Six Years of "National Emergency Strikes"', *Industrial and Labour Relations Review,* Vol. 5 (1951) pp. 12–15.
40. J.T. Sutcliffe, 'The Strikes of the 1890s', in J.E. Isaac and G.W. Ford (eds.) *Australian Labour Relations Readings,* Sun Books, Melbourne, 1966, p. 103.
41. *Ibid.,* p. 106.
42. *Ibid.,* p. 105.
43. J.E. Isaac, 'The Prospects for Collective Bargaining in Australia', in J.E. Isaac and G.W. Ford (eds.) *op. cit.,* p. 432.
44. R. Gollan, 'The Historical Perspective', in P.W.D. Matthews and G.W. Ford (eds.) *Australian Trade Unions,* Sun Books, Melbourne, 1968, pp. 14–41.
45. *Ibid.,* p. 27–8.
46. *Loc. cit.,* p. 443.
47. J. Niland, *Collective Bargaining and Compulsory Arbitration in Australia,* New South Wales University Press, Kensington, NSW, 1978.
48. *Ibid.,* p. 22.
49. Royal Commission on Trade Unions and Employers' Associations, *op. cit.*
50. *Ibid.,* p. 95.
51. *Ibid.,* p. 289.
52. *Ibid.,* p. 288.
53. *Ibid.,* p. 285.
54. Department of Employment and Productivity, *In Place of Strife,* Cmnd 3888, HMSO, London, 1969.
55. *Loc. cit.,* p. 33.
56. J. England and B. Weekes, 'Trade Unions and the State: A Review of the Crisis', *Industrial Relations Journal,* Vol. 12, No. 1 (January-February 1981) pp. 17–18.
57. *Ibid.,* p. 23.

7 Conclusion

There is a wealth of literature on strikes and industrial conflict only a proportion of which has been reviewed in this book. It is disturbing, then, that despite such wide interest and endeavour one has to conclude much more with questions than answers. In most of the areas that have been examined there remain conflicting interpretations and conflicting explanations of events.

In a way the pattern was set in the first substantive chapter (Chapter 2) when the problems involved in interpreting strike statistics were emphasised. After a rehearsal of the differences in the methods of collection, definition and presentation of strike statistics the reader could be forgiven for concluding that the problems were so severe that comparisons both over time and between nations were impossible. Such a conclusion, if understandable, would be over-pessimistic, for variations over time are less of a problem than variations between countries, and even in the case of variations between countries some useful trends can be isolated, providing the information is treated with care.

The discussion in Chapter 3 can also be seen in a similar light. The more one looks at strike trends, even in a restricted range of countries, as in this case, the more caveats one has to add to any interpretation. This issue is probably best exemplified by the difficulties involved in describing general, economy-wide trends, while recognising that changes in just one industry, like coal mining, can distort these trends enormously. There is not one simple agreed solution to this difficulty either. One possibility would be to ignore the influence of the one dominant industry throughout and, say, look at the strike trends in Australia, the USA, and the UK excluding the coal-mining industry. However, this would be open to the charge that a major area of interest was being ignored or treated as though it did not exist. The coal-mining industry is a major source of interest in its own right when discussing strikes: in practice, it is almost impossible to ignore or exclude it.

The review of explanations for variations in strike patterns and trends, in Chapter 4, showed the enormous amount of academic endeavour which has gone into this area. Studies from a variety of disciplines have tried to identify causes of patterns and variations. While some successes can be claimed, they are limited. No one explanation can be put forward which commands universal support even within its own discipline. While a move towards integrating the contributions of the different disciplines is to be welcomed it will not, by itself, solve the problem. The best one can hope for are better guides to what factors are important and what should be taken into account but this is a long way from an explanation based on a single theory or model.

The separation of material in Chapter 5 from that in Chapter 4 was, in one sense, artificial, for the discussions clearly have a point of contact. Although much of the material in Chapter 5 looked at industrial conflict broadly described rather than just at strikes, it gives a useful insight into the latter concern. Even in this instance, though, the broad claims failed to stand up and in the development of 'schools of thought' their claims became more modest. For instance, the idea that the kind of technology employed in an industry or factory will influence industrial conflict, morale, strikes and the like, is sensible and a discussion of how this will occur is valuable. On the other hand it has been recognised by most writers that the kind of technology employed is not the only factor to be taken into consideration. In other words, it does not determine the level of industrial conflict or strikes though it may influence them.

In the last substantive chapter the difficulties involved in measuring the impact of strikes were noted. While there are some simple guides to, say, the impact of a strike on production, which can be used and are used, such guides need treating with care. The position is even more difficult if one moves outside the economic arena. For example, measuring the effect of strikes in terms of the inconvenience to the public, or the impact on policy-makers, is far more difficult, especially if one is looking for anything more than a very general statement.

The problems and tensions that need to be recognised in a book on strikes, then, are amply exemplified. Of course, in many other areas of academic work similar problems arise and differences of view/interpretation can be noted. In this sense the study of strikes is not unique. The problems need stressing, nevertheless, because the subject matter is a source of frequent discussion in the media, and the discussion inevitably glosses over such problems. A corrective is needed.

It is just as important, though, to discuss the way in which advances can be made. In many of the areas discussed in this book there is much more work to be done along similar lines to that already undertaken. Ideas developed in particular contexts need further exploration and testing in other situations. For example, in the case of the impact of strikes there are many aspects of this issue which have received relatively little attention and could benefit from more. However, in other areas, while current lines of work should not be abandoned, they need complementing by others.

The best example can be taken from the work on the causes of strikes and explanations of strike patterns/trends. While such work has been useful and has given important pointers to issues that need to be taken into account in understanding strikes there is a limit to how far this can be taken. In essence, there needs to be recognition that while individual behaviour, in part, may be a reaction to economic, political or institutional conditions, and the kind of impact these conditions have on individuals is worth researching, individual behaviour is not determined by them; there is a degree of freedom which means that there may be different reactions to the same conditions.

It is worthwhile expanding on this point with an example. Certain economic conditions may be conducive to employees pressing home their demands, but while it is right to argue that labour is likely to be most aggressive in such circumstances it is not inevitable that this will be the case. It is not simply a question of differences in tactics and approach by union leaders, though that is important; it may also be a question of the perception of economic conditions. An external observer may judge conditions to be conducive to labour pressing home its demands but such conditions may be judged differently by the people involved, say by union leaders or members. In a similar way, the reaction of employers to particular economic conditions is not predictable in all cases on the basis of economic conditions. Two employers may react differently to the same economic conditions, say, because of differences in their previous experiences when they have opposed union demands. Perceptions, or even myths, may be more important than an external observer's measurement of conditions.

The same line of argument can be applied, of course, to non-economic factors. Changes in political structure, policy and power relationships may open up new ways for workers to press home their demands. It is by no means certain, though, that all workers or union leaders will view these new opportunities in the same way, or in the same way as the external observer. Inertia often plays a part: it may be difficult for individuals to accept that changes in their environment mean that they should change tactics.

Two further points also need to be made. First, attempts to relate external factors, like the economy, to strike activity need to take account not only of the differing perceptions of these external factors by participants but also of the fact that strikes are a broad classification of a number of different kinds of activity. Of course, there is a point of contact, the withdrawal of labour; but there are also major divergencies in, for example, size, duration, aim and location. This adds to the complexity of study and to the difficulty of envisaging a grand theory of strike causation. Second, it is important to recognise that strikes, anyway, are not simply creatures of the environment in which they occur because they can help to create that environment. In particular instances strikes can play a major role in re-shaping social, economic and political conditions. Relatively few strikes have a major and dramatic effect of this kind, but some do, and recognition of this emphasises the complexity of the task involved in studying strikes.

One way forward would be to place more emphasis than in the past on studying a much more restricted range of strike activity. This would allow more attention to be paid to individual reactions, perceptions and experiences, as well as to general economic, social and political conditions. Such case studies of individual strikes or a series of strikes can be particularly useful. There are a number of examples of case studies which have allowed us to learn more about the causes of strikes even though they have not allowed us to propound general laws.

Perhaps the best known case study is Gouldner's *Wildcat Strike,* in which he attempted to explain the cause of a strike at a gypsum mine at Oscar Centre, a small rural community near the Great Lakes.[1] The explanation he put forward was not one that could reasonably have been expected from a macro-level study of strike patterns in that it centred on a detailed analysis of relationships between workers and management at one particular mine. According to Gouldner, what he termed the 'indulgency pattern' was crucial to this relationship (the indulgency pattern essentially meant that management did not supervise workers too closely and also included the idea of the 'second chance' when workers transgressed).Gouldner saw the break-up of the indulgency pattern, which occurred when a new manager was appointed at the mine, as the beginning of a period of increasing resentment against management and the company. This resentment eventually led to the strike, although the strike was actually called over a wages issue: the wages issue, though, was merely a more convenient and acceptable explanation.

The ability to look in detail at working relationships has many attractions. It allows new possibilities to be examined and evaluated. Case studies can, though, also be used to take account of the same kind of factors as those considered in macro studies. There is no reason, for instance, why case studies cannot take account of the impact of changed economic conditions. For example, this was one of the factors looked at in Liston Pope's study of the Loray textile mill strike.[2] One of the 'environmental' factors that he highlighted as being important to an understanding of the cause of the strike was the severe decline in the market for cotton textiles in the 1920s. This led to a budgetary and technological reappraisal in the industry. Costs were lowered by rationalisation (including mill mergers, greater bureaucratisation of individual enterprises and changes in labour policy) and new machinery was introduced which heralded increased working speed and closer management supervision of work tasks. One of the other 'environmental' factors was the increasing power of the union, the National Union of Textile Workers. The point that is being made is that the kind of factors looked at in this case were not all that different from those examined in macro studies. The difference was in the detail with which they were examined and the ability to look at the way in which national conditions had an impact at the local level.

Case studies enable the researcher to look in much more detail at the individual histories relevant to a strike and at the particular perceptions of the people taking part in it. One of the central arguments that has been put forward in some case studies is that strikes occur in a context where different perceptions are held of the same events by different actors.[3] Perceptions, interpersonal relationships, local labour market factors, historical issues, can all be taken into account by case studies in a way that they cannot be by macro studies.

While there are a number of good examples of case studies and there are similarly good examples of other types of small-scale work there is less such work than is justified. The work is not just the province of one academic discipline. While it might be associated with the sociologist and the psychologist there is no reason why smaller-scale studies should not be undertaken by the political scientist or the economist, and some have been. This was recognised, for example, by Mayhew when he called for more attention to be paid to such work by economists and for the breaking down of disciplinary barriers.[4]

The suggestion, then, is that more emphasis on micro-level studies would repay the effort. Such studies are not an alternative to macro-level work and the need for such work is far from exhausted. The micro-level studies should also not be divorced from those conducted at a macro level. The ideas gained from macro studies can and should be used at the micro level. Work at both levels is essential and should feed, one on the other.

NOTES

1. A.W. Gouldner, *Wildcat Strike,* Harper, New York, 1954.
2. L. Pope, *Millhands and Preachers,* Yale University Press, 1942.
3. See, for example, T. Lane and K. Roberts, *Strike at Pilkingtons,* Fontana, London, 1971.
4. K. Mayhew, 'Economists and Strikes', *Oxford Bulletin of Economics and Statistics,* Vol. 41, No. 1 (February 1979) pp. 1–19.

Bibliography

Allen, V.L., *Militant Trade Unionism,* Merlin, London, 1966.

Allen, V.L., *The Sociology of Industrial Relations,* Longman, London, 1971, p. 39.

Ashenfelter, O.C. and Johnson, G.E., 'Bargaining Theory, Trade Unions and Industrial Strike Activity', *American Economic Review,* Vol. 59, No. 1 (1969) pp. 35–49.

Batstone, E., Boraston I. and Frenkel S., *The Social Organisation of Strikes,* Blackwell, Oxford, 1978, p. 18.

Bean, R., *Comparative Industrial Relations,* Croom Helm, Beckenham, Kent, 1985.

Becker, B.E., and Olsen, C.E., 'The Impact of Strikes on Shareholder Equity', *Industrial and Labour Relations Review,* Vol. 39, No. 3 (April 1986) pp. 425–38.

Bennis, W.G., *Changing Organisations: Essays on the Development and Evolution of Human Organisations,* McGraw-Hill, New York, 1966.

Blackburn, R.M. and Mann, M., *The Working Class in the Labour Market,* Macmillan, London, 1979.

Blau, P.M. and Scott, W.R., *Formal Organisations,* Routledge and Kegan Paul, London, 1963.

Blauner, R., *Alienation and Freedom,* University of Chicago Press, Chicago, 1964.

Braverman, H., *Labor and Monopoly Capitalism,* Monthly Review Press, New York, 1974.

Brown, W., (ed.) *The Changing Contours of British Industrial Relations,* Blackwell, Oxford, 1981.

Burns, A.F. and Mitchell, W.C., *Measuring Business Cycles,* National Bureau of Economic Research, New York, 1946.

Burtt, E.J., *Labour in the American Economy,* Macmillan, London, 1979.

Carey, A., 'The Hawthorne Studies: A Radical Criticism', in J.M. Shepherd (ed.) *Organizational Issues in Industrial Society,* Prentice Hall, Englewood Cliffs, N.J., 1972, pp. 297–315.

Chamberlain, N.W., Cullen, D.E. and Lewis, D., *The Labour Sector,* McGraw Hill, New York, 1980.

Chamberlain, N.W. and Schilling, J.M., *The Impact of Strikes,* Greenwood Press, Westport (Connecticut), 1954.

Chermesh, R., 'Strikes as Social Problems: A Social Matrix Approach', *British Journal of Industrial Relations,* Vol. 23, No. 2 (July 1985) pp. 281–308.

Chinoy, E., *Automobile Workers and the American Dream,* Doubleday, New York, 1955.

Clarke, R.O., 'Labour-Management Disputes: A Perspective', *British Journal of Industrial Relations,* Vol. 18, No. 1 (1980) pp. 14–25.

Clegg, H.A., *Trade Unionism Under Collective Bargaining,* Blackwell, Oxford, 1976.

Clegg, H.A., *The Changing System of Industrial Relations in Great Britain,* Blackwell, Oxford, 1979.

Collected Works of Marx and Engels, Vol. 18, Institut für Marxismus-Leninismus, East Berlin.

Creigh, S.W., 'Research Note: Stoppage of Work Incidence in the United Kingdom, 1913–1977; *International Journal of Social Economics,* Vol. 7, No. 5 (1980) pp. 296–308.

Creigh, S.W. and Makeham, D., 'Strike Incidence in Industrial Countries: An Analysis', *Australian Bulletin of Labour,* Vol. 8, No. 3 (1982) pp. 139–49.

Creigh, S.W. and Poland G., *Differences in Strike Activity Between Industrial Countries in the Post-War Period,* National Institute of Labour Studies, Flinders University of South Australia, Working Paper No. 59, 1983.

Creigh, S., Poland, A. and Wooden, M., *The Reasons for International Differences in Strike Activity,* National Institute of Labour Studies, Flinders University of South Australia, Working Paper No. 61, 1984.

Curtis, Eaton B., 'The Worker and the Profitability of the Strike', *Industrial and Labour Relations Review,* Vol. 26, No. 1 (October 1971) pp. 670–9.

Dabscheck, B. and Niland, J., *Industrial Relations in Australia,* Allen and Unwin, London, 1981.

Dahrendorf, R., *Class and Class Conflict in Industrial Society,* Routledge and Kegan Paul, London, 1959.

Dalton, M., 'The Role of Supervision', in A. Kornhauser, R. Dubin and A.M. Ross (eds.) *Industrial Conflict,* McGraw-Hill, New York, 1954.

Davies, R.J., 'Economic Activity, Incomes Policy and Strikes—A Quantitative Analysis', *British Journal of Industrial Relations,* Vol. 17, No. 2 (July 1979) pp. 205–23.

Department of Employment and Productivity, *In Place of Strife,* Cmnd 3888, HMSO, London, 1969.

Dubin, R. 'Constructive Aspects of Industrial Conflict', in A. Kornhauser, R. Dubin and A.M. Ross (eds.) *Industrial Conflict,* McGraw-Hill, New York, 1954.

Dunlop, J.T., *Industrial Relations Systems,* Holt, New York, 1955.

Durcan, J.W. and McCarthy, W.E.J., 'The State Subsidy Theory of Strikes: an Examination of Statistical Data for the Period 1956–70', *British Journal of Industrial Relations,* Vol. 12, No. 1 (March 1974) pp. 26–47.

Edwards, P.K., 'Size of Plant and Strike Proneness', *Oxford Bulletin of Economics and Statistics,* Vol. 42 (May 1980) pp. 145–56.

Edwards, P.K., *Strikes in the United States, 1881–1974,* Blackwell, Oxford, 1981.

Edwards, P.K., 'The Pattern of Collective Industrial Action', in G.S. Bain (ed.) *Industrial Relations in Britain,* Blackwell, Oxford, 1983, pp. 209–36.

Edwards, R., *Contested Terrain,* Heinemann, London, 1979.

Eldridge, J.E.T., *Industrial Disputes: Essays in the Sociology of Industrial Relations,* Routledge and Kegan Paul, London, 1968.

Enderwick, P., 'Strike Costs and Public Policy', *Journal of Public Policy,* Vol. 2, Part 4 (October 1982).

Engels, F., 'Labour Movements', in T. Clarke and L. Clements (eds.) *Trade Unionism Under Capitalism,* Fontana, Glasgow, 1977.

England, J. and Weekes, B., 'Trade Unions and the State: A Review of the Crisis', *Industrial Relations Journal,* Vol. 12, No. 1 (January–February 1981).

Evans, E.W., 'Research Note: On Some Recent Econometric Models of Strike Frequency', *Industrial Relations Journal,* Vol. 7, No. 3 (1976) pp. 72–6.

Evans, E.W. and Creigh, S.W., (eds.) *Industrial Conflict in Britain,* Cass, London, 1977.

Evans, E., 'On Some Recent Econometric Models of Strike Frequency: a Further Comment', *Industrial Relations Journal,* Vol. 8, No. 4 (Winter 1977–8).

Fantasia, R., 'The Wildcat Strike and Industrial Relations', *Industrial Relations Journal,* Vol. 14, No. 2 (Summer 1983).

Faunce, W.A. (ed.) *Readings in Industrial Sociology,* Meredith, New York, 1967, pp. 258–9.

Fox, A. and Flanders, A. 'The Reform of Collective Bargaining: From Donovan to Durkheim', *British Journal of Industrial Relations,* Vol. 7, No. 2 (1969) pp. 151–80.

Friedman, A., 'Responsible Autonomy versus Direct Control over the Labour Process', *Capital and Class,* No. 1 (Spring 1977) pp. 43–57.

Gennard, J., *Financing Strikers,* Macmillan, London, 1977.

Gennard, J., 'The Effects of Strike Activity on Households', *British Journal of Industrial Relations,* Vol. 19, No. 3 (November 1981) pp. 327–44.

Gennard, J., 'The Financial Costs and Returns of Strikes', *British Journal of Industrial Relations,* Vol. 20, No. 2 (July 1982) pp. 247–56.

Gifford, A., 'The Impact of Socialism on Work Stoppages', *Industrial Relations,* Vol. 13, No. 2 (1974) pp. 208–11.

Goldthorpe, J.H., 'Attitudes and Behaviour of Car Assembly Workers: a Deviant Case and Theoretical Critique', *British Journal of Sociology,* Vol. 17, No. 3 (September 1966).

Goldthorpe, J.H., Lockwood, D., Bechofer, F. and Platt, J., *The Affluent Workers,* Cambridge University Press, London, 1968.

Gollan, R., 'The Historical Perspective', in P.W.D. Matthews and G.W. Ford (eds.) *Australian Trade Unions,* Sun Books, Melbourne, 1968, pp. 14–41.

Graham, K., 'Union Attitudes to Job Satisfaction', in M. Weir (ed.), *Job Satisfaction,* Fontana, Glasgow, 1976.

Griffen, J.I., *Strikes: A Study in Quantitative Economics,* Columbia University Press, New York, 1939.

Hameed, S.M.A., and Homes, T., 'Measurement of Production Losses Due to Strikes in Canada: An Input-Output Analysis', *British Journal of Industrial Relations,* Vol. 15, No. 1 (March 1975) pp. 86–93.

Hansen, A.H., 'Cycles of Strikes', *American Economic Review,* Vol. 11, No. 4 (1921) pp. 616–21.

Harbison, F.H., 'Collective Bargaining and American Capitalism', in A. Kornhauser, R. Dubin and A.M. Ross (eds.) *op. cit.*

Hertzberg, F., *Work and the Nature of Man,* Stapes Press, London, 1968.

Hibbs, D.A., 'Industrial Conflict in Advanced Industrial Societies', *American Political Science Review,* Vol. 70, No. 4 (1976) pp. 1033–58.

Hibbs, D.A., 'On the Political Economy of Long-Run Trends in Strike Activity', *British Journal of Political Science,* Vol. 8, No. 2 (1978) pp. 153–75.

Hill, S., *Competition and Control at Work,* Heinemann, London, 1981.

Hudson, R., 'The Effects of Dock Strikes on UK International Trade', *Applied Economics,* Vol. 13, No. 1 (March 1981) pp. 67–77.

Hunter, L.C., 'The State Subsidy Theory of Strikes: a Reconsideration', *British Journal of Industrial Relations,* Vol. 12, No. 3 (November 1974) pp. 438–44.

Hunter, L.C., *The Economic Determination of Strike Activity: A Reconsideration,* Department of Social and Economic Research, Discussion Paper No. 1, University of Glasgow.

Huxley, C., 'The State, Collective Bargaining and the Shape of Strikes in Canada', *Canadian Journal of Sociology,* Vol. 4, No. 3 (1979) pp. 223–39.

Ingham, G.K., *Size of Industrial Organisation and Worker Behaviour: An Empirical Study,* Cambridge University Press, London, 1970.

Ingham, G.K., *Strikes and Industrial Conflict,* Macmillan, London, 1974.

Isaac, J.E., 'The Prospects for Collective Bargaining in Australia', in J.E. Issac and G.W. Ford (eds.) *Australian Labour Relations Readings,* Sun Books, Melbourne (1966).

Jackson, M.P., *Industrial Relations,* Croom Helm, Beckenham, Kent, 1985.

Jurkat, E.H. and Jurkat, D.B., 'Economic Function of Strikes', *Industrial and Labour Relations Review,* Vol. 2, (July 1949) pp. 527–45.

Kalbitz, R., *Aussperrungen in der Bundersrepublic.* E.V.A., Köln-Frankfurt, 1979. Quoted by W. Muller-Jentsch, 'Strikes and Strike Trends in West Germany, 1950–78', *Industrial Relations Journal,* Vol. 12, No. 4 (July–August 1981).

Kassalow, E.M., *Trade Unions and Industrial Relations: An International Comparison,* Random House, New York, 1969.

Kaufman, B.E., 'Interindustry Trends in Strike Activity', *Industrial Relations,* Vol. 22, No. 1 (Winter 1983) pp. 45–57.

Kaufman, B.E., 'The Determinants of Strikes in the United States 1900–1977', *Industrial and Labour Relations Review,* Vol. 35, No. 4 (July 1982) pp. 473–90.

Kennedy, T., *European Labor Relations,* D.C. Heath, Lexington, Mass., 1980.

Kerr, C., 'Industrial Conflict and its Mediation', *American Journal of Sociology,* Vol. 60, (1954) p. 199.

Kerr, C. and Siegel, A., 'The Inter-industry Propensity to Strike', in A. Kornhauser, R. Dubin and A. Ross (eds.) *op. cit.*

Kerr, C., *et al, Industrialism and Industrial Man,* Heinemman, London, 1962.

Knight, K.G., 'Strikes and Wage Inflation in British Manufacturing Industry 1950–1968', *Bulletin of the Oxford University Institute of Economics and Statistics,* Vol. 34, No. 3 (August 1972) pp. 281–94.

Kornhouser, A., Dubin, R. and Ross, A.N., (eds.) *Industrial Conflict,* McGraw-Hill, New York, 1954.

Korpi, W., 'Workplace Bargaining, the Law and Unofficial Strikes: the Case of Sweden', *British Journal of Industrial Relations,* Vol. 16, No. 3 (1978) pp. 355–68.

Korpi, W., 'Unofficial Strikes in Sweden', *British Journal of Industrial Relations,* Vol. 19, No. 1 (1981) pp. 66–86.

Korpi, W. and Shalev, M., 'Strikes, Industrial Relations and Class Conflicts in Capitalist Societies', *British Journal of Sociology,* Vol. 30, No. 2 (1979) pp. 164–87.

Kuhn, J.W., *Bargaining in Grievance Settlement: The Power of Industrial Work Groups,* Columbia University Press, 1961.

Lenin, V.I., 'Capital and Labour', in T. Clarke and L. Clements (eds.) *Trade Unions Under Capitalism,* Fontana, London, 1977, pp. 64–76.

Likert, R., *New Patterns of Management,* McGraw-Hill, New York, 1961.

Littler, C.R., *The Development of the Labour Process in Capitalist Societies,* Heinemann, London, 1982.

Maki, D.R., 'The Effects of Unions and Strikes on the Rate of Growth of Total Factor Productivity in Canada', *Applied Economics,* Vol. 15, No. 1 (1983) pp. 29–42.

Marginson, P.M., 'The Distinctive Effects of Plant and Company Size on Workplace Industrial Relations', *British Journal of Industrial Relations,* Vol. 22 (March 1984) pp. 1–14.

Maslow, A.H., *Motivation and Personality,* Harper and Row, New York, 1954.

Mauro, M.J., 'Strikes as a Result of Imperfect Information', *Industrial and Labor Relations Review,* Vol. 34, No. 4 (July 1982) pp. 522–38.

Mayhew, K., 'Economists and Strikes', *Oxford Bulletin of Economics and Statistics,* Vol. 41, No. 1 (1979) pp. 1–2.

Mayo, E., *The Human Problems of an Industrial Civilization,* Harvard University Press, Cambridge, Mass., 1946.

McGregor, D., *Leadership and Motivation,* MIT Press, Cambridge, Mass., 1966.

McLean, R.A., 'Interindustry Differences in Strike Activity', *Industrial Relations,* Vol. 18, No. 1 (Winter 1979) pp. 103–9.

Neumann, G.R. and Reder, M.W., 'Output and Strike Activity in US Manufacturing: How Large are the Losses?', *Industrial and Labour Relations Review,* Vol. 37, No. 2 (January 1984) pp. 197–211.

Nicholson, N., 'Strikes and other Forms of Industrial Action, *Industrial Relations Journal,* Vol. 11, No. 5 (November–December 1980) pp. 20–31.

Niland, J., *Collective Bargaining and Compulsory Arbitration in Australia,* New South Wales University Press, Kensington, NSW, 1978

Paldam, M. and Pedersen, P.J., 'The Macro-Economic Strike Model: A Study of Seventeen Countries 1948–1975', *Industrial and Labor Relations Review,* Vol. 35, No. 4 (1982) pp. 504–21.

Paldam, M., 'Industrial Conflicts and Economic Conditions', *European Economic Review,* Vol. 20, No. 2 (1983) pp. 231–56.

Parsons, T. and Smelser, N.J., *Economy and Society: A Study in the Integration of Economic and Social Theory,* Routledge and Kegan Paul, London, 1956.

Pencavel, J.H., 'An Investigation into Industrial Strike Activity in Britain', *Economica',* Vol. 37, No. 147 (1970) pp. 329–56.

Pizzarno, A., 'Political Exchange and Collective Identity in Industrial Conflict', in C. Crough and A. Pizzorno, (eds.) *The Resurgence of Class Conflict in Western Europe Since 1968: Volume 2, Comparative Analyses,* Macmillan, London, 1978.

Prais, S.J. 'The Strike-Proneness of Large Plants in Britain', *Journal of Royal Statistical Society,* Series A (General), Vol. 141, Part 3 (1978) pp. 368–84.

Rees, A., 'Industrial Conflict and Business Fluctuations', *Journal of Political Economy,* Vol. 60, No. 5 (October 1952).

Revens, R.W., 'Industrial Morale and Size of Unit', in W. Galenson and S.M. Lipset (eds.) *Labor and Trade Unionism,* Wiley, New York, 1960, pp. 259–300; Action Society Trust, *Size and Morale,* Action Society Trust, London, 1953; S. Talacchi, 'Organisational Size, Individual Attitudes and Behaviour: An Empirical Study, *Administrative Science Quarterly,* Vols, 1960, pp. 398–420.

Roethlisberger, F.J. and Dickson, W.J., *Management and the Worker,* Harvard University Press, Cambridge, Mass., 1939.

Ross, A.M. and Hartman, P.T., *Changing Patterns of Industrial Conflict,* Wiley, New York, 1960.

Ross, A.M. and Irwin, I., 'Strike Experience in Five Countries 1927–47: An Interpretation', *Industrial and Labor Relations Review,* Vol. 4, No. 3 (1951) pp. 323–42.

Royal Commission on Trade Unions and Employers Associations 1965–1968, *Report.* Cmnd 3623, HMSO, London, 1968.

Sapsford, D., 'On Some Recent Econometric Models of Strike Frequency: A Reply', *Industrial Relations Journal,* Vol. 8, No. 1 (1977) pp. 70–1.

Sayles, L.R., 'Wildcat Strikes', *Harvard Business Review,* No. 32 (November–December 1954).

Sayles, L.R., *Behaviour of Work Groups,* Wiley, New York, 1958.

Schneider, E.V., *Industrial Sociology,* McGraw-Hill, London, 1971, p. 92.

Scott, J.F. and Homans, G.C., 'Reflections on the Wildcat Strikes', *American Sociological Review,* Vol. 12 (1947).

Scott, W.H., *Coal and Conflict,* Liverpool University Press, Liverpool, 1963.

Shalev, M., 'Industrial Relations Theory and the Comparative Study of Industrial Relations and Industrial Conflict', *British Journal of Industrial Relations,* Vol. 18, No. 1(1980).

Sheppard, H.L. and Herrick, N.Q., *Where Have All the Robots Gone?* Free Press, New York, 1972.

Shorey, J., 'The Size of the Work Unit and Strike Incidence', *Journal of Industrial Economics,* Vol. 23, No. 3 (March 1975) pp. 175–88.

Shorey, J., 'An Inter-Industry Analysis of Strike Frequency', *Economica,* Vol 43 (1976) pp. 349–65.

Shorey, J., 'Time Series Analysis of Strike Frequency', *British Journal of Industrial Relations,* Vol. 15, No. 1, pp. 63–75.

Shorter, E. and Tilly, C., *Strikes in France 1830–1968,* Cambridge University Press, Cambridge, 1974.

Skeels, J.W., 'The Economic and Organizational Basis of Early United States Strikes 1900–1948', *Industrial and Labour Relations Review,* Vol. 35, No. 4 (July 1982) pp. 491–503.

Smelser, N.J., *Social Change in the Industrial Revolution,* Routledge and Kegan Paul, London, 1959, presents a case study of social change in the Lancashire textile industry using the systems theory perspective.

Smelser, N.J., *The Sociology of Economic Life,* Prentice Hall, Englewood Cliffs, N.J., 1983.

Smith, C.T.B., *et al, Strikes in Britain,* Department of Employment, Manpower Paper 15, HMSO, London, 1978.

Snyder, D., 'Institutional Setting and Industrial Conflict', *American Sociological Review,* Vol. 40, No. 3 (1975) pp. 259–78.

Stern, R.N., 'Methodological Issues in Quantitative Strike Analysis', *Industrial Relations,* Vol. 17, No. 1 (February 1978) pp. 32–42.

Sutcliffe, J.T., 'The Strikes of the 1890s', in J.E. Isaac and G.W. Ford (eds.) *Australian Labour Relations Readings,* Sun Books, Melbourne, 1966.

Sweet, T.G. and Jackson, D., *The Classification and Interpretation of Strike Statistics: An International Comparative Analysis,* University of Aston Management Centre, Working Paper No. 97, 1978.

Taft, P. and Ross, P., 'American Labor Violence: Its Courses, Character and Outcome', in H.D. Graham and T.R. Gurr (eds.) *Violence in America,* Bantam, New York, 1969.

Terry, M., 'Organising a Fragmented Workforce: Shop Stewards in Local Government', *British Journal of Industrial Relations,* Vol. 20, No. 1 (March 1982) pp. 1–19.

Trist, E.L., Higgin, G.W., Murray, H. and Pollock, P.B., *Organizational Choice,* Tavistock, London, 1963.

Trotsky, L., 'Marxism and Trade Unionism', in T. Clarke and L. Clements (eds.) *op. cit.*

Turner, H.A., *Is Britain Really Strike Prone?,* Cambridge University Press, London, 1969.

Turner, H.A., Clack, G. and Roberts, G., *Labour Relations in the Mortar Industry,* Allen and Unwin, London, 1963.

Walker, C.R. and Guest, R.H., *The Man on the Assembly Line,* Yale University Press, New Haven, Connecticut, 1957.

Walsh, K., 'Industrial Disputes in France, West Germany, Italy and the United Kingdom: Measurement and Incidence', *Industrial Relations Journal,* Vol. 13, No. 4 (Winter 1982).

Walsh, K., *Strikes in Europe and the United States,* Frances Pinter, London, 1983.

Warren, E.L., 'Thirty-Six Years of "National Emergency Strikes"', *Industrial and Labour Relations Review,* Vol. 5 (1951) pp. 12–15.

Whittingham, T.G. and Towers, B., 'Strikes and the Economy', *National Westminster Bank Quarterly Review,* November 1971, pp. 33–42.

Whyte, W.F., *Pattern for Industrial Peace,* Harper and Row, New York, 1951.

Wood, S. (ed.) *The Degradation of Work?,* Hutchinson, London, 1982.

Wood, S. and Pedlar, M., 'On Losing Their Virginity: the Story of a Strike at the Grosvenor Hotel, Sheffield', *Industrial Relations Journal,* Vol. 9, No. 2 (Summer 1978) pp. 15–37.

Woodward, J., *Industrial Organisation: Theory and Practice,* Oxford University Press, London, 1965.

Woodward, J. (ed.), *Industrial Organisation: Behaviour and Control,* Oxford University Press, London, 1970.

Wright Mills, C., *New Men of Power: America's Labor Leaders,* Harcourt, New York, 1948.

Wright Mills, C., *White Collar,* Oxford University Press, London, 1959.

Yoder, D., 'Economic Changes and Industrial Unrest in the United States', *Journal of Political Economy,* Vol. 48 (1940) pp. 222–37.

Index